To my father, Julio, and my mother, Gail, for inspiring me, and to my sons Zan and Cameron for inspiring me as well.

—Joey Rive

To my wife, Candace, and our children, Jasmine and Jaden Williams. To coach Jack Bailey for 20 plus years of service to Scots tennis.

—Scott Williams

CONTENTS

TENNIS
SKILLS & DRILLS

JOEY RIVE

SCOTT C. WILLIAMS

HUMAN KINETICS

Library of Congress Cataloging-in-Publication Data

Rive, Joey.
  Tennis skills & drills / Joey Rive, Scott C. Williams.
      p. cm.
  ISBN-13: 978-0-7360-8308-9 (soft cover)
  ISBN-10: 0-7360-8308-1 (soft cover)
  1. Tennis--Training. I. Williams, Scott C. II. Title.
  GV1002.9.T7R58 2012
  796.342--dc23

                                                2011027132

ISBN-10: 0-7360-8308-1 (print)
ISBN-13: 978-0-7360-8308-9 (print)

Acquisitions Editor: Laurel Plotzke Garcia; **Developmental Editor:** Heather Healy; **Assistant Editor:** Claire Marty; **Copyeditor:** Joanna Hatzopoulos; **Permission Manager:** Martha Gullo; **Graphic Designer:** Keri Evans; **Graphic Artist:** Tara Welsch; **Cover Designer:** Keith Blomberg; **Photographer (cover):** Clive Brunskill/Getty Images; **Photographer (interior):** Neil Bernstein; **Visual Production Assistant:** Joyce Brumfield; **Photo Production Manager:** Jason Allen; **Art Manager:** Kelly Hendren; **Associate Art Manager:** Alan L. Wilborn; **Illustrations:** © Human Kinetics; **Printer:** Versa Press

We thank T Bar M Racquet Club in Dallas, Texas, for assistance in providing the location for the photo shoot for this book.

Human Kinetics books are available at special discounts for bulk purchase. Special editions or book excerpts can also be created to specification. For details, contact the Special Sales Manager at Human Kinetics.

Printed in the United States of America   10 9 8 7 6 5 4 3 2 1

The paper in this book is certified under a sustainable forestry program.

Human Kinetics
Website: www.HumanKinetics.com

United States: Human Kinetics
P.O. Box 5076
Champaign, IL 61825-5076
800-747-4457
e-mail: humank@hkusa.com

Canada: Human Kinetics
475 Devonshire Road Unit 100
Windsor, ON N8Y 2L5
800-465-7301 (in Canada only)
e-mail: info@hkcanada.com

Europe: Human Kinetics
107 Bradford Road
Stanningley
Leeds LS28 6AT, United Kingdom
+44 (0) 113 255 5665
e-mail: hk@hkeurope.com

Australia: Human Kinetics
57A Price Avenue
Lower Mitcham, South Australia 5062
08 8372 0999
e-mail: info@hkaustralia.com

New Zealand: Human Kinetics
P.O. Box 80
Torrens Park, South Australia 5062
0800 222 062
e-mail: info@hknewzealand.com

E4810

CONTENTS

ACKNOWLEDGMENTS

I would like to thank T BAR M Racquet Club and the entire staff for being so patient with me through this process, especially Glen Agritelly, Darren Boyd, Chris Wade, and Doug Kruger.

Thanks to Bobby Bernstein, Dave Licker, Greg Alexander, and Doug Kruger for their technical help.

Thanks to Laurel Plotzke Garcia, Heather Healy, and all the folks at Human Kinetics for giving me a chance.

Thanks to Scott Williams for his help and for the opportunity to collaborate with him through the final stages of the book. Finally, I would like to thank all my friends and coaching buddies for their interest in the book and their continued support throughout.

—Joey Rive

Thank you to Joey Rive, Laurel Plotzke Garcia, and Heather Healy for making this book special. A special thanks goes to Cindy Newman and coach Jack Bailey.

—Scott Williams

KEY TO DIAGRAMS

X   Any player

S   Server

SP   Server's partner

R   Returner

RP   Returner's partner

K   King

CO   Coach

⟶   Path of player

– – – –⟶   Path of ball

– **1** – –⟶   Shot number

•   Bounce

       Cone

CHAPTER 1

FOREHAND SKILLS

The forehand has become the weapon of choice for most tennis players today. How well a player hits this shot forecasts the style of play. The forehand is often central to the game plan for both sides of a match; a player can build a game plan around using it or combating it. A good forehand has power, consistency, accuracy, and variety. It enables a player to overpower an opponent, go from defense to offense with a single shot, or put an opponent on the defensive in order to transition to the net. Players with a strong forehand include Andy Roddick, Roger Federer, Rafael Nadal, Venus Williams, and Serena Williams.

The forehand plays a large part in the process of a balanced groundstroke attack. Depending on individual strengths and weaknesses, a player can use it offensively to stay in a point until the right opportunity comes around or even to play a strong defense. An effective forehand is not only about power, it is also about the way the player uses it, such as to set up net play or a killer backhand down the line.

Over the last 40 years the forehand has evolved from the classic Continental grip into more choices such as the Eastern, semi-Western, and full Western grips. Players have used classic forehand styles within an attack style strategy—flat balls or balls hit on the rise—but they focused on placement and finesse. Today the way players strike the ball is considerably different. Racket technology and advances in proper technique have made hitting the forehand more of a full-body workout designed to deliver a striking blow. This is apparent in the professionals and young juniors of today. The modern-day forehand strategy is more aggressive and designed to hit a winner from the backcourt or take time away from an opponent in an effort to control play.

Today's forehand also depends on a big serve. Modern tennis could be called the serve-and-forehand era. When technology and sport science advanced greatly from the mid- 1980s through the 1990s, the conventional ways of winning points, such as the serve-and-volley, or the Swedish way, of outlasting an opponent on the court, became less effective. The return came back faster and the ball was struck with greater velocity. Thus, the forehand became a weapon. Instead of a chess match, tennis became a power game and, consequently, the emphasis changed toward the first strike.

This chapter covers offensive and defensive styles as they relate to the forehand, the various forehand shots, the technique for those shots, and the characteristics of a good forehand. Chapter 3 provides drills needed for developing a great forehand weapon.

CHOOSING A FOREHAND

Today's game is ruled by the forehand first. Even if a player's most powerful weapon is the backhand, the forehand must be strong. The player needs to develop the forehand well in order to counter the opponent's forehand long enough to use the backhand effectively.

The quality of the forehand shot determines the player's offensive and defensive nature and provides the player with the basis for the resulting game style and plan. So, when learning or reviewing technique, it is vital that the player stay current. The goal is to have great technique for every shot, so the player should constantly try to improve. All players must be able to execute a variety of both offensive and defensive forehands.

Technique is important in a player's development, and it dictates what the player's better shots will be. A player should choose a grip, stance, and stroke (swing path) that correspond to the goals for the forehand and can help the player develop to the highest levels.

There are five types of forehands: the Eastern forehand, the semi-Western forehand, the Western forehand, Continental forehand, and the slice forehand. Each shot is characterized by its grip and has a different technique for its use. The player should first choose the most comfortable grip, which in turn dictates the type of forehand and the technique for hitting it. Still, it is important to master multiple grips in order to shift between forehands, such as the defensive slice versus an offensive winner or a forehand rally shot.

The Eastern and semi-Western forehand grips are the most versatile. The Continental and Western forehand grips are used less often because they have limitations in hitting certain shots, such as high and low balls. The Western grip can be used aggressively on higher bouncing surfaces such as clay or hard court. A person using the Western grip has to be proficient at quickly changing to other grips for certain shots, such as from a Western forehand to an Eastern backhand grip on a one-handed backhand (see Forehands and Grips, p. 5).

FOOTWORK AND BODY POSITION

No matter what forehand technique a player chooses, the player needs to use proper footwork and body position to get set to hit the ball. Knowing how to move quickly and efficiently results in greater choices for controlling the ball.

Movement

Movement to the forehand side is vital to the success of the shot. The player should keep the feet moving at all times when the ball is in play and split step when the opponent hits the ball. A *split step* is jumping an inch or two (2.5 to 5 cm) off the ground and landing on the balls of the feet, ready to move (see figure 1.1). For balls hit to the right side, the player should step out with the right foot (see figure 1.2) and try to line up the right foot behind the incoming ball. For balls hit to the left side, the player should step out with the left foot and line it up behind the incoming ball. Once lined up on the ball, enough weight should be loaded on the leg and foot to establish balance as the player begins to push off and transfer weight into the shot. In other words, the first step gets the player to the ball quickly and efficiently, making the execution of the whole shot easier.

Figure 1.1 Split step.

Figure 1.2 Step to the right after split step.

Figure 1.3   Open stance.

Figure 1.4   Semi-open stance.

Stances

Three types of stances are used in tennis: open, semi-open, and closed. A player's stance is dictated by the shot being hit and by personal preference. The player should use a stance that creates the best platform for the player's legs to push off and hit a powerful shot. As long as a player knows the proper technique for the different stances, all three can be effective.

Open Stance

In an open stance (figure 1.3), the player uses the back leg to load and set the feet in a manner that keeps the body relaxed, balanced, and open to the shot. A player should experiment with the open stance to see what feels the most comfortable for control and power. The grips and strings used today are based on topspin and allowing the arm the maximum ability to swing freely. The degree to which a player uses an open stance depends on shots hit by opponents. Strong, high-bouncing shots hit out of the player's strike zone may require more of an open stance because of the lack of time to prepare and to line up the feet on the ball. Windy conditions, playing left-handed servers who swing wide, or playing great right-handed kick serves on the ad side of the court can require an open stance as well.

Players can use the open stance on all of the forehand shots. It can be used on shots hit directly to the player or on tougher balls that require stretching. The open stance gives the player the advantage of getting to more balls and hitting them aggressively. It gives the arm ample space to strike the ball and swing freely, especially on those tougher, higher balls. Drawbacks of hitting with an open stance relate to the amount of power a player achieves through the hitting zone. A shot hit from an open stance relies on angular momentum (created by rotation only), which produces less power compared with a square stance that combines linear and angular momentum.

Semi-Open Stance

The semi-open (also known as semi-closed) stance, shown in figure 1.4, is a form of the open stance and is used regularly when players move around their backhand to hit a forehand. Some players like to hit with an open stance regardless of the oncoming ball but others prefer to use a semi-open stance for a shot that is hit directly to them, giving them the option to hit through the shot more by using linear and angular momentum. This stance is especially useful on shots where the player is pulled away from the center of the court and needs balance through contact. The back leg loads as it does with the open stance, but the front leg comes a little more in front and to the side. A player can use this stance on all forehand shots.

Closed Stance

When using the closed stance (figure 1.5), a player sets the back leg in the loaded position but brings the front leg directly in front of the back leg to effectively close the hips and shoulders to the net. It is also known as the *square* stance. The use of this stance depends on a player's preference and how quickly the player moves to the ball. If a player can get to the ball in plenty of time and prefers to set both legs (one in front of the other), the closed stance is more powerful. A closed stance is best used on shots that are hit directly to the player. It becomes increasingly difficult to hit a closed stance when stretching out for wide shots.

FOREHANDS AND GRIPS

Figure 1.6 shows a view of the bottom octagon of a racket and, for the purposes of grip discussion, numbers each of the bevels of the racket handle. All of the grips are based on how a player positions the bottom knuckle of the index finger, or the index knuckle (see figure 1.7), on the bevels. Figures 1.8*a* and *b* on page 6 show the placement for the index knuckle for a right-handed and a left-handed player for all of the forehand grips.

Figure 1.5   **Closed stance.**

Figure 1.6   **The eight bevels of the racket.**

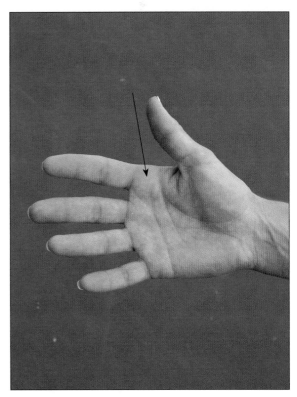

Figure 1.7   **The index knuckle.**

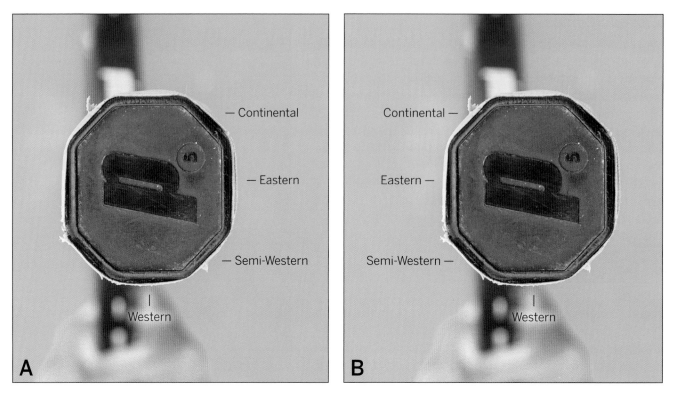

Figure 1.8 The location of the index knuckle on the racket for *(a)* right-handed players and *(b)* left-handed players using the forehand grips.

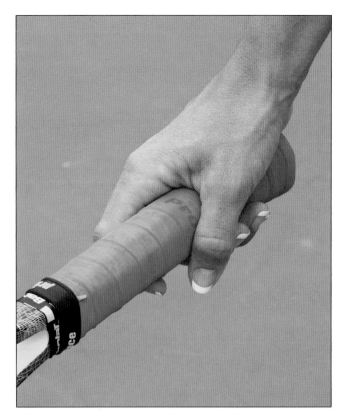

Figure 1.9 Continental grip.

All current grips can be traced back to the Continental grip shown in figure 1.9. Tennis pioneers used the Continental grip because the game was originally played on grass, where the ball bounced low. This grip is now primarily used for slice forehands, backhands, the serve, forehand and backhand volleys, and the overhead. The Continental grip is a great grip for low balls and balls hit at hip level. To find this grip, the player puts the dominant hand flat on the strings and moves the hand down to the grip. The top part of the grip is in the V between the thumb and forefinger, and the index knuckle is on bevel 2 of the racket handle for right-handed players and bevel 8 for left-handed players (refer to figures 1.6 and 1.8).

One limitation of hitting with this grip is that it can be difficult to combat the heavy topspin that most players use. Rather than having to switch grips to cope with various ball heights and spins, most players transition to using the Eastern or semi-Western forehand grips, which can be used to play any forehand. Using a hybrid grip (somewhere between the Eastern and semi-Western grips) is an option that allows players to tailor their grip to match their swing.

Eastern Forehand and Grip

The Eastern forehand (see figure 1.10) is one of the most versatile grips in modern-day tennis. For the Eastern forehand grip, the index knuckle is on bevel 3 of the racket handle for right-handed players and bevel 7 for left-handed players (refer to figures 1.6 and 1.8). As shown in figure 1.10, the racket begins to close if the player holds the arm in front of the body.

The use of this grip depends on the player's swing and how much topspin the player wants to put on the ball. The Eastern grip does not automatically create as much topspin as the semi-Western grip. A player needs to develop strong wrists and a higher loop (to sweep under the ball more) to achieve the same topspin with the Eastern grip that is already built into the semi-Western grip. The Eastern forehand grip is popular with players who like to drive their forehands (flat) as well as use topspin.

The main disadvantage of the Eastern grip is the reduced ability to counter (defend) against a ball that bounces high. The Eastern grip has a slightly more closed face on the takeback, so to use this grip for countering high-bouncing balls, a player needs accurate timing and strong wrists to be able to impart topspin back to the opponent.

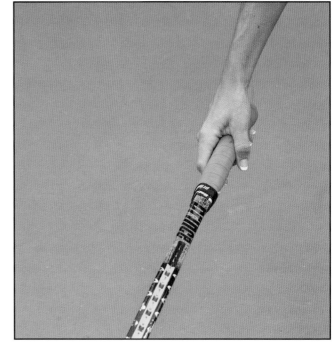

Figure 1.10 Eastern grip.

Semi-Western Forehand and Grip

The semi-Western forehand (see figure 1.11) is the most popular forehand technique in today's game. Top professionals, such as Rafael Nadal and Venus Williams, as well as juniors use the semi-Western forehand grip. For right-handed players, the index knuckle is placed on bevel 4 and bevel 6 for left-handers (refer to figures 1.6 and 1.8). The racket face if you were to hold the racket in front of you would be slightly more closed than the Eastern forehand.

The semi-Western grip is designed for players who are trying to produce a lot of topspin on their shots. Because the racket face is slightly more closed than in the Eastern forehand, it allows the player more flexibility to counter an opponent's high-bouncing shot. The main disadvantage of this grip occurs when countering a low or slice shot. If a player is not properly loaded and low enough to accept the oncoming shot, then it is a struggle to get under the shot in an appropriate fashion.

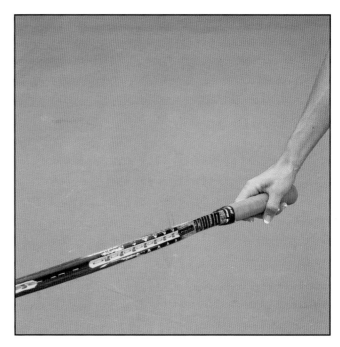

Figure 1.11 Semi-Western grip.

Western Forehand and Grip

The Western forehand technique uses a grip that is more extreme than the Continental, Eastern, and semi-Western forehands as shown in figure 1.12. For this grip, both right-handed and left-handed players place the index knuckle on bevel 5 of the racket handle (refer to figures 1.6 on page 5 and 1.8 on page 6). This grip puts the palm of the hand completely under the racket handle.

The main advantage of the Western forehand grip is the amount of topspin it can generate. This grip is the choice for a player who wants to hit the ball with a lot more topspin (especially on higher balls) than the other two more modern grips. Players who play on clay courts or slow, hard courts may gravitate toward this forehand grip. Usually the player who uses it is used to slower-paced or higher-bouncing shots. If the player exclusively uses slower surfaces against the same types of opponents, then perfecting the Western forehand could be an advantage.

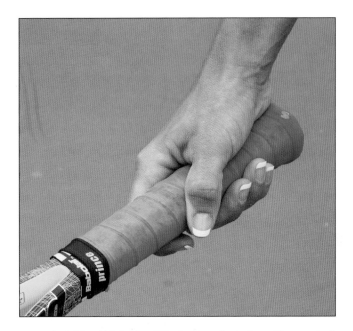

Figure 1.12 With the Western grip, when the racket is turned over to playing position, the palm will be completely under the racket.

Unfortunately, the disadvantages of this grip can be numerous, especially for players who play on various surfaces. A player using this grip is susceptible to lower shots and slices from an opponent, which, if played on a faster surface, can present a challenge. On a faster surface the ball doesn't bounce as high, so a player has to make different swing adjustments. It is more prudent to develop a stroke that can adapt to all surfaces. Also, because of the many grip changes that can occur during a point, the extreme nature of the grip makes it harder to switch to other grips.

In addition, the technique required to hit a Western forehand can be too extreme. The grip causes the wrist to lay back more than with the semi-Western or Eastern forehand. This makes it difficult to extend the wrist through the point of contact. Because the grip is so far under the racket handle, the elbow bends more and becomes almost in line with the bottom of the butt cap of the racket. This sometimes causes swing problems for a player, such as dragging the racket head, and hampers the player's ability to smooth out the swing.

FOREHAND AND STYLES OF PLAY

Tennis has five styles of play: aggressive baseline play, all-court play, serve-and-volley play, rallying baseline play, and defensive play. Aggressive baseline play and all-court play are considered offensive and are built around the forehand. Serve-and-volley players build their games around their serve and attacking style, but they can still use the forehand as a weapon. Rallying baseline play and defensive baseline play use the forehand as a rally ball or in a defensive manner.

A player's style is based on what forehands are the player's favorites, the technique for those shots, overall on-court personality, and the player's aggressive or defensive nature. A player can change or improve playing style by adding shots to the repertoire and improving technique. A player should try to establish one particular forehand shot as a weapon, then add and develop other shots to complement the particular style. One of the main goals of choosing a grip is to use one that corresponds with the player's style of play. Table 1.1 shows the type of forehand technique that players can use in each style of play based on grip choices.

Table 1.1 Techniques for Styles of Play

Type of technique	Style of play				
	Aggressive baseline	**All-court**	**Serve-and-volley**	**Rallying baseline**	**Defensive baseline**
Eastern forehand grip	X	X	X	X	X
Semi-Western forehand grip	X	X	X	X	X
Western forehand grip	X	With good use of different grips		X	X
Continental forehand grip			X		X

POINTS OF CONTACT AND STRIKE ZONES

Players should know the correct contact point and strike zone for the shots they want to execute. Their court position, movement, and racket preparation should match that contact point. Three points of contact are possible: attack, rally, and defensive. They fall in a horizontal plane (see figure 1.13). Although players must address each individual ball in a groundstroke, the style of play sets the tone for the types of shots they want

Figure 1.13 The points of contact include the *(a)* attack, *(b)* rally, and *(c)* defensive.

to execute. For example, aggressive baseline players predominantly want their contact points in front to maintain the attacking style of play. The strength of the opponent's shot also dictates a player's contact points. A player needs to use shot selection and contact points together to keep a rally going and to help establish control of a point.

The attack point of contact is in front of the body or in front of the front foot. The attack point of contact is usually a crosscourt shot or any shot that is played from a position of strength in the court. This position is usually inside the baseline. For example, a down-the-line forehand may be contacted a little late, but it is attacking if the court position is inside the baseline. However, a player can possess a weapon that is hit with an early contact point but from deeper in the court; as long as the success rate stays high, it is attacking.

The rally point of contact is between the hips and is offensive if a player hits with heavy topspin. The later contact point allows for maximum load to be drawn from the legs in the execution of the shot. A rally point of contact is used to neutralize a player and increase the chance to get a better opportunity later in the rally. Rally shots are usually played crosscourt or as a high, heavy down-the-line shot, and they are usually executed from the baseline or just behind it.

The defensive point of contact is in line with or behind the back hip and is usually played as a high, heavy shot to get back into the point or a ball hit with a higher trajectory. This contact point suggests a good shot from an opponent or possibly poor movement to a shot. Players usually use a defensive contact point when they are behind the base-line and playing defensively.

The three strike zones—lower-level, midlevel, and upper-level—fall in a vertical plane (see figure 1.14). Great players can hit winners from all three strike zones. The mid- and lower-level strike zones are especially preferred for hitting topspin. Most players should attempt to meet the ball in the ideal, midlevel strike zone.

Figure 1.14 The strike zones include the *(a)* lower-level, *(b)* midlevel, and *(c)* upper-level.

The upper-level strike zone is at shoulder level or higher. Usually a ball hit from this strike zone is hit with heavy topspin or a higher trajectory. In today's game, a common offensive strategy is to step back from a high-bouncing shot to let it come down farther into the preferred strike zone so the player can answer with an effective shot. Players from earlier generations may have scoffed at this idea; they would have taken this ball earlier to prevent giving up court position. Ultimately, though, a player's goal when hitting in the upper-level strike zone is to execute a quality shot that gives a better opportunity on the next shot.

The mid-level strike zone is between the shoulder and the knee (as is the strike zone in baseball), and it is used for shots with a rallying type trajectory that gives the player depth on the shot. Because most shots can be executed well in this strike zone, players need to be able to move and play in a court position that allows them to hit as many shots as possible in it. An aggressive player who moves well can do this. An opponent who hits high-bouncing and penetrating shots to a player near the baseline can make hitting balls in the midlevel strike zone difficult because they can force a player backward in the court.

The lower-level strike zone is below the knee and down to the ground. This strike zone is usually used for a low ball from the opponent or a ball that a player is late getting in position for. It can still be aggressive if the player attacks the ball with power from the legs and takes it early. A player who perpetually hits balls in this zone is usually relegated to playing defensively. A player who tries to be aggressive from a defensive position is playing low-percentage tennis.

The strike zone depends on where a player feels most comfortable executing a shot, the depth of an opponent's shot, and the potential bounce of an opponent's shot. Players who do not like to hit high-level shots around shoulder level must learn to take the ball earlier in their preferred strike zone. The styles of play also influence strike zones. Players using aggressive baseline and all-court styles need to be able to attack from all three strike zones. Because of the nature of the transitioning style, players using the serve-and-volley style must be able to aggressively hit balls low in the strike zone because many of their shots are taken on the rise. Rallying baseline players are more comfortable hitting balls in a midlevel strike zone, and defensive players hit shots from a mid- to lower-level strike zone because of their defensive nature or poor movement to the ball.

STROKE TECHNIQUE

After choosing a grip to suit individual game style and goals, the player is ready to take a closer look at the technique needed throughout the stroke pattern. The following text breaks down the different actions that make up the phases of the forehand stroke: preparation and backswing, forward swing and contact, and follow-through. The breakdown presents the technique and chain of events for executing a successful Eastern forehand.

Two of the other forehands, semi-Western and Western, require some slight modifications to accommodate their grips but otherwise follow the same pattern. The stroke-specific modifications are noted. The fourth type of forehand, the slice forehand, can actually be executed with two different grips (Continental and Eastern, though most commonly Continental) and requires a bit more modification. The counterattacking slice approach is addressed in Playing the Forehand on page 27.

Preparation and Backswing

In the ready position (between shots), the arm is comfortably to the side with the elbow bent and placed midway between the waist and shoulders. The racket head is up and pointing slightly backward with the wrist taut. The core of the player is low and comfortable and getting ready to rotate for loading. As the ball approaches, the shoulders and trunk begin the unit turn and loading process. The player makes a half turn of the shoulders backward (see figure 1.15) for a rally ball or a quarter turn (45 degrees) for a ball hit deep or if the player is in a hurry (that is, in open stance).

As the shoulders and trunk rotate, the wrist and racket face also begin to pull backward and loop in a high-to-low fashion. The player must comfortably bend the elbow behind the body to allow a fluid full swing that loops under the ball to create the desired low-to-high movement (see figure 1.16). The racket head is up and the face of the racket is outward. The racket should set in the same direction of the back leg that is loading for the shot.

As the shoulders and racket pull back, the front arm goes forward to provide balance and to track the oncoming ball. How far in front to pull the arm depends on the player's comfort and balance. The arm can be held out straight in front or a little farther back, but no farther than the potential contact point. At the same time, the player's weight starts to shift easily backward; the back leg bends. The player should keep the body weight toward the back foot and with the knees bent until the loop begins.

Players should experiment with the grip to find the proper amount of loading for the legs. They should find a comfortable core position that provides the desired power and topspin. It is helpful to think of the load in terms of how much power and topspin the player is trying to generate. Too much loading of the legs followed by an upward unloading of the legs creates topspin and not as much power. Loading lightly on the legs to push upward and outward to the target area produces a more powerful shot.

Figure 1.15   Unit turn.

Figure 1.16   Preparation and backswing.

COACHING POINTS

The following problems are common in the forehand preparation and backswing, and players should work to avoid them:

- **Overrotation.** Overrotation issues occur when a player competes against an opponent who hits hard or high-bouncing deep shots. Overrotation can cause mistimed or late contact shots. A lack of timing or a late contact reduces the power a player can generate and may cause the player to shank the ball. Players should be careful not to overrotate the hips and shoulders or have the racket set behind the back.

- **Poor front arm position.** A front arm positioned too far back causes a player to contact the ball late and be improperly balanced backward. Another problem, which coaches call *dead arm*, happens when a player prematurely drops the arm before contact or does not use the arm at all, leaving it to dangle next to the body.

- **Two-part backswing.** In this situation, a player sets the racket in a quarter turn initially until the ball bounces and then brings it all the way back to a half turn while preparing to swing. When players make the early preparation and then make another preparation farther back, they hit the shot with a late contact point.

Semi-Western Forehand Modifications

- This grip usually functions better with an open stance. The open stance allows the arm to swing more freely through the shot.

- As the racket is taken back, the racket head should tilt backward slightly more than with the Eastern grip. Because of the laid-back position of the racket, the wrist lays back slightly more than with the Eastern grip.

- The player needs good trunk rotation and loading of the legs (weight is back, the feet are set, and ready to move forward), but because this grip turns the racket face farther down, a little more load of the legs is needed to come under and hit the ball squarely.

Western Forehand Modifications

- Because the wrist lies back far in this grip, the elbow comes in line with the wrist. The elbow can hamper a fully extended swing, thus reducing power.

- The Western grip reduces power, so the trunk rotation and loading of the legs needs to be more pronounced than even the semi-Western grip.

- The stance for this shot is more open than the open stance used with the semi-Western grip. With this grip, the player needs more room to properly swing through the ball.

Forward Swing and Contact

As the trunk rotates forward, the arm starts to extend in a low-to-high fashion out toward the oncoming ball. The size of the loop the player can take while swinging depends on the oncoming ball. A deep ball requires a quicker takeback, a smaller loop, and perhaps initially a lower preparation of the arm. A slow-paced ball allows for a full or longer takeback with a bigger loop and possibly a higher-set position. On a slower-paced shot, the player has the opportunity to time the loop to gain maximum acceleration.

As the racket is prepared on the backswing, the player starts to transfer the body weight from the back leg to the front leg, using the back leg to push forward and transfer evenly and fluidly to the front leg and eventually the front toe. Performing the loading drills in chapter 3 can help keep the weight back and provide a stronger base to more effectively push off the back foot onto the front foot.

The path of the swing is dictated by the position of the elbow, so it is important to keep it bent comfortably at the beginning of the loop (elbow a few inches lower than 90 degrees) and straighten as the swing progresses toward contact (see figure 1.17). If the elbow is positioned properly, the path of the racket head starts to lead the elbow and the racket face starts to square up to the oncoming ball.

The front arm has been comfortably taut in the location of the preparation phase throughout the backswing, but as the player rotates the body forward, the front arm starts to pull away naturally with a little tension in the arm. The front arm pull-away is smooth, not abrupt or jerky, and should be at or near waist level of the player.

The manner in which the racket arm is extended upward and toward the shot depends on the particular grip, stance, and loop of the player and the type of shot the player is trying to hit. A flat ball has a straighter trajectory, and a heavier-topspin or loopier ball has a higher trajectory. The swing should be natural and fluid.

Just before contact, the wrist and racket head begin to accelerate upward and outward to square up to the ball. An attacking contact point should be slightly in front of the front foot at the level of the oncoming ball, slightly behind (or farther back) for a rallying shot, and even farther back for a defensive shot or shot hit in a more open stance. The player's head remains still and focused on the ball through contact as shown in figure 1.18.

CRITICAL CUE:

Players should focus the eyes slightly before the contact point and use it as a guide for when to swing the racket head powerfully.

Figure 1.17 Forward swing.

Figure 1.18 Contact point.

Semi-Western Forehand Modifications

- The forward swing is slightly more upward to catch the shot squarely on the racket head.
- Because the grip turns the racket head farther down, the wrist must generate more acceleration in order to get brush on the ball. The contact point is slightly behind the front foot of the player, allowing for the racket head to stay through the contact a little longer, which will impart topspin on the ball.
- The legs come from a more loaded position and explode upward, holding the weight as long as possible.

Western Forehand Modifications

- An open stance is used, and the legs uncoil from a more pronounced loaded position than with the semi-Western forehand.
- Because of the severity of the grip, the racket head must come from a lower position and sweep under to hit the ball squarely. The arm extends out farther and sweeps from an even lower to higher path to generate power. The elbow is closer to the body because of the laid-back wrist, so the pathway of the swing flows closer to the body than with the semi-Western and Eastern grips. Because of the extra topspin imparted on the ball, this modification uses the rally point of contact and the mid- and upper-level strike zones.
- The elbow eventually extends, but it is in line with the wrist as the loop begins its forward swing and extends outward after contact.

Follow-Through

After contact, the arm and racket head keep extending out toward the intended target until the racket head starts to go toward the opposite shoulder (see figure 1.19). The height of the ball dictates the follow-through. Hitting a higher oncoming ball means the player is likely to follow through with the racket head lower on or near the opposite shoulder. A flatter oncoming ball brings the racket head higher up.

Figure 1.19 Follow-through.

COACHING POINTS

Rafael Nadal has perfected a new follow-through that goes straight up and finishes on the same side as the defensive point of contact. This follow-through is known as the *reverse forehand*. This is a very advanced follow-through for imparting extra spin on the ball, and it is particular to Nadal's swing. Beginners should use the follow-through that ends up over the opposite shoulder and then experiment with lower follow-throughs as they advance.

The wrist is in line with the elbow, allowing the racket face to extend upward and outward. The proper extension and flow of the arm determines the depth and power of the shot.

The trunk rotation continues throughout the shot. It is what drives the racket head and it concludes when the follow-through is complete. The player should hold the follow-through for a split second to complete the swing.

Semi-Western Forehand Modifications

- The player should try to keep wrist cocked a little longer on the follow-through and then flip or snap it with the focus on the thumb turning over.

- The weight transfer is not from backward to forward as with the closed stance. The open stance used with the semi-Western grip requires a weight transfer to a front foot that is turned open (or facing the opponent). The weight should transfer with the hips turning toward the target in a balanced fashion. Transferring too fast or too much toward the open leg causes flaws in the mechanics of the stroke.

- The finish is out in front and should settle toward the opposite shoulder but slightly lower than with the Eastern grip.

Western Forehand Modifications

- The main points of the Western forehand are discussed in the semi-Western section.

- Because the grip is so turned over, the player can't help but feel the elbow becoming involved with the swing on this grip. The elbow does jut out, but the player should still try to lead with the racket head. This can cause some issues for the elbow, so players should monitor their swing closely.

- The follow-through usually ends across or slightly above the waist of the opposite side of the body. Because of the lower preparation, the follow-through is extended higher, and the arm is extended to just above waist level or slightly higher.

SPINS AND LOCATION

Forehands can use topspin ranging from no spin to extreme topspin (high and heavy), and they can place the ball short, deep, angled, and down the line. Using the different spins and placements can develop the forehand into an all-around weapon. As already mentioned, the different grips correspond to differing degrees of difficulty in executing the various forehand techniques. The following text presents the techniques required for maximizing the player's range and effectiveness across the various spins and court placements of the ball.

Flat or No Spin

To hit a flat ball, the player must find the proper wrist position that squares up the racket head. This differs among players' swings and how they use their legs, but the goal is to have the arm and wrist in position behind the ball to extend the wrist out straight forward at contact. Good use of pushing off from the legs provides the depth on the shot. Because of the position of the semi-Western and Western grips, the wrist would have to lie back accordingly to get the correct racket head placement. The player should feel as if he or she is throwing the wrist out toward the shot. It should feel as if that wrist is going through the ball.

CRITICAL CUE:

To produce the optimal swing path, players should imagine hitting through three balls instead of just hitting one.

Topspin

To hit topspin on a shot, the player brings the racket head underneath the ball (visualize the top of the racket head when the racket head is at the side of the body) and brush up on the ball with acceleration; the racket head extends and the wrist turns at the same time. The player uses the legs to come under the ball and aid in the brushing up of the ball. How the racket face strikes the ball determines how much power and topspin will be on the shot. A slight closing of the racket face produces some additional topspin but it is not a major contributor to topspin, although it is commonly mistaken as one. It helps for the player to envision the ball hitting the top of the racket head with the thumb turning over rapidly during the hit. The swing path of the racket contributes to topspin by going upward to brush the back of the ball for topspin and going outward for power. The modern-day forehand has a slightly closed racket face and is swung outward and upward.

High and Heavy Topspin

This shot is similar to the topspin shot but it creates a higher trajectory, or arc, that combines power and topspin. Greater emphasis is on leg strength going upward for this shot. The player wants to sweep under the ball and extend the arm and wrist outward and upward. To create arc, the player must stay balanced a little longer, strike the ball upward, and brush the ball with the racquet face.

Backspin, Sidespin, and Underspin

Players can add variety to their game by adding backspin, sidespin, and underspin to their shots. The trajectory for the backspin shot is usually higher because it is meant to barely go over the net and bounce back toward the net. A player creates backspin by using a severe slice—a very strong high-to-low movement of the arm. The player has balanced forward momentum up to contact and then the arm cuts down on the shot with the racket face open and staying open past contact. The body stays balanced to provide stability for the swing.

Sidespin is used when a player tries to get a ball to go or slide away from the opponent. Sidespin should be hit with a lower trajectory. A player creates sidespin by using the same movement as on a blocked approach shot (see page 134), but instead of using only slightly higher-to-lower arm movement, the player uses the wrists to open the racket face and push the racket head out in an inside-out fashion. The player keeps the momentum forward after contact.

An underspin shot is a slice. This ball is meant to cut but, depending on the strength of the shot, it stays low and makes the opponent hit up. The racket head is slightly open and should be directly behind or slightly above the pathway of the ball. The player moves through the shot with balance and contacts the ball with the racket head coming down on the shot and slowing or stopping immediately after contact. The player should keep the momentum forward after contact.

Crosscourt

The contact point for a crosscourt shot is in front of the front foot (the attack point of contact). The player should square up the racket head to encourage the feeling of hitting straight through the ball. It may help to imagine slightly contacting the outside of the ball. The wrists snap across the outside of the ball. The player should focus on the thumb creating an arc through the ball with proper extension. This ball is hit flat or with topspin and is meant to land in two main areas of the court: deep—2 to 3 feet (0.6 to 0.9 m) from the baseline and alley, or midway between the baseline and service line on the outside third of the court. The hips also rotate toward the target area, not too quickly, but smoothly and with acceleration.

CRITICAL CUE: Because this shot is hit with such force upward, the players should imagine their bodies and feet leaving their shoes.

Down the Line

The player aims to contact the ball later in the rally contact point. The body positions itself with the shoulders slightly squared to the net. They are slightly less squared for a ball hit from a crosscourt shot and more squared from a ball hit from a down-the-line shot. The player extends the arm out toward the target with the body flowing in the same direction. The front toe of the player should turn toward the down-the-line target. This shot should be hit with the feeling of coming around the outside of the ball (or the contact point).

Deep

To hit an area deep in the court—2 to 3 feet (0.6 to 0.9 m) from the baseline, the player extends the arm out to the intended target. The swing depends on the coordination of the arm, wrist acceleration, and follow-through. The emphasis is on extension and keeping the arm extending outward until it finishes the swing. The body and swing weight of the racket is used to help extend the arm, which is the reason movement and weight loading is so emphasized.

Short

When a player hits the ball short—on or near the service line, the player should focus on an extension to the target but might use a more accelerated wrist snap to hit topspin that will bring the shot in before the alley. The player uses a shorter backswing and then extends out and across the body on the finish. The wrist snaps down on higher balls in upper-level and high midlevel strike zones.

COACHING POINTS

If players have trouble hitting to any of the following specific locations, a number of troubleshooting tips can help.

- **Hitting crosscourt.** A crosscourt shot that goes wide may mean the player came around too fast, turned the hips too soon, or caught the ball too far in front and on the outside. A ball hit toward the middle signifies a late contact point, hitting on the inside of the ball, or improper body position.

- **Hitting down the line.** If the ball is consistently being hit wide, the player should adjust the feet or the contact point. The player may be late getting prepared and with the contact. When a ball is hit out or past the baseline, it usually signifies that the ball was not hit with the proper amount of topspin or arc. It could also mean the stroke was not completed.

- **Hitting deep.** Balls hit too deep (past the baseline) usually indicate too much power and not enough spin, improper body position, or a miscalculation of arc and trajectory. Other possible problems include having the racket face too open on contact or loose strings on the racket. When balls consistently land too deep, players should first check their footwork and then add more topspin to their shots.

- **Hitting short.** Balls that land short indicate a few possible problems: The body was not in proper position to execute the shot, the player lifted the head during contact to cause a weaker shot, the player mistimed the shot, or the player miscalculated the arc or trajectory needed for the shot.

PLAYING THE FOREHAND

All players want to be able to hit great forehands in any situation. To approach that level, they need to be aware of their own performance and work to improve it. It is important for players to understand the strengths and weaknesses in their forehand to help decide what types of shots and strategies to use. A good forehand is a weapon, a rally ball, a shot that is hit aggressively to help set up other shots, and a defensive tool.

As previously mentioned, a player's style of play combined with the player's favorite shots dictates the shots that are best to master first. Table 1.2 shows which shots can be hit with each of the forehand techniques. Practicing and perfecting the technique with these shots helps the player hit deeper and more penetrating shots, gain control of the point, and reach higher levels. Regardless of which shots are a player's favorites, it is important to know how to hit every forehand shot because there will be a time in every match when the player must use every shot in this book.

The phase of play during a game affects how a player plays the forehand. Anywhere in the court from the baseline to the net, a player may need to be in an offensive, transitional, rallying, counterattacking, or defensive mode. Combining these phases of play with a combination of locations, spins, and tactics gives a player many options to construct and win the point. A player has five shot options for playing the forehand: a putaway, an attack, a rally, a counterattack, and a defensive shot. In the putaway phase, the player is hitting a winner. With an attack shot, the player is setting up to finish the point or put it away. A rally is for neutral shots. With a counterattack a player is in a defensive situation but manages to go on the offensive. The defensive shot is for getting out of trouble.

Table 1.2 Technique for Forehand Shots

Forehand shots	Type of technique			
	Eastern	**Semi-Western**	**Western**	**Continental***
Forehand crosscourt drive	X	X	X	
High, heavy crosscourt and down-the-line shot	X	X	X	
Down-the-line forehand drive	X	X	X	
Short-angled forehand crosscourt	X	X	X	X
Inside-out forehand	X	X	X	
Inside-in forehand	X	X	X	
High-to-low forehand	X	X	X	
Reverse forehand	X	X	X	
Stretched-out-wide forehand	X	X		X
Moonball forehand	X	X		X
Counterattacking slice approach	X			X

*Although hitting some groundstrokes with the Continental grip is possible, doing so will not help players develop their game.

Offensive Forehand Shots

Generally it is better to be on offense than defense. Playing offensively is advantageous because it allows for more options, which can help the player take control of the court. Offensive forehands are hit from the backcourt with one of two goals in mind: to end the point with a winner or to put an opponent on defense or out of position with the depth and placement of the shot. A player's best offense is attacking with the forehand in various ways. The following text describes all the different shots that should be in each player's arsenal.

Forehand Crosscourt Drive

Maria Sharapova makes it look easy when she drives her opponent deep into the corner with her flat crosscourt forehand. Her strategy is to drive the ball hard crosscourt with little topspin, getting her opponent to either make an error or simply back up in the court. This allows Sharapova the opportunity to step in and control the court.

How The forehand drive is hit in an open stance with the Eastern grip for a potentially flatter ball and the semi-Western grip for more built-in topspin. How open the stance is, depends on the player's positioning. The crosscourt flat shot requires the attack contact point and the midlevel strike zone. This shot can be hit flat with no spin or with spin and some arc to the ball (topspin that makes a shot get up and down quickly and gets off the court). Acceleration of the racket head and the arm still goes from low to high but extends outward just before contact.

Where Because of the degree of difficulty associated with this shot, the player should try it only when prepared and properly behind the ball. Being behind the ball means that body movement to the ball and racket preparation is efficient and proper, so the player is balanced enough to execute the shot. Poor execution can lead to errors and a loss of control of the shot. The crosscourt drive is usually executed when a player is standing between 2 feet (0.6 m) to the right or left of the hash mark and the alley. When positioned outside the alley, the player should hit the ball higher to allow recovery time. The player should aim for the far corner on the opposite side (the box behind the service line and in front of the baseline), and the trajectory over the net should be lower but still carry to the deep part of the court.

When A player usually hits this shot when in a position of strength. A forehand crosscourt drive can be a weapon that pushes an opponent deep in the court and helps set up the player's game style. One of the most common strategies of a strong crosscourt drive is to look for a weak reply and attack down the line to end the point, help transition to the net, or play strategically.

The player's position affects the timing of the shot. Usually, the player is positioned near the baseline or inside the baseline and anywhere within 4 feet (1.3 m) in from both sidelines. This position can vary for each player; it depends on how effective the player's drive is.

High, Heavy Crosscourt and Down-the-Line Shot

Caroline Wozniacki has an effective high, heavy shot that she uses strategically. Wozniacki is fast and moves well around the court, but the high, heavy topspin forehand gives her time to reset and push an opponent back. This shot is not built for power, but more as a good use of variety.

How Players can hit this shot with an Eastern, semi-Western, or Western grip. Because of the height the shot creates, the player must get under the ball more, so the player's loading ability is emphasized. Executed effectively, this shot gives the opponent a higher arcing ball with extra spin that feels heavy and difficult to control. The trajectory of the shot requires the hips to explode upward and outward and the legs to drive up under the ball. A player that loads too much on the shot requires extra effort to be fluid on the swing. The ideal strike zones for this shot are the lower-level and midlevel strike zones. The best points of contact are the rally and defensive points of contact.

Where This shot should be hit when the player is in a technically good position to execute the shot. This shot is usually executed deeper in the court or behind the baseline and on a higher-bouncing ball. Because the high, heavy ball is a high-percentage shot and has more loft, it is an ideal shot to execute from a deeper or wider position on the court.

This shot is meant to land deep crosscourt or down-the-line (behind the service line and before the baseline) and bounce higher in the court. Sometimes a player with heavy topspin can get away with hitting a shorter-landing high, heavy shot because the bounce is so great. A poorly executed high, heavy shot that lands short could spell trouble for the player if the opponent is adept at taking the ball on the rise or has an effective down-the-line shot.

When Players usually hit this shot for offensive purposes, but they can use it for defensive purposes also. Currently Rafael Nadal is the best at this shot, and he frequently uses it when up in the score to create weaker responses from his opponents. Because this shot is hit with a higher trajectory than the drive, the bounce is higher. This forces an opponent to choose whether to hit the ball while standing close to the baseline or move back in the court to hit it in the midlevel strike zone. In the first option, the ball will land in the opponent's upper-level strike zone, and most players don't like to hit this type of reply. In the second option, the player has more time to set up the next attacking shot because the opponent has backed up to meet the looping ball in the midlevel or lower-level strike zone. Either option is likely to cause a weak reply, giving the attacker the opportunity to continue offensively in the rally.

Down-the-Line Forehand Drive

Venus Williams is known for her down-the-line forehand drive. She can effectively change the ball's direction to her advantage. When she is in a crosscourt rally, she constantly looks for a down-the-line forehand she can rip and then transition forward.

How Players use the usual groundstroke grips for this shot, and it is in the midlevel strike zone. The contact point is one to two ball widths behind the flat drive, but it is still considered an attacking point of contact. The player charges in the direction of the oncoming crosscourt or diagonal shot, which requires waiting to meet the ball slightly later in the attack point of contact to take the ball up the line. The player's movement is also slightly different from hitting the flat drive because on this shot, the front toe is turned slightly in the direction of the down-the-line shot.

Where As a drive, this shot should be hit between the service line and the baseline. A down-the-line drive hit short of the baseline can cause errors if hit with underspin or backspin. The end location of the shot depends on what the player is trying to accomplish in the rally. A shot hit to the sideline is meant to end the rally. For a player changing the direction of the oncoming shot, a ball hit farther away (2 to 4 feet, or 0.6 to 1.3 m) from the sideline is desired in order to establish a favorable pattern in a rally (such as a down-the-line drive that the opponent answers with a crosscourt to the player's stronger side) or because the opponent's weakness is on that side.

When This shot functions as a weapon that hits to the open court to take advantage of an opponent's weak crosscourt shot or poor movement, or as part of a strategy to dictate play by keeping the opponent running. Most down-the-line shots are hit in an effort to change or end the point. This shot develops when the player has backed up an opponent in the court, the opponent has hit a weaker crosscourt shot, and the player wants to end the point with an aggressive down-the-line shot to open the court or to change the pattern of the rally.

The degree of difficulty for this shot is greater than for many other shots because a down-the-line shot goes over the higher part of the net and because the distance of the shot must be shorter than a crosscourt shot. Additionally, changing the direction of an oncoming ball is tough. A player should hit this shot when receiving a short or slow ball or when the player is so far off the court that this is the last option.

Forehand Crosscourt Short-Angled Shot

Serena Williams has an attacking game that uses the forehand crosscourt short angle to open up the court so she can get her opponent on the defensive and attack to her advantage.

How   This shot is hit with topspin, slice, sidespin, or no spin. The topspin shot is more common and aggressive; the slice, flat, and sidespin shots are more for finesse. The contact point of the angled shot varies. If the player is creating the angle, the contact point is slightly in front of the crosscourt flat drive (attack). If the player is reacting to an angle, the contact point is later than that of the down-the-line shot because the player has extra movement for this shot and is trying to create a greater angle (rally to defensive). The height of the contact point is in the mid- to lower-level strike zones. Throughout this shot the player must have good balance and early racket head preparation. The player must also have greater racket head acceleration in the event that a topspin shot on or near the alley sideline is needed.

Where   The player hits this shot while standing on one half of the court, inside or near the baseline. The player aims to hit diagonally crosscourt, for or near the opponent's service line on the opposite side of the court.

When   The main purpose of hitting an angled shot is to pull an opponent off the court. The deeper angled shot (landing past the service line crosscourt and bouncing off the court and into the alley) and the shorter angled shot (landing crosscourt near the service line or before it) should be included as part of every game style. This shot is a good way to keep an opponent on the defensive. After a player hits either a crosscourt hard drive or a high and heavy ball and the reply is weak or hit at an angle, the player has the perfect setup for the forehand crosscourt angled shot. Most tennis rallies are played lengthwise through the court (using deep or short balls). So, a player who can use an angled shot is able to test an opponent's variety of shots, ability to angle a shot back, and movement to the ball.

The player can hit this shot more or less aggressively depending on the desired result. The more aggressive version is created from either the opponent's angled shot, allowing the player to create an angle off the reply, or from a weak ball, allowing the player to strike the ball earlier and create the desired angle. Either way, the shot is hit with a lot of topspin. The goal is to have the shot move up over the net and then drop fast with spin on the opponent's side, heading out toward the doubles alley. The less aggressive approach uses more placement and finesse when replying to an angle or creating an angle. This shot is generally effective, but especially effective—and even essential— against an opponent who does not like to move side to side or is tired after a long match.

Inside-Out Forehand

Andy Roddick has a great inside-out shot that pulls the opponent off the court so he can dictate play. The angle he creates, plus the power his game is centered on, puts his opponent on the defensive.

How The movement and execution of this shot requires practice because the player runs around the backhand and creates space between the body and the ball. The player can hit this shot in different ways, including hitting a high and heavy ball inside out, hitting a flatter ball, and hitting a sharper angle. All of these options are effective if a player can execute them effectively. The sharper-angle version is the most difficult, but it is especially effective on clay courts because they give more time to run around to the next shot.

The proper technique for the inside-out forehand starts with the player making a semicircle around the incoming ball on the backhand side. This movement can be done in a variety of ways:

- **Step-back method.** The back leg steps behind the front leg, turning the player's hips and shoulders as they begin to make a semicircle and move forward.
- **Lateral shuffles.** Similar to the step-back method, here the player does a number of lateral shuffles to cover more ground before stepping behind or in front of the body. Andre Agassi used this technique.
- **Backpedal steps.** The player simply turns and backpedals with both feet to get into position to move into the shot. Roger Federer is known for using this movement.

The stance is open or semi-open and, because the body is running around the backhand, the shot is hit in the midlevel strike zone and contacted at the rally point of contact. The arm and wrist extend, and the wrist contacts the ball in an inside-out fashion. The body maintains its balance and drives to the inside-out corner or angle.

Where The inside-out forehand is hit diagonally crosscourt. This shot should be hit from about 1 foot (0.3 m) off the center of the court to the backhand side to approximately midway between the center and the alley. The player aims for a shorter inside-out forehand to land near the service line and deeper in the court about 2 to 3 feet (0.6 to 0.9 m) from the baseline and alley.

When The main purpose of the inside-out forehand is to be able to use the forehand to the opponent's backhand. This shot is one of the most effective forehand shots used today because it can be a part of the overall inside-out, or three-quarter court strategy (mainly using the forehand to control the court or to create an angle for the next shot). This shot gives the player's game more variety than just hitting crosscourt or down the line. Many coaches teach the inside-out forehand as part of a strategy, so a player's ability to hit the shot becomes imperative. The impetus of this strategy derives from maximizing a player's forehand opportunities.

Inside-In Forehand

Roger Federer uses this inside-in shot to perfection. His movement is so smooth that he makes this sometimes difficult shot look easy. This shot, hit off a returned inside-out shot, keeps the player on the run and is also considered a winning shot.

How This shot takes a great amount of movement and is hard to hit, but with the proper technique and timing, it is one of the best attacking forehands. This shot is hit in the midlevel zone and is contacted in the attack or rally point of contact. It requires the player to get in a better position to change the direction of the ball.

Where A player usually hits this as a second shot off an opponent's weaker crosscourt reply or off an easy second serve. Similar to the location for the down-the-line shot, a player hits the inside-in shot near the sideline for a winner and farther away from the sideline to keep the opponent moving or to change a pattern. The depth of this shot determines its success. A ball hit behind the service line allows the opponent less time to respond and sets the player up to hit another forehand.

CRITICAL CUE:

Getting to the side of the ball is not good enough. The player must think, *to it and through it.*

When A well-placed inside-in forehand keeps the opponent running and on the defensive. This shot is also an aggressive shot and is meant to create an opening to advance to the net or hit a winner.

COACHING POINTS

Two problems are common with the inside-in forehand:

- **Contact timing.** If the player contacts the ball too far in front, the player's balance will be off, causing errors. Late contact also defeats the purpose of the shot: taking time away from an opponent.
- **Poor positioning.** When the player is not in a good position to strike the ball or hurries it by trying to hit too big of a shot, problems arise. The ball must be hit precisely because the player is working with a smaller court area and the shot is hit over the higher part of the net.

High-to-Low Forehand

Venus Williams uses the high-to-low forehand especially well. Her attacking style of play mandates that she hit this shot well. For her, it is the type of shot where she can move up to a ball and take it at high level of contact and still drive through the ball.

How The footwork incorporated for this shot necessitates a move forward. The ball is either at its maximum height or heading in that direction, so the player's positioning is critical. The preparation of the racket should be slightly higher to accommodate the upper-level strike zone. The player loads backward, focused on keeping the chest balanced through the shot. The player should focus on hitting straight through the ball and using an extension that starts high and finishes lower to the target because of the height of the ball. The contact point varies depending on the ball hit by the opponent, but generally it is in the upper level strike zone and in front of the front foot (attacking). On this shot, a player hits the ball straight because gravity and spin bring the ball down automatically. The follow-through goes toward just beneath the shoulder level on the opposite side of the body. This is a timing shot because the player is incorporating swing with the bounce of the ball and extending the arm out and slightly downward.

Where This shot is usually hit inside the baseline, but it could also mean a killing shot that is inside the service line. The shot is either hit to the outer thirds of the court (putaway), deep in the court (2 to 3 feet, or 0.6 to 0.9 m, from baseline and alley), or down the middle deeper (2 feet, or 0.6 m, from the baseline) to transition to net. Usually, a player hits this shot because to avoid moving backward and giving up ground in the court. The player focuses instead on taking time away from the opponent and hitting an attacking ball.

When To hit this shot, a player must be able to hit a high ball aggressively and be able to hit the high-to-low swing path. This shot is important to hit when the player feels able to take advantage of the opponent's positioning. This is a good ball to attack on when an opponent has hit crosscourt and the player wants to step up and hit it down the line. It can work as a down-the-line shot that the player wants to hit behind the opponent or crosscourt to the open court. It is a great way to go on offense and transition to the net.

Reverse Forehand

This shot has developed through the years for retaliating against deep topspin shots. Rafael Nadal has revolutionized the use of the reverse forehand. Even though he doesn't use it on every forehand, he does use it to hit an offensive ball from a defensive position in the court or when he wants to increase the intensity of his attack. He may be answering a deep ball hit by the opponent and wants to hold his ground or he is deep in the court and wants to establish offense.

How A player hits this shot with the normal groundstroke grips. The player hits with a hurried swing and focuses on accelerating the racket head quickly through the hitting zone without moving back in the court. The motion itself is a great upward thrust that brings the swing behind the head instead of out in front. The reverse forehand hit on the baseline is usually contacted in the defensive point of contact and on the rise off the ground in the lower- and midlevel strike zones. When hit from deep behind the baseline, the reverse forehand is the turbo version of the high and heavy forehand with added spin and arc.

Where This shot can be hit to any location, although it is favorable to hit it to a spot that doesn't allow the opponent to keep the player on the defensive. The fact that the player is staying near the baseline and handling a deep shot from the opponent can cause frustration, causing the opponent to go for more on the shots and make an error.

When This shot is mainly used when the opponent hits a deep ball and the player wants to counter it. Usually, the player is near the baseline and does not want to give up court positioning. The player's goal is to hold that court position and use great acceleration (topspin) to return the ball deep to the backcourt.

Defensive Forehand Shots

A defensive shot usually means a player is on the run, on the defensive, or can't hit with pace or depth, in which case a player is reacting to an opponent's shots. This is a necessary skill because defensive shots can eventually lead to more offensive shots. The stretched-out-wide forehand shot allows a player time to get back in the rally and keep the point going. The moonball forehand shot is used as a tactic to allow for more time on the recovery or to upset an impatient opponent.

Stretched-Out-Wide Forehand

This shot, also known as the squash shot, is Kim Clijsters' signature shot. It is disheartening to a player who thinks she has hit a great shot only to have Kim run over and get it back. Clijsters is good at turning the shot into an offensive shot because the shot she normally hits is well struck and well placed, thus allowing her more time for a recovery so she can get back into the point and regain court positioning.

How The best grip to use for this shot is the Continental or Eastern forehand grip—whichever gives the player the best cut at the ball. This shot looks like what it is, a desperation shot. The strength of the outside leg is of major importance because it gives the player the balance to take a good cut at the shot. The player whips the wrist and racket head to a location behind the oncoming ball. The contact point in this scenario is either in front or behind, depending on the desperation level. The player tries to swat at the ball from a high-to-low position and on the outside of the ball, making enough contact to slice the ball back into the court. The contact point is as far out as the arm will extend and wrist will allow to snap down and across the ball. The player tries to hold position as long as it takes to gain balance before recovering. The strike zone for this shot depends on the positioning of the player. When the player is on the run, the lower strike zone is usually used.

Where   Where to hit this ball depends on the player's movement and how out of position the player is in a rally. Usually, the player is in the alley hitting this shot. The location of the shot can be anywhere back in the court. It would be great if players had so much control that they could actually place this shot to a specific location, but frankly, anywhere in the court makes it a successful shot.

When   This shot is hit when a player is on the run and out of position on the court. When a player is out on a full stretch, it is sometimes easier to hit a slice forehand than a regular forehand. This slice forehand is a great defensive tool because it can surprise an opponent who thinks they have hit a winning shot, only to have it returned in an unusual manner.

Moonball Forehand

The moonball forehand by definition is a ball hit high with little or no spin. Today's professionals occasionally use it, but only when they are desperate and want to have time to recover and throw off their opponent's rhythm.

How   Players should use their usual forehand grip for potential topspin on this shot, and the Continental grip for a flatter shot. This shot is hit high into the air to any location with a flat ball or topspin ball that goes at a very high trajectory; the height is up to the player. The player essentially lifts the ball up and follows through upward. Position of the contact point on this shot is rally to defensive point of contact. It is really more of a push shot with more loft. The angle of the racket face is open. The shot is struck in the midlevel or upper-level strike zone if the player is out of position and not able to establish proper preparation, or in the lower-level strike zone if the player is desperate and getting to the ball late. This shot is meant to be pushed up and as deep as possible.

This shot is especially effective for beginners because opponents have not acquired the skills necessary to combat it. The difference between the moonball shot and the lob is that the player is in a better strategic position on the lob. The lob is hit defensively or offensively for placement and to put an opponent out of position. The moonball is more desperate and should be hit when the player can barely get to the ball.

Where   The player can hit this shot from anywhere in the court. Toward the alleys is best for defensive purposes, and in the center of the court is best for strategic purposes. The ball should land as close to the baseline as possible for full effect and to keep the opponent from hitting an easy volley or overhead.

When   This shot is used when the player is trying to get back in the court off an opponent's offensive shot. The player can also use it if an opponent doesn't know how to handle this shot and is becoming impatient with the pace. Using the moonball may upset an opponent; it is often referred to as pushing, or getting the ball back without much pace. As a player improves and competition improves too, this shot becomes less successful as a strategy.

Counterattacking Slice Approach

Though the counterattacking slice approach is an offensive shot, any good tennis player must be able to adapt to varying situations. A player may need to counterattack a ball when he or she is in trouble because the ball is too low or because, perhaps, the wind has blown the ball into the player's body. This shot is seldom used as a first choice because topspin prevails in today's game, but when a player is forced to come up with an answer, this shot can work really well.

How   This shot is hit with a Continental or Eastern forehand grip. This shot should be hit on the rise, and the backswing must be short to maximize the player's movement forward. How much time the player has to move forward dictates how far back to take the racket. The player uses a deeper takeback for more time and a shorter takeback for less time. Whenever possible, it is always best to take the ball on the rise, giving the opponent the least amount of time possible.

   To hit with a slice, the racket head should be at the level of the oncoming ball or slightly higher. The racket face is open and moves in a slight high-to-low action for more under-spin and straight through for a flatter slice. The player's stance is more closed or going toward closed as the player moves through the shot. The contact point can be anywhere from the attack to defensive point of contact. A ball hit on the rise as an approach is struck in the lower- to midlevel strike zones. The racket head continues through contact and finishes down and across the ball, thus creating underspin. For a slice that has a lot of spin on the ball, the racket head moves more down and across; for a more penetrating but flatter slice, the racket head moves slightly downward and outward. The feet adjust around the ball to achieve balance and proper striking distance. The feet continue to move through contact and toward the target.

Where   The counterattacking slice approach is usually played near the service line and is hit down the line to the open court, either deep in the court or shorter in the court to surprise an opponent, or crosscourt to wrong-foot an opponent. The shorter-approach version should be used when an opponent does not like to move forward.

When   This approach is used when a player does not have enough time to swing on the shot or is moving too fast through the ball to take a topspin swing. This type of approach is used against speedy opponents when time is of the essence. It may also be used strategically when an opponent shows a lack of skill hitting low balls or balls on the run (in the backcourt or shorter in the court). A transitioning slice forehand stays low over the net, which can help the player get better positioning at the net.

BACKHAND SKILLS

Whether it's a one-handed shot hit crosscourt, a two-handed shot ripped up the line, a flat or high and heavy shot that lands on the baseline, or a low slice that barely makes it over the net, the backhand is a beautiful shot. Players can use the backhand to hit for a winner, defend, add variety to shots, and raise the game to another level. For some, the backhand is a weapon and a stroke to build the game around; for others, it complements the forehand or provides balance.

Players can use two types of backhands: the one-handed and the two-handed backhand. Until the 1970s, the backhand was played almost exclusively with one hand. The classic one-handed backhand was among the most beautiful, delicate, and overpowering moves ever. Legends of the game such as Ken Rosewall, Stefan Edberg, and Justine Henin are all noted for their beautiful backhands and have built their games around the backhand weapon. With the success of Jimmy Connors, Tracy Austin, Chris Evert, and Björn Borg (all two-handed backhand specialists), the number of two-handed players exploded. Coaches liked the added power and greater control of using two hands instead of one. Now players are taught both styles, and the choice is theirs: the compact feel and built-in power of the two-handed backhand, or the added reach and flexibility of the one-handed backhand.

Each backhand has a distinct style, yet they both can have the same goal: to attack, to set up the player's better side, to defend. Depending on how well the player develops it, the backhand can be a great strength or major weakness. Often players learn the forehand first and neglect properly learning the nuances of the backhand. The player should focus on developing the backhand just as seriously as the forehand—playing an individual style, executing the shots within that style, and hitting them technically correctly. Players should try to develop a backhand weapon, but if that is not possible, the backhand should at least be used to complement the forehand and overall game.

This chapter discusses backhand styles, possible shots, and the grips and technique to hit them properly. Chapter 3 presents drills to bring out the best in any player's backhand.

DEVELOPING THE BACKHAND

Both the one-handed and two-handed backhands are popular and effective, yet both have their unique advantages. As discussed in chapter 1, the offensive and defensive characteristics of a player's shots determine the player's style and the shots that player masters. This same approach can be applied to the backhand.

Advantages of the one-handed backhand include the following:

- It is easier to hit with greater power.

- It is easier to reach for more shots, including out-of-reach shots and low balls.

- It is easier to hit good angles created by the topspin.

- It is easier to switch to a one-handed slice. (The one-handed slice is preferable to the two-handed version.)

Advantages of the two-handed backhand include the following:

- It is easier to use the grips because the player uses two hands.

- It is easier because two arms can more easily manage the strength needed to hit a shot.

- It is easier to hit a higher-bouncing ball and take it in on the rise.

- It is easier to disguise.

Players decide which backhand to use based on body build, foot speed, natural feel with two hands instead of one (or vice versa), and potential game style. If the player's style is more comfortable at the net, then using a one-hander may be a good option. If the player prefers to hit from the baseline, a two-handed backhand might be appropriate.

- **Build.** A player's build can make a big difference on the quality of the backhand. If the player has broad shoulders or a large frame, a one-handed backhand could be a better option because of the needed fluidity of the two-handed backhand. The movements of players with broader frames may not be as fluid as smaller players. The most important consideration, though, is the mobility (or foot speed) of the player.

- **Foot speed.** This characteristic is essential to the two-handed backhand because the player has limited reach with this shot. If either movement or speed around the court is a weakness, the one-handed backhand may be the best choice because of the extra reach the one-handed backhand provides.

- **Natural feel.** Most coaches start out teaching the two-handed backhand. If that shot is not progressing and doesn't feel natural, trying a one-handed backhand may be an option. Players should try to hit some one-handed backhands to get a sense of whether it can develop into a reliable shot. If it doesn't work, the worst-case scenario is that hitting a one-handed backhand can help the two-handed backhand either by developing a slice or getting stronger with the dominant arm on the two-handed backhand. Initially when a player tries the one-handed backhand, arm strength can be a challenge. The player may feel that the arm is not strong enough, but may like the freedom of the shot. Through repetition, the arm eventually becomes stronger.

- **Potential game style.** The player should look at the backhand with an eye toward potential. If all signs indicate that the style of play will be aggressive shots (such as serve and volley or hitting lots of slices), the player may want to consider the one-handed backhand.

BACKHAND AND STYLES OF PLAY

It is important to recognize the differences between the one-handed backhand and the two-handed backhand and how each fits into the player's style of play. Table 2.1 on page 32 summarizes this information.

- **Aggressive baseline play.** Because of the heavy groundstrokes hit in this style, most players who use this style of play would use a two-handed backhand because of the combination of control, power, and solidness of the two-handed backhand. Although the two-handed backhand fits this style best, an aggressive baseline player still needs to develop a one-handed backhanded slice and, in some cases, it is possible for a player with a powerful one-handed backhand to play with an aggressive baseline style.

- **All-court play.** The all-court player can be proficient with either the two-handed backhand or the one-handed backhand. While a few professionals in the world do have a two-handed backhand slice, most hit a one-handed backhand slice for reasons of increased range of motion and comfort.

- **Serve-and-volley style.** This style definitely leads the player to a one-handed backhand. The quickness needed to play this style would be hard to develop for a two-handed backhand player. It would be difficult to try and incorporate an extra

Table 2.1 Techniques for Styles of Play

Type of technique	Style of play				
	Aggressive baseline	**All-court**	**Serve-and-volley**	**Rallying baseline**	**Defensive baseline**
Eastern-Eastern	X	X	Rare but possible	X	X
Continental-Eastern	X	X	X	X	X
One-handed Eastern	X	X	X	X	X
One-handed wrist-behind-the-grip	X	X	Not recommended	X	X
One-handed Continental	Not recommended	Not recommended	X	Not recommended	Not recommended
One-handed backhand slice	X	X	X	X	X

arm into the swing when the player's reach is of the essence. The extra range of movement of the one-handed backhand is maximized with all the quicker movements around the net.

- **Rallying baseline play.** The rallying baseline player would lean toward a two-handed backhand because this style is based mainly on hitting groundstrokes. This player should also learn the one-handed backhand slice. This player probably hasn't developed a strong enough two-handed backhand to upgrade the game to the aggressive baseliner status.

- **Defensive play.** The defensive player probably uses both the one-handed and two-handed backhands. The main reason this player is defensive is because of court positioning, so the likely scenario is that the defensive player hits one-handed backhand slices or not very effective two-handed backhands from too far back in the court.

FOOTWORK AND BODY POSITION

Most players try hard to hit big forehands. Often that means their movements are big and therefore the backhand may be exposed. Adding power and variety to the backhand helps the player make it an effective weapon. Proper footwork and positioning are essential for doing this.

Movement

Proper movement allows the player to get into position for more balls and to be balanced while striking them. The backhand requires essentially the same movement as the forehand. The primary focus is on the outside leg and four basic moves: a step out with the outside leg for a ball landing on the baseline, a step back with the back leg for a deeper ball, a step forward with the outside leg or back leg for a short ball, and a step behind diagonally with the back leg to get out of the way of a shot or if the player has a backhand inside out (this shot is not common).

It is not advisable to run around a forehand to hit a backhand. It increases a player's court movement and makes recovering more difficult. Today's tennis is so dominated by the forehand that most players' forehands are better than their backhands. Therefore, this type of movement may not be worth the problems it could cause. It is fine for a player to take balls hit through the middle with the backhand if doing so is preferable, but crossing too far over that line means that the player better be able to hit a lot of winners with the backhand or have a tremendous inside-out backhand.

Following are key movements that are specific to the two backhand types:

- **Two-handed backhand.** A common problem for two-handed backhand movement is that at times the back leg can become underused. If a player makes a habit of properly stepping out with the outside leg to line up behind the ball, that player will always be in balance while striking the ball.

- **One-handed backhand.** Movement for the one-handed backhand is similar the two-handed backhand up until the outside leg slides out for balance. For the one-handed backhand, once the back leg has been set for loading and balance, the player steps toward the incoming ball with the front leg and swings. The step forward toward the ball provides ample power and control. A one-handed player can also hit an open-stance backhand in an effort to improve movement and recovery, but it will not create as much power as stepping forward.

  For a slice using the one-handed backhand, the movement is similar. However, the front leg may cross over or beyond the back leg a little more, especially if the player is on the run. The reach on the two-handed backhand is limited because the other arm is being used, but if a player uses a one-handed slice effectively, it can make for a very effective style of play that incorporates variety and versatility into the game.

Stances

For the backhand, players mainly use the closed stance (see figure 2.1) and the open stance (see figure 2.2 on page 34). The use of the back leg and position of the front leg dictate the stance. For a closed stance, the front leg crosses over an imaginary line drawn

Figure 2.1 Closed stance for the *(a)* one-handed and *(b)* two-handed backhand.

Figure 2.2 Open stance for the *(a)* one-handed and *(b)* two-handed backhand.

from the back leg to the front leg. For an open stance, used on wider shots, the body faces more toward the net and the back leg reaches out to the side, away from the front leg. The closed stance is predominantly used when a player has time to step into the shot. When the player is stretched or has less time, the open stance is necessary.

GRIPS

As with the forehand, backhand technique hinges on the player's grip. Two grip options exist for both the two-handed and one-handed backhands. Options for the slice backhand are also covered here. All players, no matter what type of primary backhand they use, can employ the slice backhand.

Two-Handed Backhand

For the two-handed backhand, players should pay careful attention to the use of the arms while executing a shot. The playing arm is dominant and the other arm is nondominant. So, for a right-handed player, the left arm is nondominant and for or a left-handed player, the right arm is nondominant. On the two-handed backhand, a player needs to coordinate the use of both arms by developing the use of the nondominant arm.

For most players, the main source of strength for a backhand shot is the nondominant arm. The bottom hand on the racket (the dominant arm) provides stability and extension while the top hand on the racket (nondominant arm) provides the majority of the acceleration. For these reasons, players often develop and rely on the nondominant arm more than the dominant arm. However, for a powerful shot, players must have some strength in the bottom (dominant) arm. To create more balance between the two arms on the backhand, players should hit one-handed backhands with each hand placed as it would be in the two-handed version. Hitting with each arm individually allows players to see how much power each arm contributes to their regular two-handed shot.

The two main grips used when hitting the two-handed backhand are the both-hands Eastern (or Eastern-Eastern) grip and the bottom-hand Continental and top-hand Eastern forehand (Continental-Eastern) grip. These grips allow varying degrees of power and topspin. Figures 2.3 and 2.4 show the placement of the index knuckles for right- and left-handed players. (Refer to figure 1.6 on page 5 for bevel numbers.)

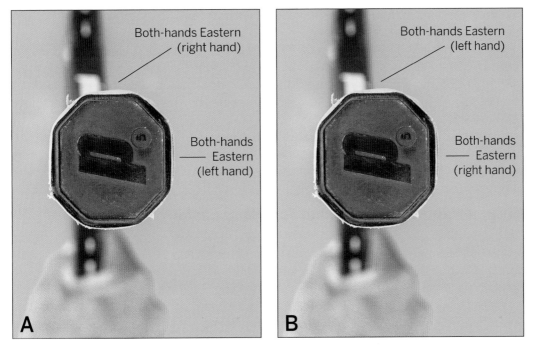

Figure 2.3 Location of the index knuckles on the racket for *(a)* right-handed players and *(b)* left-handed players using the both-hands Eastern grip.

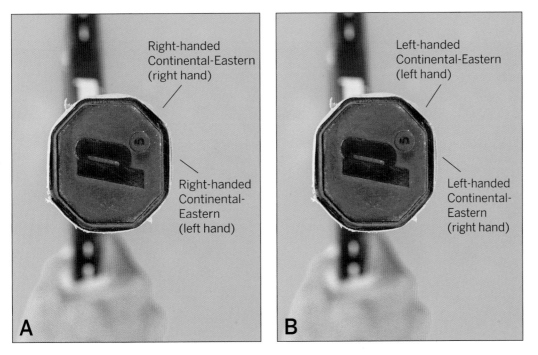

Figure 2.4 Location of the index knuckles on the racket for *(a)* right-handed players and *(b)* left-handed players using the bottom-hand Continental and top-hand Eastern forehand grip.

Both-Hands Eastern Grip

The both-hands Eastern grip is a common two-handed backhand grip. It allows the player to hit with topspin, power, or both. In this grip, the dominant hand uses the Eastern backhand grip and the nondominant hand uses the Eastern forehand grip. Right-handed players place the index knuckles of the right and left hands on bevels 1 and 7 respectively (see figure 1.6 on page 5). Left-handed players place the left hand on bevel 1 and the right hand on bevel 3 (see figure 2.5). The top hand presses against the bottom hand without the fingers intertwining.

The amount of topspin depends on the size of the loop when preparing for the shot and how well the player uses the wrists before and during the ball strike. (For more information, see Stroke Technique on page 38.) The only drawback to this grip is that it is built for topspin and thus requires wrist flexibility to square the racket head for a flatter, more powerful shot.

Any player who likes to incorporate topspin into the game can use this grip. The aggressive baseline player would definitely consider this grip. So might the all-court player with good use of the slice as well as the rallying baseline player and the defensive player.

Bottom-Hand Continental and Top-Hand Eastern Forehand Grip

For the Continental-Eastern grip, the right-handed player places the bottom (right) hand in the Continental grip and the top (left) hand in the Eastern forehand grip. The left-handed player uses Continental for the left and Eastern for the right (see figure 2.6). The hands press together without the fingers intertwining. The racket face is slightly closed.

When using this grip, the player can hit the two-handed backhand flat or with topspin. This grip does not have the added benefit of a grip already in a topspin position, so topspin must be generated with strong wrists that can hit a shot with acceleration and a strong upward thrust of the shot itself. The player can use this grip for all styles of play. It can provide the perfect balance of power and topspin needed when staying on the baseline or transitioning to the net.

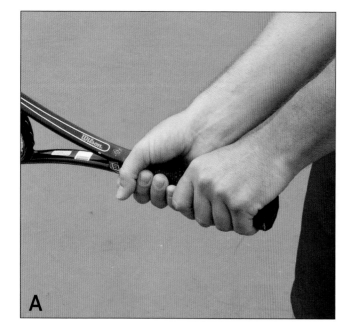

Figure 2.5 Left-handed two-handed backhand grip using the Eastern-Eastern grip.

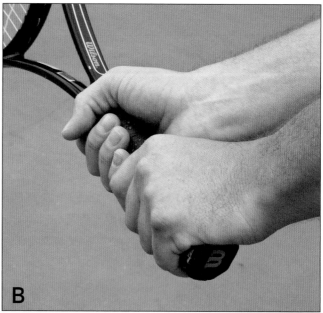

Figure 2.6 Left-handed two-handed backhand grip using the Continental-Eastern grip.

One-Handed Backhand

The two main grips for the one-handed backhand are the Eastern backhand grip and the wrist-behind-the-grip backhand grip. The Eastern backhand grip is the most popular grip used for the one-handed backhand. Roger Federer uses the Eastern backhand grip to great success. The wrist-behind-the-grip or the semi-Western backhand grip is also widely used. A player might also choose the Continental grip for the backhand, but it is rarely used today, except with the backhand slice. Figures 2.7a and 2.7b show the placement of the index knuckle for right- and left-handed players. (Refer to figure 1.6 on page 5 for bevel numbers.)

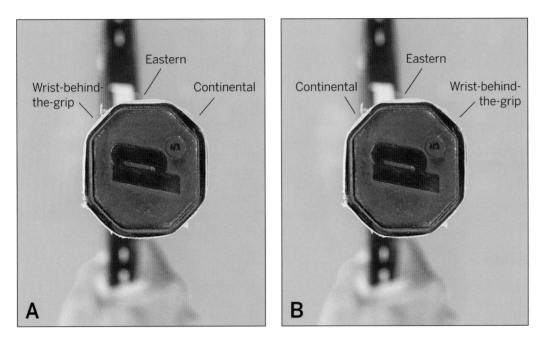

Figure 2.7 The location of the index knuckle on the racket for *(a)* right-handed players and *(b)* left-handed players using the one-handed backhand grips.

Eastern Backhand Grip

For the Eastern backhand grip (see figure 2.8), both right- and left-handed players place the index knuckle on bevel 1 of the racket handle (refer to figure 2.7a–b). If a player uses the wrist effectively and accelerates the racket head up through the ball, this grip can generate a great deal of topspin and power. The player uses the wrist to make adjustments in the spin or to flatten out the shot. When hitting a flatter shot with this grip, the player hits the shot through the ball, but with minimal wrist snap upward. Also, changing from this grip to the slice grip is relatively easy.

This type of grip is fine for all styles of play, especially an offensive style such as the aggressive baseline style. The all-court and serve-and-volley player may also use this type of grip. The rallying baseline and defensive player would most likely use the two-handed, not one-handed, backhand. A player can use this grip to hit topspin and flat shots effectively.

Figure 2.8 Left-handed eastern backhand grip for one-handed backhand.

Figure 2.9 Wrist-behind-the-grip backhand grip for the one-handed backhand.

Wrist-Behind-the-Grip Backhand Grip

The wrist-behind-the-grip backhand grip (see figure 2.9) is also known as the far-Eastern backhand grip and sometimes the semi-Western backhand grip. The right-handed player places the index knuckle on bevel 8 (the bevel just to the side of the Eastern grip but rotating the forearm to the opposite side as for the forehand; see figure 2.7a). The left-handed player places the index knuckle on bevel 2 (see figure 2.7b). This grip position squares up the racket head and builds in topspin with a straight extension of the arm. This grip is good for balls hit at normal chest height and above and taking a ball on the rise. Because the hand is turned farther on the racket, switching to the Eastern or semi-Western forehand grip is slightly more difficult.

Players can use this grip for all styles, but this backhand is a get-up-and-go grip because it uses the attack point of contact. This grip is perfect for taking balls early because of the more straight forward extension of the arm, so it makes sense that an all-court, a serve-and-volley, and to a lesser degree an aggressive baseline style player would use this grip. The rallying baseline and defensive player may want to use this grip as a good form of built-in defense, because they can use the early contact point as a means to take time away from an attacking opponent.

Slice Backhand

The slice backhand is a beautiful shot and a useful tool. Topspin shots are prevalent in the game, so possessing an effective slice sets a player apart from the rest. The slice backhand is meant to be kept low with a flat trajectory, barely go over the net, and dip down after crossing the net. Used offensively, the shot can provide variety. It can also be used as an excellent defensive shot. A player who does not move well or does not prepare adequately might overuse this shot.

The slice backhand is hit with either the Eastern forehand grip or the Continental grip. The grip players choose depends on whether they want to build in more slice to the stroke or use more wrist to produce the slice. The Continental grip requires more cut, or wrist snap, downward and requires flexible wrists. The Eastern forehand grip has more built-in underspin.

The advantage of the Eastern grip is that the player does not have to change grips when hitting an Eastern forehand followed by a backhand slice. The Eastern grip allows the player to get more slice on the ball as long as the wrist is pronated slightly downward. The Continental grip produces a flatter, more penetrating shot, and it requires less wrist pronation. The disadvantages become apparent when the player is in poor position for the shot. An Eastern forehand grip may produce too much underspin, thus causing the ball to land short, and the Continental grip may not provide the desired loft needed on the shot to get the ball over the net.

STROKE TECHNIQUE

After choosing the one-handed or two-handed backhand grip to suit preferred game style and goals, the player is ready to take a closer look at the technique needed throughout the stroke pattern. The following text breaks down the technique needed to execute each type of backhand. Each of these strokes consists of a particular preparation and backswing, forward swing and contact, and follow-through.

Two-Handed Backhand

As noted previously, the two-handed backhand combines power and topspin. To execute it successfully, players need to coordinate the movements of the arms and the body.

Preparation and Backswing

The shoulders make a half turn, or unit turn, as the racket is taken back (see figure 2.10). The elbows, arms, and racket head should be set comfortably behind the player—not too steep and not too low. The racket is about 1.5 feet (0.5 m) away from the side of the body and the wrists are slightly firm. The grip dictates how far under the shot the player will have to loop and brush up on the ball. The trunk and hips rotate backward to load properly with the legs. Just as in all shots, the back leg should load primarily to provide a platform for the swing and to provide adequate balance (see figure 2.11).

Eastern-Eastern Grip
- More brush is required for the Eastern-Eastern grip. The trunk and hips rotate backward a little more.

Continental-Eastern Grip
- This grip requires that the player square the racket head.

Forward Swing and Contact

The weight transfers forward while the racket makes a loop; the racket head dips lower for more topspin and waist high or slightly higher for a flat ball. The loop and swing pattern is also dictated by the choice of grip. As the loop takes place, the hips will rotate backward. As the hips begin to rotate forward, the wrists pronate downward to sweep under the ball, and the arms extend outward for contact and the desired brush on the ball (see figure 2.12).

Figure 2.10 Two-handed backhand unit turn.

Figure 2.11 Two-handed backhand preparation and backswing.

Figure 2.12 Two-handed backhand forward swing and contact.

The ball is hit in the mid- to lower-level strike zones. The higher-level strike zone would also require a loop and sweep under the ball for a better extension of the arms. It is preferable that the player hit the two-handed backhand in front of the front foot to allow the player to be able to eventually handle tougher balls, more easily transition to the net, and maintain an aggressive position on the court. For the swing, the player should focus on hitting through the contact zone and accelerating the racket head to create topspin or to hit a more effective ball. Shots hit later in the rally zone are hit down the line as a disguise or as a desired effective shot, or they are hit with a defensive point of contact as a disguise or as a means to produce more topspin and brush on the ball.

Eastern-Eastern Grip

- The pathway of the swing sweeps upward for topspin but more outward for drive.

- The wrists in this phase snap up during contact with equal pressure. The wrist on the nondominant arm is laid back and must snap up and on the outside of the ball to create topspin. The player should have the feeling of brushing up on the ball while hitting the shot and extending the arms out through contact in a smooth fashion under the ball.

- To achieve topspin, the player should get into a more loaded position with the knees bent before transferring the weight forward.

Continental-Eastern Grip

- The pathway for this grip is pretty flat; it has little sweep under for flatter balls and slightly more sweep under for topspin. The racket head on this grip squares up as the player hits it, so in order to create topspin, the wrists must sweep under and drive upward.

- Both wrists apply snap and pressure. The nondominant arm is slightly laid back so it can snap up more to create topspin or slightly less for a flat ball.

- No extra load is required for this shot.

Follow-Through

During this phase, the racket head continues outward as the wrists turn over. The hands finish over the other shoulder or at shoulder level (see figure 2.13). The player can hold the body position or bring the back leg forward to assist in recovery. One recent technique for making the two-handed backhand more effective is for the player to feel as though the back leg is flowing through the shot and settles in line with the front foot. From this position, the player can use that outside leg to push back toward the middle of the court for recovery.

Eastern-Eastern Grip

- On the follow-through, the arms extend outward and upward a little more to square up the racket head for the shot.

- The arms should extend out to the opposite shoulder.

- To help square up the racket head, the weight transfer is usually a little more exaggerated upward.

Continental-Eastern Grip

- The arms extend outward and, based on the shot, they are flatter if driving the ball and more upward if imparting topspin.

- To aid in acceleration, the nondominant arm accelerates upward as well.

Figure 2.13 Two-handed backhand follow-through.

One-Handed Backhand

The one-handed backhand combines power and topspin with an expanded reach for the player. Because the player uses one hand instead of two, it is likely that strength is a concern. On the other hand, the player's reach and flexibility for hitting more difficult one-handed shots can increase.

Preparation and Backswing

The player makes a unit turn (see figure 2.14), making a half turn with the shoulders. The racket is taken back comfortably behind the body (not too steep, between waist and shoulder height). The other arm aids in the takeback and holds the position. The racket head is above the wrist, and the wrist is firm. The weight transfers backward, and both legs establish preferred stance (either closed or slightly open), while loading on back leg. Today's coaches try to establish an initial back leg load to get behind the ball. This back leg load helps the player maintain some balance through the shot, especially when fewer steps are required.

The racket face is squared on the takeback (see figure 2.15). The arm is comfortably bent at the elbow, the palm is positioned down, and the hand is set level with the back leg. The strike zone for normal shots is at midlevel. For shots hit with depth and pace that require a quicker takeback area, it is toward the lower-level strike zone.

Eastern Backhand Grip

- This grip requires a preparation to loop the racket upward before going down, but it prepares the player for a slightly steeper takeback if hitting with topspin.

Wrist-Behind-the-Grip Backhand Grip

- This grip has built-in topspin, and the arm sets in the normal midlevel strike zone position as it does for the Eastern backhand. The load toward the back leg is similar.

- The main difference in the preparation is that the racket face position is squared with the use of this grip, so the preparation to sweep under the ball for added topspin is eliminated. The player may still like to load toward the back leg and thrust upward, but in that case most of the topspin is incorporated with a steeper loop and a greater snap of the wrist.

Figure 2.14 One-handed backhand unit turn.

Figure 2.15 One-handed backhand preparation and backswing.

Forward Swing and Contact

The knees bend, and the load is set with the back leg. The hips begin to rotate backward before rotating forward and starting the loop. The wrists stay firm during the loop, and the racket face should stay squared or slightly closed downward. The arm and racket face extend outward to meet the ball at the attack point of contact, in front of the front foot, and at the midlevel strike zone (see figure 2.16). To hit a ball in the lower-level strike zone requires a deeper knee bend as well as a little more loop and sweep upward. The hips rotate forward as part of the swing. The player should feel as though the hips are holding the body's balance. The hand begins to pull backward. The head stays still on impact.

Eastern Backhand Grip

- The wrist accelerates slightly upward and forward for a flat ball and more severely upward for a topspin shot.

Wrist-Behind-the-Grip Backhand Grip

- Contact is made with the racket head already square so wrist needs to slightly accelerate upward.

- The loop is not as steep as is required for the Eastern backhand grip.

Follow-Through

As the racket extends upward using acceleration, the front arm goes toward the ball, and the back arm pulls farther backward. The wrist naturally begins to turn; the backhand will hold as far back as is comfortable. A more extended back arm gives greater balance. Near the end of the follow-through the player flicks the wrists up and out toward the opposite shoulder; the thumb essentially turns over and flows through the follow-through. The follow-through is out in front, and the racket head finishes above the wrist. The finish is over the opposite shoulder (see figure 2.17).

Figure 2.16 One-handed backhand forward swing and contact.

Figure 2.17 One-handed backhand follow-through.

Eastern Backhand Grip

- The wrist snaps upward on the follow-through, and the focus is on the arm and thumb flipping over and the racket head finishing up. The player should think, thumb up.

Wrist-Behind-the-Grip Backhand Grip

- The wrist in this grip snaps more outward and the palm of the hand stays slightly down. The thumb can still turn over, but not as much.

Backhand Slice

The backhand slice is a very effective tool for staying in a rally, especially when in a vulnerable position on the court and as an important use of variety. The lower trajectory of the ball allows for greater recovery time and a tough ball for an opponent to hit.

Preparation and Backswing

The shoulders make a unit turn as the body and racket head load backward (see figure 2.18). The weight should be transferred to the back leg for balance before using the stance. The player should focus on preparing the racket slightly above the level of the oncoming ball or directly behind it. The player should use a higher racket head preparation for more slice imparted on the ball and directly move it behind for a flatter, more powerful slice. The nondominant arm provides balance by assisting in the takeback (see figure 2.19). The fingers of the nondominant hand can hold the throat of the racket on the takeback.

The hip moves backward and the proper loading occurs depending on the stance and the movement. If the player puts the front foot across the line of the back leg, the stance is closed; if the player positions the front leg in front and toward the opposite shoulder, the stance is open. The racket face is open and up over the wrist.

Eastern Forehand Grip

- This grip has built-in underspin. The outside edge of the racket head is slanted toward the player. For this grip to work, the player needs to swing straight through the shot or slightly from high to low.

Figure 2.18 Backhand slice unit turn.

Figure 2.19 Backhand slice preparation and backswing.

- To hit a more powerful flat slice, the player drives through a little more with the legs. For a slice that floats or lands short in the court, the player may load up a little more with the legs.

Forward Swing and Contact

As the body moves forward the shoulder is kept in place. The front arm begins to move in a high-to-low fashion without going too steep. The player should imagine hitting on a plate of glass: dipping down too much would break the glass. As the front arm moves forward, the back arm releases and begins to move backward (see figure 2.20). Contact is possible in all three points of contact.

Using a carioca step can help a player's execution of the backhand slice because it keeps the body balanced and the shoulders turned just before and directly after contact. To perform a carioca step, the player loads on the back leg. Immediately before contact, the back leg comes around the back of the body and sets in front of the front leg (see figure 2.21). As the shot is hit, the player must either take another carioca step behind and in front of the front foot again or pull out of the shot and recover for the next shot.

Eastern Forehand Grip

- This grip pronates or cocks backward and accelerates downward more at contact.

Continental Grip

- This grip pronates slightly less and accelerates outward more at contact.

Follow-Through

The player should try to keep the shoulder closed as long as possible, but as it does so the arm pulls to the other side of the body, and the back arm gets into a similar extended position as with the one-handed backhand (see figure 2.22).

Figure 2.20 Backhand slice forward swing and contact.

Figure 2.21 Backhand slice carioca step.

Figure 2.22 Backhand slice follow-through.

Eastern Forehand Grip
- The follow-through on the Eastern grip travels in a more high-to-low fashion, and the wrist pronates downward.

Continental Grip
- The Continental grip extends more outward in a slight high-to-low fashion.

PLAYING THE BACKHAND

So far this chapter has covered the core techniques of the two-and one-handed backhands and analyzed the natural tendencies of each one. Next, the chapter discusses the backhand shots that all players need to learn and feel comfortable hitting. All of these shots can be hit with the two- or one-handed backhand, with slight differences. Regardless of which backhand the player chooses, it is important to have confidence in the backhand and be able to hit a variety of shots with it. Weaknesses in a player's backhand shots can hinder the player's progress. The shots presented here use a variety of spins and locations on the court. (See pages 16–19 for a review of spins and placements.) Table 2.2 shows which shots can be hit with each of the backhand techniques.

Table 2.2 Technique for Backhand Shots

Backhand shots	Type of technique			
	Two-handed backhand		One-handed backhand	
	Eastern-Eastern	Continental-Eastern	Eastern	Wrist-behind-the-grip
Backhand crosscourt drive	X	X	X	X
High, heavy crosscourt shot	X	X	X	X
High, heavy backhand down the line	X	X	X	X
Down-the-line backhand drive	X	X	X	X
Short-angled backhand crosscourt	X	X	X	X
Offensive backhand slice	rare	rare	With a change to the Continental grip	With a change to the Continental grip
Defensive backhand slice			With a change to the Continental grip	With a change to the Continental grip
Moonball backhand	X	X	With a change to the Continental grip	With a change to the Continental grip

Offensive Backhand Shots

An offensive backhand is a great weapon. This shot could be a winner, a ball to use to keep the opponent running, or a shot that takes time away from the opponent. Another offensive tool using the backhand is a shot that a player hits to a specific location, hoping for a certain reply from the opponent. For example, a player might hit a backhand down the line hoping for a crosscourt reply so the player can use the forehand on the next shot. The slice can also be considered an offensive backhand, especially if it is hit with power, spin, a low trajectory, and aggressive intent. The most offensive backhand is the backhand down the line. Most players start a match assuming their opponent has a better forehand than backhand and that the opponent will use the backhand defensively. Thus, a player with a powerful and well-placed down-the-line backhand can open the court and have more options.

Offensive backhands make a big difference in a player's game. Most people try to perfect their forehands, so when a backhand is effective and becomes a strength, it can take a player to a new level. The sections that follow discuss when to hit the different options for offensive shots, where to hit them, and how to hit them. Any necessary modifications needed for the one-handed or two-handed techniques are provided.

Backhand Crosscourt Drive

Justine Henin is considered to have one of the best one-handed backhands of all time. Her ability to hit penetrating backhands deep in the court, as well as her use of angles, gives her the perfect combination to help her overall game. Maria Sharapova has one of the best two-handed flat drives on the tour. Her forehand flat crosscourt drive is also excellent, so her main groundstroking style is offensive and flat from the ground, designed to overpower an opponent.

How   The method for creating the crosscourt drive varies between the two-handed and one-handed versions.

Two-Handed Shot   The player uses the preferred stance or stance dictated by the movement to the ball. In a good position, the player can use a closed stance. When out of position, the player should use an open stance. However, a player should avoid hitting a flat crosscourt shot from a wide-open stance because, unless the player's skill is perfect, the result is a flat ball that lands short in the court, prohibiting proper recovery time and giving the opponent an easier shot.

Using one's preferred grip, the contact point of the shot is usually in the attack point of contact and the midlevel strike zone. The player is trying to drive the ball with power and depth, so it can be considered a control shot. The loop on this shot is full and the player accelerates the arms and wrists first outward and then upward for the follow-through. To produce a flat ball and maximum momentum, the angle of the racket head should be square.

One-Handed Shot   For the one-handed version, a player should use a slightly closed stance. The player should be in very good position for the shot, otherwise controlling the shot could be a problem. This shot is executed with either the Eastern backhand or wrist-behind-the-grip backhand grip. The contact point in is the attack point of contact and the midlevel strike zone. This shot can be hit flat or with more spin to give some shape to the ball, making it go up and down quickly and get off the court. Acceleration of the racket head and the arm still goes from low to high but extends outward immediately before contact.

Where   A player hitting a crosscourt drive should be between the alleys. Getting near the alleys or outside the alleys requires a high, heavy ball (see the next shot) to try to get back in the point. The optimal landing location for a crosscourt drive is between the service line and baseline, generally closer to the baseline, approximately 2 to 3 feet (0.6 to 0.9 m) from the baseline and alley. In general, the player should place the ball in any location deep in the court that pushes an opponent back in the court.

When   The appropriate time to use the backhand crosscourt drive differs for the two- and one-handed versions.

Two-Handed Shot   This shot is hit flat and deep. The goal is to get the opponent moving backward in the court, allowing the player to hit either an aggressive forehand or backhand on the next ball. The player can accomplish this with power or a flat, deep ball.

One-Handed Shot   The one-handed backhand player uses the crosscourt backhand for two reasons. The shot can be hit when an opponent has hit a weak shot down the line and wants to use the backhand to be aggressive with the crosscourt shot. It can also be used to set up the forehand by hitting a deep backhand that gives the player enough time to get around the next backhand.

High, Heavy Backhand Crosscourt

A high, heavy backhand is a topspin shot that bounces high and is difficult for the opponent to retrieve. Rafael Nadal uses the high, heavy backhand to push an opponent back in the court, allowing more time for him to recover and hit his forehand. The high, heavy backhand crosscourt is one of his most effective shots.

How   The two- and one-handed versions are hit the same way. A player executes the high, heavy backhand crosscourt by trying to get under the ball with as much power as possible to hit up on the ball. The ball feels heavy (the reason for the name) as the opponent receives it. The contact point for this shot is in the rally point of contact and in either the mid- to upper-level strike zone.

   The high, heavy backhand crosscourt can be hit from an offensive position or a defensive position on the court.

Where   This shot can be used strategically when the player isn't comfortable hitting a flat crosscourt drive and is in an offensive position on the court (midway between the center hash mark and the alley) or in a defensive position on the court (behind the baseline or in the alleys). This shot is hit deep in the court (midway between the service line and the baseline or near the baseline) and to mainly the outer thirds of the court or possibly to the middle. This shot is hit strategically to push an opponent back in the court or to give a player more time for recovery.

When   This shot usually has an opponent reaching up to strike the ball, which is effective if that opponent is short or doesn't like hitting balls with a higher strike zone. This shot also allows the player more time to run around the backhand to hit a forehand, if that is the player's preferred style. This shot is hit when a player is on the run and trying to play a safer shot or when a player wants to push an opponent backward and gain time to recover or to create an angle for the forehand.

High, Heavy Backhand Down the Line

Justine Henin uses a one-handed backhand to hit this shot. It is extremely valuable to her game because it keeps her opponent on the defensive long enough for her to hit a more angled backhand or an aggressive forehand.

How   This shot requires a preparation with more load in the legs, and it is hit with a lot of topspin and a high trajectory. This ball is meant to bounce high and out of the opponent's strike zone. It is a great setup shot to hit before transitioning to the net. The contact point for this shot is normally in the rally point of contact and the mid- to upper-level strike zone.

Two-Handed Shot Both the Eastern-Eastern grip and the Continental-Eastern grip can execute this shot. A player using the Eastern-Eastern grip will have to extend slightly more outward to provide power and depth. The Continental-Eastern grip requires a little more wrist snap upward to create more topspin on this shot. This shot is played with a closed stance if the player is in good position or slightly open if not in a good position or if this is the player's preferred stance.

One-Handed Shot Both the Eastern backhand and wrist-behind-the-grip backhand grip can execute this shot. The Eastern backhand grip requires more wrist snap and loading of the legs to hit this shot high and heavy. The wrist-behind-the-grip backhand grip requires more loft and extension outward. This shot is hit with a slightly closed stance and hit with loft and power generated from substantial leg loading and upward swing.

Where This ball should land deep in the court behind the service line and before the baseline, but it has the added benefit of possibly landing short and jumping up on a player to accomplish the same objective as the flat drive.

When The goal of this shot is twofold: get the opponent to hit crosscourt to the player's better, more aggressive shot (a backhand hit down the line high and heavy may make an opponent go crosscourt where the player can establish control of the point) and hit a ball that allows the player to recover or get in a better position for the next shot.

Two-Handed Shot The player hits this shot when on the run in the backcourt, near the baseline, and trying to play a safer shot or push an opponent backward to gain ample time to recover. It is used strategically to an opponent's weakness or to have the opponent hit back to the player's strength. It may also be used if the player has a weak crosscourt shot.

One-Handed Shot The shot is hit when the player is in a favorable position in the court (midway between the center hash mark and alley). If on the run, the player may want to use the slice backhand. Either way, the goal is the same: push the opponent back in order to recover and hit a more aggressive shot.

Down-the-Line-Backhand Drive

The down-the-line backhand drive is one of the most beautiful displays of power and finesse in the game. Serena Williams has a powerful down-the-line backhand drive. Opponents constantly look for this shot to come, and they are fearful of hitting a shorter ball that she can get behind and unload on the shot.

How The player can use a preferred backhand grip for this shot. To hit this shot successfully, the player needs to be inside the baseline, thus in a more offensive position. This grip is used with a closed stance or a slightly open stance if out of position. A player makes contact at the rally point of contact and the midlevel strike zone, but this shot's contact point is one ball later than the crosscourt shot and is driven for power.

Two-Handed Shot This shot requires good body preparation because the shot changes the direction of the oncoming shot, the player has a smaller area to work with when hitting up the line, and the wrist snap is out toward the outside of the shot. The big toe on the lead foot points toward the target.

One-Handed Shot This version is effective, but the one-handed player must be very skilled to accomplish the same result as the two-handed player. For the two-handed player, the extra arm provides more control, allowing time to turn or close the shoulders more, and the wrist must snap toward the outside of the shot. The one-handed player needs greater control and must extend the arm outward upon contact. The big toe on the lead foot points toward the target.

Where   This shot is hit deep in the court to anywhere between the service line and baseline. The player should aim to place the shot 2 feet (0.6 m) from the alley for a winner and 2 to 4 feet (0.6 to 1.3 m) from the alley when changing the pattern. This shot should be from a position either midway between the center hash mark and the alley to almost in the alley. The down-the-line-backhand hit from the alley would have to be exceptional to recover in time for the next ball.

When   This power shot should be hit when the player is in great position and trying to hit a winner or keep the opponent running. It is also an effective way to change the direction of the oncoming ball or to break up or change the rhythm of the point; in other words, the player hits down the line to have the opponent hit crosscourt to the player's better side. The success of this shot relates directly to the player's positioning and the timing of the contact point (slightly later than with the crosscourt drive), so it is important to be in good position for it.

Short-Angled Backhand Crosscourt

Jo Wilfried Tsonga effectively uses the one-handed version of this shot. His goal is to pull the player out of position on the backhand side so he can do more with his forehand, his weapon. Andy Murray uses the two-handed version effectively; he uses his speed around the court to look for opportunities given to him off this shot.

How   The main grip for this shot is the player's usual backhand grip. This shot is usually hit with an open stance. The player can hit this shot earlier if trying to roll it crosscourt or slightly later to get into a more loaded position to hit with more topspin.

Two-Handed Shot   The two-handed, short-angled backhand crosscourt shot is hit with a rally contact point in either the low- or midlevel strike zones. The angle of the racket head is slightly toward the outside of the shot and is dictated by the wrist snap. The player extends the arms outward—but not as far out as the crosscourt drive—and rolls over the wrists in a more accelerated fashion to get the ball to cross the net and then dip downward.

One-Handed Shot   The execution of the one-handed version is similar to that of the two-handed version, but the player needs a strong and flexible wrist to perform this shot. The shot uses any of the contact points, and it is hit at the midlevel to lower-level strike zone. Though it is possible for a player to hit the two-handed version of this shot successfully from a bad position, the one-handed version must be hit in an optimal position and with great skill. The player extends outward, and the wrist snap dictates the dip after crossing the net.

Where   The player should aim for the service line crosscourt toward the alley. The goal is for the ball to bounce away from the opponent or through the alley and off the court, making the opponent run or hit a defensive shot. This goal is accomplished with a lot of topspin and great acceleration of the racket head. In order to hit this angle shot, the position of the player on the court should be midway between the center hash mark and the alley or farther out toward the alley.

When   This shot is used to pull an opponent off the court and as a lead-in to other shots. It challenges an opponent's ability to run and to hit while off balance. It also challenges the opponent's perspective because the ball must be hit either close in the alley or outside the alley. The player's best opportunity to hit a short-angled backhand crosscourt is as a reply to an opponent's short-angled shot. Another short-angled backhand shot is created off a short or weaker ball. The player moves up aggressively and takes the ball more in the attack point of contact and creates another angled shot.

The shorter angle with a rally or defensive contact point is used to counter and create a greater angle from the opponent. The shorter angle hit from an attack contact point is used strategically to wrong-foot or put an opponent on the defensive. Both shots are effective and, if used properly, can cause real headaches for the opponent, giving the player an easy next ball.

Offensive Backhand Slice

Samantha Stosur uses this shot effectively. She uses her backhand slice to complement her good kick serve. Combining variety with a shot (kick serve) that pushes her opponent back in the court, she can use a backhand slice (low ball). This tactic is a great way to confuse an opponent.

How This shot is hit with one hand. The arm extends out from a slightly high-to-low position. The best grip for the offensive backhand slice is the Continental or slightly Eastern forehand grip. This shot should be hit with a closed stance or a slightly open stance. A player can also slide into this shot with balance. An offensive backhand slice is designed to stay low and needs a lot of power. The player should use the attack point of contact and move through the ball more aggressively with a carioca step. The strike zone is mainly in the midlevel strike zone and the path of the racket is straighter and more directly through the ball. The offensive slice has a little less underspin than the defensive version.

Where This shot is hit from anywhere in the court from the center hash mark to the alley. A player can hit this shot crosscourt to keep the opponent from getting in good position on the shot (a form of defense) or hit it down the line to keep the opponent running or change the pattern to better suit the player. The player can try to have the ball land deep in the court to push an opponent back in the court, or slightly lower and shorter crosscourt if the player doesn't more forward very well. The player should hit the down-the-line version low, but with a little carry so that the player can recover for a more aggressive shot. This offensive shot can be hit toward the line; the defensive version can be hit farther toward the middle of the court (midway between the alley and center).

When The offensive backhand slice is a very effective shot. It results in a low ball that can change the opponents' rhythm, put the opponent on the defensive, or induce fatigue or errors. A shot that stays low is valuable because an opponent may not like hitting low balls. This could be because the opponent just doesn't move that well, is big in stature and has trouble getting low enough, or has a severe grip that doesn't allow effectively playing that shot. Most offensive shots are hit with topspin, so an offensive slice can frustrate an opponent. It can lead the opponent to try to change the variety of shots. These unexpected changes can sometimes make the difference in gaining offense.

Defensive Backhand Shots

Players are forced to use the defensive backhand when their contact point is late or when they don't properly recover after a shot. Defensive backhands are also designed to mix up an opponent's rhythm or to get a player out of trouble and recover for the next shot. The proper execution of these shots dictates whether the player stays on defense or can shift to a more offensive position. Strategically, the player can hit the defensive backhand in a location that gets the opponent to answer with a shot to the player's strength, such as the player's forehand.

Defensive Backhand Slice

Fernando Verdasco uses the defensive backhand slice to get out of trouble and keep the ball low, allowing him more time to recover and set up for the forehand.

How   This one-handed shot uses a closed stance, but if the player gets to it late or if it is the player's preferred style, a more open stance can work successfully. Using a Continental or slightly Eastern forehand grip, the player takes the ball behind the back leg in the defensive contact point; the player usually is on the run or moving backward. The ball is met in the mid- to lower-level strike zones. The angle of the racket face is similar to the angle for the offensive backhand slice, but greater emphasis is on keeping the body balanced through the shot. To keep the ball low, the player must extend through the ball with a slicing motion in a high-to-low fashion. The player can visualize the slice being executed on a horizontal sheet of glass: cut too low and the glass breaks, extend through and the glass stays intact.

The technique differs from the offensive backhand slice because the latter shot is usually hit while the player moves forward for an attack. When hitting the defensive slice the player is just trying to keep it low and get out of trouble. The carioca step may not be used on the defensive backhand slice. Usually, the player is on the run and is not able to bring the back leg around through contact.

Where   This shot is hit anywhere in the court, but preferably to the opponent's weaker side or angled away from the opponent.

When   This shot is hit when the player is on a dead run, the player is getting pulled out of position, or the player's aggressive backhand is not that strong. When a player gets on a dead run, sometimes the only chance to stay in the point is to hit a defensive slice. The player tries to surprise an opponent into an error with speed, tenacity, or an unbelievable shot. This shot can also be used to mix things up and make the opponent work just a little harder by keeping the shot low.

Moonball Backhand

This shot is not used often in the professional game unless the player is totally out of position and just trying to get enough time to recover for the overhead that is surely coming on the next ball. This shot is much more effective in league play where the execution of the shot is erratic or not as powerful. Played against poor overheads, the moonball backhand can be used offensively.

How   This shot is usually hit with one hand because the player is on defense and doesn't have the reach with the other arm. For this reason, players should learn the one-handed version. For the two-handed version, a player extends the arms out as far as possible and uses a push stroke.

The grip for this shot depends on court positioning. On the run, a player may be able to hit this shot with only a Continental grip. Otherwise, the player's usual grip can be used. The stance is usually open and on the run. The goal is to hit this shot high in order to recover quickly. The racket face must be open. The contact point for this shot is defensive, and the ball is hit in the lower-level strike zone.

Where   The player can hit this shot from anywhere in the court to keep the rally going. Your best possible location is in the middle so that no angle is created.

When   This is a defensive shot, but it can cause problems for some opponents. The shot is hit high in the air when the player is on a dead run and totally out of position on the court. The goal is for the player to get back in the court and try to stay in the point. This shot can cause problems for an opponent who is impatient and may get frustrated having to hit one more ball, an opponent who is not adept at taking a ball out of the air and attacking, or an opponent who does not like high balls and has to move back in the court to hit the shot. The difference between this shot and a lob is that this shot is played higher and less offensively.

FOREHAND AND BACKHAND DRILLS

The ball controls of an effective forehand or backhand are acceleration (for power and offense), accuracy (for control of shots), consistency (for making shots repeatedly), and variety (for the ability to hit various types of shots, including defensive shots). To achieve these qualities, players should focus on the fundamentals. The fundamentals include focusing on movement and balance as a player hits the ball, which are covered in chapters 1 and 2. This chapter helps players make acceleration, accuracy, consistency, and variety an integral part of their game, and it helps players maximize the effectiveness of the forehand and backhand. The qualities of effective forehands and backhands are discussed next.

- **Acceleration.** Acceleration is how the player creates racket head speed and momentum through shots—using the legs and extending the dominant arm before and after contact and through the follow-through. The acceleration adds power and spin to the player's shots. For example, a player hits a ball with topspin and it bounces out of the opponent's strike zone, keeping the opponent off balance; now the player can play the preferred style more easily. Groundstrokes today are designed for power and for hitting an opponent off the court. How well a player strikes the ball can be directly related to how well the player ultimately plays, so hitting shots with good acceleration is an important goal. Accelerating the racket head helps the player create a shot that is both smooth and powerful and a shot that is overpowering.

- **Accuracy.** Shot accuracy relates directly to skill level. The ability to place the ball where it is intended to go gives players confidence and separates them from their peers. Achieving this command of their strokes takes great skill and technique, and it is invaluable to players developing a style of their own. Players need to have a good vision of how they should play (their own game style) to advance to higher levels of play. When players begin thinking more strategically about what shots they will need as part of that style, their accuracy becomes even more important.

  Knowing how and when to hit shots that land deep in the court, shots that are angled shorter or deeper, and short shots that fit within a player's game style gives the player a huge advantage. It is also the difference between playing an offensive shot to effectively finish off a point and hitting a defensive shot that merely keeps a rally going. Every tennis player should think with this attention to detail.

- **Consistency.** Consistency and accuracy go hand in hand. A consistent player can accurately place shots where intended and can rely on those shots for the duration of a match. A consistent player can alternately be a *grinder*, which means the player gets a lot of balls in play, as well as a player that performs at a high level day in and day out.

  Consistency is the model for every tennis player. As a player develops strengths and shores up weaknesses, consistency develops. Good coaches try developing a player's skill first, and then help them become more consistent with that new skill. A long-term plan of development and consistency results in improvement throughout a player's career.

- **Variety.** It is important that players develop weapons, such as a forehand or backhand, and also add variety to their game. When players possess good offensive and defensive shots, variety can become a weapon. A forehand that can overpower an opponent or slice backhand that can serve as a defensive shot are good examples of how variety can be a valuable tool, even a weapon. Players must learn the shots associated with their preferred style of play. Then, as play improves, they can add a variety of shots to enhance that style.

  Variety in shot selection can disguise weaknesses, throw off an opponent's rhythm, and affect both the player's and opponent's confidence. Picture an opponent who doesn't know what is coming next and struggles because of the variety of shots the player possesses. Being able to execute a good lob at an opportune

Drilling With the Backboard

Many of the drills in this chapter offer a solo variation that can be practiced on a backboard. This strategy is helpful for players without a practice partner or coach. It is also good for players who want to get in some extra practice on their own. The backboard is an excellent tool for stroke development because the ball is always coming back at the player, which helps establish a rhythm from the ball just hit against the backboard. The following are tips for successful backboard drilling.

- **Setting the aim.** To start, the player stands 12 feet (3.7 m) from the wall and aims for the middle of the backboard in an area above the net line (if the wall has a net line and target areas painted on it). If no lines or targets exist the player can visualize them. Moving forward and backward in this area gives the player different bounces and different trajectories, so the player should be challenged to work on technique in the different areas.

- **Determining the trajectory.** To begin with, players should use higher, heavier shots that have a high trajectory to give the ball loft. Focus on loading underneath the shot and producing topspin to give the ball proper loft. A flatter ball produces a bounce with less loft, causing the player to have to move more. A ball hit flat against a backboard comes back flat and fast, so players should use flatter balls with greater depth when they practice backcourt grooving drills.

- **Using repetition.** An effective way to practice grooving drills on a backboard is to focus on a certain number of repetitions (e.g., 10, 20, 30, 100) on the forehand or backhand side. This type of repetitive drilling sets the stage for developing consistency (hitting shot after shot), acceleration (hitting with spin and trajectory), accuracy (location of the shot provides a higher bounce to maintain repetitions), and variety of shots (slice, flat shots).

moment and being able to hit a slice that confuses an opponent are powerful tools. Variety in shots is also helpful for recovering back in the court. Players should predominately hit shots that allow for a quick recovery and allow them to play more aggressively.

As players progress, they should work daily on acceleration, consistency, accuracy, and variety. The drills in this chapter help the player zero in on specific ways to improve these skills. A complete player concentrates on improving weaknesses, but also works to perfect strengths, too. Noting the player's strengths and weaknesses in these skills during practice is a good way to develop strong work habits. Ultimately the player should incorporate the objectives of practices into the game plan. (See chapter 10 for more on game plans.)

The following progression of drills works through the identified characteristics for a great groundstroke. The drills start from basic and progress to advanced. They first work on consistency of the core techniques and then expand the playing area with movement, speed, and depth of shot. They progress into drills for learning and fine tuning the different shots and finally drills that mimic match play. To be the best player possible, it is mandatory that the player learn all the proper technique shots and styles in a progressive fashion.

1. Grooving drills to warm up and ingrain the fundamental core techniques

2. Movement drills to work on footwork and balance

3. Acceleration drills to work on hitting through the zone for increased topspin and power

4. Specific shot drills to work on consistency, accuracy, and variety

5. Live ball drills to work on shot recognition and match play skills

GROOVING DRILLS

The goal of grooving drills is to practice the basics of the game and to prepare for more complex and intense practice. These partner drills are effective for both the forehand and backhand and can be practiced in two ways:

1. **Short court.** These drills are for preparation and execution.

2. **Backcourt.** These drills are for overall technique and movement.

Alternatively, the backboard can be used to groove strokes, as directed in the solo variations of the following drills. The straight-ahead short court and backcourt drills are best for backboard drilling because the bounce off the board is straight back as opposed to angled, allowing for easier grooving.

Using the backboard for crosscourt drilling is predominately for more advanced players and for working on speed, movement, and desperation shots. Because of the low trajectory of the flat crosscourt shot, the bounce off the wall is lower and angled outward, requiring hustle to the next shot. The easiest shot for working on crosscourt is a high, heavy shot. The bounce off the wall is higher and allows more time for proper recovery and the ability to groove the shot.

Whether drilling with the backboard or with a partner or coach, it is important to focus on preparation. One way to do so is by playing the call-out game. This technique works with any of the drills in this chapter, but is especially beneficial to practice during the grooving drills.

CALL-OUT GAME

Purpose: Identify and practice early preparation for the correct stroke.

Procedure: The player watches the opponent's racket and shot, and then calls out *forehand* or *backhand* as soon as possible. The player should try to be fast at this and pick up the nuances of the opponent's strokes. The player should notice whether the opponent takes the ball early or late and consider what the opponent's grip suggests about the type of game the opponent has.

Variation: The player calls out the shot and then freezes in position. While frozen, the player should check that his position is the correct preparation for the oncoming ball.

Short Court Grooving Drills

A great deal of tennis players warm up with short court drills. This type of warm-up is designed to help check technique, warm up the body, test different grips, and generally get a feel for the racket. Three short court drills can help in grooving the game. The first drill is done straight ahead, the second drill is done diagonally, and the third is a point situation. All these drills set the player up for later drilling, so the player should master these first, equally using the forehand and backhand.

STRAIGHT-AHEAD SHORT COURT

Purpose: To practice preparation and execution technique.

Procedure: Both players start at the service line. Keeping the ball inside the service box, they rally back and forth lightly, becoming progressively more aggressive depending on the level or intensity of the practice. The players focus on different grips and stances to test variety, a strong first step to the ball (foot closest to the ball first on all shots), and proper stroke execution. The focus here is on technique, not power.

Coaching points: The players should focus on one technique component at a time, starting with grip, then movement and stances, and finally on the technique desired for the different phases of the swing (preparation, forward swing and contact, and follow-through).

Solo variation: Grooving this drill on a backboard is a great tool for warming up. The player stands about 5 feet (1.5 m) away and at first hits the ball softly with a high trajectory to establish a rhythm and to work on technique. When warmed up, the player moves back 2 feet (0.6 m) at a time and begins to flatten out the shot, progressing toward a normal groundstroke. The player continues to move back to a maximum of 10 feet (3 m), which produces a deeper-bouncing ball. The player works on greater acceleration from a deep location by hitting this ball harder. Standing closer than 10 feet (3 m) and hitting the ball harder produces a quicker shot and forces a player to have a quicker preparation and acceleration.

DIAGONAL SHORT COURT

Purpose: To practice preparation and execution technique as well as movement, acceleration, and accuracy of location.

Procedure: The drill is the same as the Straight-Ahead Short Court drill, except players rally crosscourt. They should make sure the ball lands in front of the service line.

Coaching points: In this drill, the player tries to make contact while brushing the outside of the ball. This crosscourt rally focuses on the accuracy and acceleration needed to hit the ball to a specific location within the service box.

Solo variation: To groove crosscourt strokes off a backboard, the player uses a high trajectory to allow time to run to a shot and get into the desired position to hit crosscourt. The player stands about 6 to 10 feet (1.8 to 3 m) in front of the backboard. The player alternates hitting forehands and backhands crosscourt, and the ball returns off the wall either straight or down the line.

CRITICAL CUE:
The player should be sure to line up and load the foot closest to the ball first before contact.

COMPETITIVE SHORT COURT

Purpose: To create a competitive situation, testing movement, strategy, and execution at an accelerated pace.

Procedure: Players compete for points using only the short court area. They should use regular tennis scoring and play a set or points to 11, 15, or 21.

Coaching points: Using and covering both boxes emphasizes an accelerated version of normal backcourt rallies, so this is a perfect time to check and practice strategies. To be successful in this drill, good strategy, movement, touch, and the ability to spin or shape the ball are needed. This is a fun but challenging game. Players should use the opportunity to work on developing a little touch.

Backcourt Grooving Drills

These drills are universal to most warms-ups. In addition to helping groove strokes, they help develop the basis for a player's game style. Performing these drills with an emphasis on not missing a shot, recovering properly, and being in position for each ball, helps the player's focus and intensity.

STRAIGHT-AHEAD BACKCOURT

Purpose: To lengthen strokes and add more power.

Procedure: Players rally from the baseline or move progressively to the backcourt by moving back step by step. They hit down the middle and focus on perfect technique and movement while adding length on the shot. Players should pay attention to the execution and resulting length of the shots, while experimenting with hitting flatter and adding more spin, to get the desired depth.

Coaching points: Players can improve their focus by zeroing in on the ball and trying not to be out of position for any shot. They should focus for a fixed time and recognize when fatigue or loss of focus occurs. Timing how long a player can focus allows for gradually and systematically increasing this ability for longer periods.

Solo variation: The player stands 15 feet (4.6 m) away from the board and hits flat balls to work on forward movement and high, lofty shots to work on backward movement. The amount of forward and backward movement depends on the pace of the shot, so the player should use a variety of speeds to work on different amounts of movement. If a player is unable to sustain a rally using flatter shots, shots with higher loft can be used to start, and then the flatter ball can be slowly incorporated.

CROSSCOURT BACKCOURT

Purpose: To incorporate movement, accuracy, and variety from the back-court while hitting to a specific spot on the court.

Procedure: Players rally crosscourt. They should set goals for depth and placement, zero in on hitting to a specific area, such as past the service line and before the baseline, and then broaden the hitting area by using the alleys.

Coaching points: This drill can test a variety of shots because each player must adapt to the shot hit by the other and counter with the best shot to stay in the rally.

CRITICAL CUE:

For each shot, the player recovers back to the center and prepares for the next shot. Accelerating through the shot provides more depth and time for recovery.

RELEASE TECHNIQUE DRILL

Purpose: To work on stroke extension. This technique can be implemented with any of the backcourt grooving drills.

Procedure: As two players rally, each player, after making contact with the ball, practices the follow-through by releasing the racket gently into the other hand at the end of the extension.

Coaching points: On the forehand side, the nondominant arm catches the racket. The player should experience a stretch in the back of the shoulders while swinging upward and outward, pausing for a brief second after each hit. The racket should be in the opposite hand in front of the body with the butt cap facing toward the net and the other player (see figure 3.1). This drill exaggerates the follow-through to help highlight the use of the arms at full extension.

Figure 3.1 Proper release position.

HANDCUFF DRILL

Purpose: To check for overrotation. During the preparation and subsequent swing, a common mistake on the backswing is to overrotate and take the racket too far back.

Procedure: A great method to correct overrotation tendencies is for the player to grab the playing arm on the forearm or higher (sort of like wearing handcuffs) with the nondominant hand on the forehand side and keep this position while playing. On the backhand side, the player places the index finger of the nondominant hand on the strings of the racket when preparing for a one-handed shot. This helps to increase sensory awareness of where the racket head is letting go as the racket is swung forward to meet the ball. The same may be done with a two-handed shot, and then the hand slides down on the handle.

MOVEMENT DRILLS

Movement is a huge key to success in tennis, so it is imperative to include movement drills among the list of must-do's when practicing. Efficiency in movement has always been recognized as essential to hitting good shots. The most elite players practice the following types of drills daily.

1. **Loading step drills.** Players practice stepping into the ball using the forehand and backhand.

2. **Specific movement drills.** Players practice proper movement to the ball and proper recovery, whether moving side to side or moving backward and forward. Drills should be practiced using the forehand and backhand.

3. **Combination movement drills.** Players practice maintaining good movement through a combination of shots with the forehand and backhand.

All of these types of drills give heightened awareness to proper movement throughout a point or to a specific shot. Plus, each drill has many variations to make it specific to one shot or one movement, and it can be executed in combination with different shots or different movements. These drills are technical in nature and invaluable to develop and succeed as a tennis player, so players should strive for proficiency in all of them.

It is common to find the drills difficult to master if the movements are quite different from the player's already established movement patterns. Most players are unaware of using inefficient movement because developing a shot in spite of bad movement is possible. They should experiment with these drills to improve the shot by incorporating efficient movement. Players can perform each drill using the forehand or backhand.

SOLO VARIATIONS FOR THE LOADING STEP AND SPECIFIC MOVEMENT DRILLS

Players can also use the backboard to work on the loading step and specific movement drills. (For the combination movement drills, specific instructions for solo variations are provided within each drill.) Initially, the player can practice the loading step drills with slower-paced shots within a smaller area of the short court (within 5 feet, or about 1.6 m), and then speed up the pace of the shots and move back deeper in the court (10 to 15 feet, or about 3 to 5 m). The player should practice the specific movement drills from this deeper position in the court, too. When comfortably warmed up for either type of drill, the player can start counting repetitions (10, 20, 30 . . .) to work toward a specific goal.

Loading Step Drills

CRITICAL CUE:

Players should picture the middle instep of the foot closest to the ball landing in the pathway of the oncoming ball.

Loading step drills are important for practicing getting the foot closest to the ball lined up and loaded to transfer the body weight into the shot. Incorporating this first step is difficult and does throw off players' timing if they have been doing it incorrectly, but players should practice and carefully implement this first move.

For each of the following loading step drills, the drilling player should be on the baseline at the center hash mark, and the partner or coach should be in the middle of the court at the service line or a couple of feet (0.6 m) toward the baseline. The partner or coach feeds balls by throwing them like rally balls, using a similar pace and trajectory for each ball. For more advanced players, a racket feed may work better. The pace of the feeds should allow enough time for the drilling player to recover back to the original position prior to receiving the next ball. The drilling player should incorporate a split step before the partner feeds the next ball.

ALTERNATING OPEN AND CLOSED STANCE

Purpose: To achieve a full transfer of weight and power when hitting shots in open and closed stances.

Procedure: The coach or partner feeds balls with varying degrees of difficulty that require the player to take only one or two steps of sideways or forward movement to reach the ball. To practice a closed-stance groundstroke, the player takes two steps: one step out to line up the foot closest to the ball and then a step forward to the incoming ball to transfer weight from the lined-up position. To practice the first step and open stance, the player takes only one step out with the foot closest to the ball and loads that leg, hitting from an open stance. The first step should be a strong yet comfortable step—the player should remember to visualize having the ball hit the middle instep of the foot stepping out.

Coaching points: **The player should put full weight on the leg lining up on the ball. To check weight placement and balance, a player can line up on the incoming ball and then, just prior to contact, lift the other (front) leg. The player should hold the leg up for one count before placing it back down. An inability to keep the leg up indicates imbalance. A player who predominately uses the front leg feels as though the back leg is weak during this exercise, but continued practice leads to improved balance.**

> **CRITICAL CUE:**
> Players who prematurely step away from the path of the ball just hit should try to stay balanced longer on the leg they just finished hitting on. This requires good use of core strength and trunk rotation.

BACK LOADING STEP

Purpose: To achieve a full transfer of weight and power when stepping backward to return a ball hit deep.

Procedure: The first move is diagonally backward with the foot that the player is trying to line up with the ball. The step is strong, and the emphasis is on loading the leg. The coach or partner must feed high and deep balls to force the backward step. The feeder should throw (or hit, if needed) at different speeds to incorporate all the possible shots in a match and target the player's upper-level strike zone.

Coaching points: **Players can check for loading and balance by lifting the front leg to make sure the weight is transferred fully back before moving forward to hit the ball.**

Specific Movement Drills

Specific movement drills are designed to teach players exactly what steps to take to a shot. Moving to a ball correctly affects speed around the court and subsequent recovery to get in good position for the next shot. The goal is to be efficient with all movement and to run in a balanced fashion. For the specific movement drills, the drilling player should be positioned on the baseline at the center hash mark, and the partner or coach should be in the middle of the court at the service line. The partner or coach drills with eight balls and feeds the balls by hand or by racket, depending on the level of the player. The pace of the feeds should allow enough time for the drilling player to recover and split step just before receiving the next ball.

FORWARD MOVEMENT

Purpose: To improve footwork to a ball hit inside the baseline and toward the service line.

Procedure: The partner or coach feeds the balls with varying degrees of difficulty so that the drilling player must take more than two steps forward to hit the ball. Tosses can range from just in front of the baseline to all the way inside the service line. The drilling player runs forward quickly and turns sideways a couple steps before striking the ball. The player should focus on turning the body and shuffling forward, being careful to not cross the legs. Then, the player strikes the ball and recovers quickly back to the baseline.

Variation: The partner or coach can push the drilling player back with a deep feed and then throw a ball near the service line. The drilling player hits the first ball off the back leg and then runs forward and makes the adjustment turn just before hitting the shorter ball off the front leg.

SIDE MOVEMENT

Purpose: To incorporate efficient lateral movement needed in a rallying situation and an efficient recovery.

Procedure: The coach or partner feeds balls toward the alley so that the drilling player must move 3 to 5 feet (0.9 to 1.5 m) laterally to hit the ball. The tosses should include balls that are slightly diagonal forward and backward. On the toss, the drilling player immediately pivots with the outside foot, moving first toward the shot. Then, the player takes as many crossover steps as needed before sliding the outside foot out toward the oncoming ball for an open-stance groundstroke. If time allows, the player may step in for a closed-stance stroke.

Coaching points: Players should focus on a big, strong first step because it is more efficient and creates better balance at the end of the shot.

BACKWARD MOVEMENT

Purpose: To improve the backward footwork needed to get behind a deep ball.

Procedure: The coach or partner feeds the balls deep to force the drilling player to move backward beyond the baseline and take multiple steps to get behind the ball. The drilling player takes a big first step backward and then incorporates a crossover step before setting the back leg, keeping the hips facing forward. The player should then pivot the hips in preparation for hitting the ball and recover by thrusting the back leg forward quickly to move back into the court in preparation for the next ball.

Coaching points: To prevent the hips from turning, the player can visualize a piece of tape on the chest that should remain visible until pivoting the hips. The player should focus on stepping in a diagonal direction backward, followed by a crossover step and another drop step to avoid the tendency to get too close to the oncoming ball and have to make extra moves to adjust.

Combination Movement Drills

Combination movement drills simulate real match play situations and maximize the movement for each shot. The drilling player is positioned on the baseline at the center hash mark, and the partner or coach is positioned in the middle of the court at the service line. Eight balls are fed by hand or racket depending on the level of the player, and the pace of the feeds should allow enough time for recovery to the center and a split step just before receiving the next ball.

SIDE-TO-SIDE MOVEMENT

Purpose: To maximize side-to-side movement and to simulate a live ball rally.

Procedure: The coach or partner feeds balls that require the drilling player to move 3 feet (0.9 m) or more to the side. The tosses should vary the amount of movement to the side and should alternate between requiring forehand and backhand shots from the player. The player hits the ball either crosscourt or down the line, depending on the area of focus. The player makes a quick hip turn for recovery toward the center of the court by using a crossover step and taking a split step to prepare for the next ball.

Coaching points: The player should start the hip turn for recovery when making contact with the ball and continue it until the completion of the groundstroke. By rotating the body more fully, the hips and shoulders face the net, saving the player additional steps on the recovery.

Solo variation: The player hits crosscourt so the ball returns down the line. The player starts 8 to 12 feet (2.4 to 3.6 m) from the backboard to work on smaller movement ranges and progresses to 15 feet (4.6 m) or more to cover a larger area of court and use a greater range of combinations.

BACKWARD-TO-FORWARD MOVEMENT

Purpose: To maximize forward and backward movement and to simulate a live ball rally.

Procedure: Starting with a deep feed, the coach or partner alternates tossing short and deep balls that require the player to move 3 feet (0.9 m) or more forward or backward. Throughout the drill, the feeder should vary the amount of movement needed. The player should start hitting crosscourt and then later switch to down the line. On the first toss, the player moves back with a strong first step and shuffles as needed to get behind the ball, loading onto the back leg. After making the shot, the player split steps and runs quickly forward to get the next ball.

Coaching points: The player should avoid turning the hips in the movement leading up to striking the ball. Instead, the player should make a slight hip turn at the end of the stroke to speed up recovery for the next ball.

Solo variation: The player starts 8 to 12 feet (2.4 to 3.6 m) from the backboard to work on smaller movement ranges and progress to 15 feet (4.6 m) or more to cover a larger area of court and use a greater range of combinations. To work on forward and backward movement, the player alternates hitting a high ball with loft (for a deep ball and backward movement) with a harder, flatter ball with a low trajectory (for a short ball and forward movement).

INSIDE-OUT FOREHAND MOVEMENT

Purpose: To practice the inside-out forehand movement pattern. This shot is used widely in today's game.

Procedure: The coach or partner feeds balls toward the player's body, forcing the player to move out of the way and set up behind the ball. The player needs to create space to rip the ball. The player should focus on using a drop step back diagonally and turning the shoulders during the preparation.

Solo variation: The player focuses on moving around each ball to hit the ball inside out against the backboard. Off the wall, the ball returns straight and the player must run over and hit the next forehand crosscourt to set up the run around forehand again.

RANDOM MOVEMENT

Purpose: To practice all movements in a live game simulation, to practice different movement combinations, and to emphasize the proper use of the split step.

Procedure: The coach or partner is positioned on the forehand or backhand side of the court and feeds balls to random locations on the court, allowing the player enough time between shots to recover. The player hits each shot back to the coach, recovers back to the middle of the court on the baseline, split steps, and responds to the next ball. The player should do repetitions hitting everything to the forehand side and then the backhand side of the court.

Solo variation: The player starts 8 to 12 feet (2.4 to 3.6 m) from the backboard to work on smaller movement ranges and progresses to 15 feet (4.6 m) or more to cover a larger area of court.

ACCELERATION DRILLS

One of the successful traits of a good forehand or backhand is acceleration. The speed of the racket head through the contact of a shot produces acceleration. Good acceleration of the racket head adds weight to a shot. From start to finish, the swing should be fluid, without hitches in a player's racket preparation. Players can practice each of the drills in this section using either the forehand or the backhand.

Keep in mind the following tips for performing the acceleration drills:

- The player should load the back leg to set the stage for a continued swing through the shot and then push from the back leg to the front leg in conjunction with the swing.

- The elbow should be close to the body for power and stability. The player should focus on the swing path coming closer to the body as the dominant arm loops down to swing up and forward and extends toward the follow-through.

- The player should imagine the area 2 to 4 inches (about 5 to 10 cm) before the contact point as the acceleration zone and swing aggressively upward through this zone, trying to hit with the top of the strings.

- The player should throw the racket arm toward the target, making sure that the racket head comes through first, followed by the elbow. The elbow coming through first is often seen with a more Western grip, but this approach should generally be avoided.

- If not in use, the nondominant arm should provide balance. The player holds the arm comfortably in front or to the side in preparation and gradually pulls away or to the side upon contact.

- The player needs to follow through, visualizing hitting through the ball, with the goal of extending the arm outward and finishing to maximize the effect on the shot. For most players this means finishing on the opposite side of the body anywhere from waist level to shoulder level. The most common finish is around the opposite shoulder, depending on the stroke, but it is important to experiment with different finishes to find the one that produces the most power. The finishing movement needs to be strong, consistent, and a smooth continuation of the swing path.

Recently, advanced level players have started trying to finish around the chest on the opposite shoulder. Rafael Nadal, however, has tweaked the formula and changed modern tennis with the acceleration he gets by swinging up and staying on the same side. The massive amount of topspin that he puts on the ball makes this swing effective; players should try adding it to their game.

SOLO VARIATIONS FOR ACCELERATION DRILLS

The backboard is a great tool for working on acceleration, but players need to modify the pace of shots. Because hard-hit balls come back hard and fast, sustaining a rally can be difficult. Players should stand 10 feet (about 3 m) from the backboard and use slower-paced shots initially to see the differences in the depth and pace of the shot coming back, then gradually begin to add pace, adapting movement accordingly.

Another way to practice acceleration is to self-feed a bucket of balls. The player drops balls lightly, alternating landings slightly in front, behind, and to the side of the body. Once warmed up, the player lightly throws the balls a little farther away to incorporate movement. The player can initially work on the swing and acceleration down the line, then start to hit crosscourt and angles to see the differences between each shot. This solo variation can also be part of the practice court warm-up before a match to prepare the body for maximum acceleration right away.

BASIC ACCELERATION DRILL

Purpose: To develop racket head acceleration through strokes. Players should do this drill at the beginning of each practice.

Procedure: The player stands 5 feet (1.5 m) from the net near the middle or slightly to the side of the shot being drilled. The coach or partner is on the opposite side and close to the net. About every 2 seconds, the feeder tosses balls diagonally, approximately 2 feet (0.6 m) to the front and side of the stroke being drilled. The player hits up on the ball as fast as possible while extending the racket head and arm toward the shot. The player focuses on hitting up through the attack point of contact with as much force as possible.

Coaching points: The goal for this drill is to hit with force and depth, producing a ball with a lot of topspin and a low trajectory (as low as the player can hit without hitting the ball into the net). The player should experiment with different trajectories to see which one produces the deepest shot. Signs of a good stroke include a ball that lands near the baseline (just outside works for this drill) with shape and moves quickly through the court.

Variation: To check extension, the player uses the technique of releasing the racket described in the Release Technique Drill (see page 59).

CRITICAL CUE:

Pay attention to preparatory technique. The player must load the arm (preparation loop) and body (balanced with weight predominantly on the back leg) to maximize acceleration and extension of the racket head and arm toward the ball.

SWINGING VOLLEY DRILL

Purpose: To develop or improve swing or stroke mechanics with acceleration. A properly hit swinging volley (that lands near the baseline) requires a full swing and proper trunk rotation. This is the same technique needed for groundstrokes. Taking the ball out of the air simulates a ball off a bounce, allowing the player to practice the swing needed to create or counter power. The extension needed to perform this drill successfully, naturally improves swing mechanics.

Procedure: The player stands on the center hash mark of the baseline. The coach or partner feeds ball diagonally with loft into the upper to mid strike zone: toward the shoulder and approximately 2 to 3 feet (0.6 to 0.9 m) to the side of the swing path. The feeds should allow the player time to recover and get in good position for the next swing. The player sets the outside foot and swings fully, hitting the ball out of the air and focusing on the elements of good acceleration throughout the shot. The loft of the feed causes the player to hit under the ball, using topspin to give the ball some shape and keep it in the court. The player should try to get each shot near the baseline and then switch to sharp crosscourt shots off the court. The player should alternate hitting balls flat (drives) and with shape (higher bouncing). The player repeats the drill standing at the center of the baseline.

Variation: The player can test for improved acceleration from time to time by decreasing the time between tosses. A player who is able to recover and swing faster with force and acceleration while maintaining form is developing a powerful and consistent stroke pattern.

MOVING ACCELERATION DRILL

Purpose: To develop or improve racket head speed while hitting a low shot on the move.

CRITICAL CUE:

The player needs to use core muscles to accelerate on each ball and good balance in the legs for the shuffle forward while striking the ball. The player should be low and loaded throughout each repetition.

Procedure: The player starts on the baseline midway between the center hash mark and the alley. The coach or partner stands in front and a few feet toward the alley of the extended stroke and throws low balls that bounce 0.5 to 1 foot (15 to 30 cm) high. The tosses should come immediately after each ball is hit, and the feeder moves 2 feet (0.6 m) away from the player with each new toss. The player follows the feeder, who is walking backward toward the net while feeding, swinging from low to high as fast as possible through the strike zone, and producing balls with a great deal of topspin and power.

Coaching points: Proper placement and timing of the feeds is mandatory to push the player to accelerate on each ball. The rapid-fire succession of tosses can be slowed down if needed or thrown at different heights if the player desires. The end locations of the shots are not as important as the speed of the racket head through the contact point. The movement toward the net simulates a short ball, and the sustained loading helps improve a player's core strength.

Variation: This drill can also work on backward, diagonal, and side-to-side movements. Backward movement reverses the steps the feeder and player take. For diagonal movement, the balls are tossed in a line diagonally forward toward the alley. To practice side-to-side movement, the partner or coach moves to about 2 feet (0.6 m) directly in front of the player and tosses the ball side to side, requiring anywhere from 2 to 4 feet (0.6 to 1.3 m) of movement in either direction. Ample recovery time is needed on the side-to-side movement so that the contact point remains the same.

HARD HITTING: OUT OF THE BALLPARK

Purpose: To increase acceleration and power in the forehand or backhand.

Procedure: The player start on the middle of the baseline. The coach or partner feeds balls from the middle of the other side of the court. The feeds should land approximately 4 to 5 feet (1.3 to 1.5 m) in front and 2 feet (0.6 m) to the side of the stroke being drilled. The feeds should be easy, bounce to shoulder height, and come at a frequency that allows the player ample time to recover and prepare for the next ball.

The player prepares with a big windup and swings as hard as possible, culminating with a forceful follow-through. Where the ball lands is not important; even hitting the fence is fine! When the player is used to striking the ball with force, the drill continues. Now, while focusing on acceleration and topspin, the player needs to hit hard and aim to get the ball to land before the baseline. The ball should have shape (height and spin) and get off the court quickly.

Coaching points: A ball that lands past the baseline usually indicates a lack of acceleration or improper shot technique. The player can correct the problem by adding more acceleration, experimenting with the grip, emphasizing a more pronounced follow-through and finish, or a combination of these adjustments. For more acceleration, the player needs to focus on using a low-to-high swing path with the racket head leading the elbow. The arm and racket face need to extend as quickly as possible toward the shot. The Eastern, semi-Western, or a hybrid of the two grips may be used. On the follow-through, the elbow should be pointing in the desired direction of where the player wants the ball to go.

Variation: The player can also start at the middle of the service line to work on accelerating from the midcourt. In this version the feed lands 1 to 2 feet (0.3 to 0.6 m) away from the player, and the player hits the ball toward the service line with an emphasis on lining up the foot closest to the ball and loading the leg.

HARD HITTING: KILLER SHOTS

Purpose: To simulate a live game situation and develop or improve the ability to hit a hard-hit ball and transition to the net.

Procedure: Player 1 starts on the center hash mark on the baseline and faces players 2 and 3 who are positioned on the opposite side of the net on the baseline. One of the two other players feeds a ball so that it lands 4 to 5 feet (1.3 to 1.5 m) in front and 2 feet (0.6 m) to the side of the forehand or backhand being practiced. Player 1 hits the ball aggressively (the killer shot), focusing on the elements of acceleration, and approaches the net. The players play out the point. They should score the game to 11, 15, or 21 and then rotate positions.

Coaching points: The execution of the transition shot determines how easily the next shot can be put away at net. If the transition shot lands short, the player should check for a balanced stance, maximum speed, and full arm extension on the swing and that the racket is facing properly out toward the target. If a player's balance and execution are fine and the ball still lands short, the grip (possibly a Western grip) may have too much topspin and isn't allowing for a fast enough pace.

Variation: This drill can be frustrating if the skill level of player 1 is lower than those of players 2 and 3. To accommodate skill level differences or add variety, players should use the drop-off game. In this version, the player who returns the killer shot keeps playing, and one of the other players (2 or 3) drops off the court; the point is completed in a one-on-one situation.

SPECIFIC SHOT DRILLS

Specific shot drills provide the opportunity to zero in and improve on a particular ground-stroke shot. Each shot is important to have for a balanced game with variety. Drilling specific shots can also provide the opportunity to improve the skills discussed in chapters 1 and 2 in a more specific scenario. Each of these drills can be used to drill both the forehand and backhand side.

The drills in this section highlight first the successful execution of a shot and then hitting to a target to help develop focus and accuracy within the shot. For the technique and target portions of the drills, the beginning court position is the same. The player starts on the middle hash mark on the baseline. A coach or partner, who is on the service line on the opposite side, feeds 8 to 10 balls by racket. The coach or partner can start with closer feeds to allow the player to master the proper movement before progressing to wider feeds that require more advanced movement. The tempo of the feeds can also speed up to improve recovery technique and time. The feeds can have varying tempos based on the skill being practiced. For example, players might want slower feeds for grooving and faster feeds for focusing on more challenging movement and learning to hit tougher shots.

The target drills require some equipment. The player or coach places a court squeegee with a hook on the net so that the pole is perpendicular to the ground, as shown in figure 3.2. If a squeegee is not available, a broom handle or similar object may serve as an effective substitute. A cone is placed over the top of the handle to provide a target (see figure 3.3). It is best to use cones with varying heights to work on the different trajectories and angles of the shots. Often the squeegee will have a hook attached, allowing a target to be raised and lowered.

A cone can also be placed deep in the court (see figure 3.4). In this setup, a player's goal is to try to hit the primary cone (the one on the squeegee). A secondary goal is to hit the deep quadrant cone if the player misses the primary cone. The cone on the squeegee can also be used as a target to hit over when trying to use the deeper cone as the primary target. Players should use the setup that works best for the shot they are practicing.

Figure 3.2 A squeegee pole can be attached to the net.

Figure 3.3 Target cone placed on the squeegee handle.

Figure 3.4 Cone and squeegee setup with a cone in the deep crosscourt quadrant.

CROSSCOURT FLAT SHOT

Purpose: To develop a shot played for power and a show of strength.

Technique practice: The coach or partner feeds balls diagonally to the mid strike zone toward the shoulder and approximately 2 to 3 feet (0.6 to 0.9 m) to the side of the swing path. To produce a flat ball and a low trajectory, the player accelerates from low to high but extends the arm outward just before contact. The player makes contact slightly in front of the front foot and hits the outside of the ball, aiming for a trajectory of approximately 1 to 2 feet (0.3 to 0.6 m) over the net. Between shots, the player recovers back to the middle and split steps to prepare for the next shot.

Coaching points: Players should experiment with different contact points to find the best spot for executing the crosscourt shot. Contacting the ball too late makes the ball go more down the line.

Solo variation: See the solo variation of the Diagonal Short Court drill on page 57.

Target practice: Set up the pole 7 to 12 holes to one side of the net strap and anywhere from 1 to 5 holes below the top strap. Move the pole to different positions to work on different angles. The cone can be set up higher or lower to add height variety to the shot. A lower target is the most aggressive form of the shot, and a higher target provides control (comfortable rally shot) for a safer shot. A cone placed deep in the court can add an additional target.

CRITICAL CUE:

To assist the aim for the deep crosscourt corner, the player should extend the racket arm through the shot and imagine the arm going through the court to the opposite corner.

DOWN-THE-LINE SHOT

Purpose: To develop a weapon that can be played for power to the open court, keeping the opponent on the run or taking advantage of the opponent's weak crosscourt shot or poor movement.

Technique practice: The coach or partner feeds balls diagonally to the mid strike zone and approximately 2 to 3 feet (0.6 to 0.9 m) to the side of the swing path. The player accelerates from low to high but closes the shoulders. The player makes contact a little behind the contact point of the crosscourt flat shot and aims for a trajectory of 2 to 3 feet (0.6 to 0.9 m) over the net. Between shots, the player recovers back to the middle and split steps to prepare for the next shot.

Coaching points: This shot has a high risk of error because of the small target area, high net clearance, and the difficulty associated with changing the direction of the ball. To change the direction of the oncoming crosscourt or diagonal shot it is necessary to wait a little longer for the ball to get in the strike zone. The player should experiment with contact point and racket face angle to establish the best combination for executing the shot with power. Also, ball feeds can progress outward to practice this shot from a range of locations, anywhere from midway from the baseline hash mark to the alley.

Solo variation: See the solo variation in the Straight-Ahead Backcourt drill on page 58. Instead of standing centered to the backboard, move to one side.

Target practice: Set up the pole and cone about 2 feet (0.6 m) from the alley toward the net strap and anywhere from 1 to 5 holes below the top strap, moving the pole to work on different trajectories and angles. Then, place a cone on the court 4 to 5 feet (1.3 to 1.5 m) from the baseline and the alley if hitting for placement or 2 to 3 feet (0.6 to 0.9 m) from the baseline and alley if practicing winners.

CRITICAL CUE:

Control of the shot is determined by the ability to keep the ball on the strings longer (to change the direction of the ball) and hit fully through the ball. The player should focus on hitting around the ball and using different degrees of spin and then work toward hitting a flatter ball to produce a more effective shot.

HIGH, HEAVY CROSSCOURT AND DOWN-THE-LINE SHOT

Purpose: To develop a heavy shot that will push or keep an opponent back in the court while creating room to step farther into the court and play more offensively.

Technique practice: The coach or partner feeds balls diagonally with spin and increased velocity to create a higher ball that bounces up high with topspin. The player prepares for the shot in one of three ways: back up and let the ball drop into the midlevel strike zone, move in and take the ball on the rise, or take the ball out of the air. The shot is like the normal groundstroke but with more upward arc on the ball. After the shot, the player split steps to prepare for the next shot.

Coaching points: A high, heavy ball is often played off a high-bouncing ball, leaving ample time to establish a proper load. Players should practice this shot from offensive (inside or near the baseline) and defensive (behind the baseline) positions. Note that hitting from a defensive position may require a slightly later contact point because the player arrives late, which requires more effort to get under the ball.

Variation: The high and heavy shot can also be hit down the line. The player can adjust the footwork, body position, and swing pattern accordingly, while adding the lower loading, increased top spin, and higher arm extension.

Solo variation: Since the bounce is high, the high and heavy shot is easy to drill on the backboard. The player stands 15 feet (4.6 m) away from the backboard to either the forehand or backhand side. The player picks a starting groundstroke (forehand or backhand) and hits one ball down the line with loft so that the ball bounces back high. On the next ball, the player hits a high, heavy crosscourt shot. The player should initially use a limited angle. The player runs over to meet the ball and executes the high, heavy crosscourt shot from the other side. To advance the drill, the player can widen the angle to incorporate more movement.

Target practice: Drilling this shot requires a target placed higher than the net strap. One option is to set up a pole on each net post by connecting a rope between the poles at a height of 3 to 4 feet (0.9 to 1.3 m) above the net. After a player has mastered hitting over the rope at this height, the player can raise the rope height. Another option is to set up an obstacle (bench, chair, bucket of balls, or other object) a few feet in front and to the side of the swing, forcing the player to hit up and over the object. The player should stand far enough back to avoid swinging into the object and enough to the side of the object to avoid a ball ricocheting backward. Finally, the player can place a cone approximately 2 to 3 feet (0.6 to 0.9 m) from the alley and baseline on the appropriate side of the court for either a crosscourt or down-the-line shot and practice the shot.

SHORTER- AND DEEPER-ANGLED SHOTS

Purpose: To develop a range of angled shots designed to pull an opponent off the court.

Technique practice: Two players hit balls diagonally with spin toward each other's doubles alleys. Each player tries to hit seven balls into the alley. The drill can start with players hitting diagonally crosscourt and then moving backward toward the baseline after each point. Players should aggressively brush the outside of the ball, accelerate the racket face in a shorter arc across the body, and aim to clear the net by 1 to 2 feet (0.3 to 0.6 m) for shorter angles and 3 to 5 feet (0.9 to 1.5 m) for balls landing past the service line. Between shots, the player recovers back to the middle and split steps to prepare for the next shot.

Coaching points: Using the rally and defensive points of contact helps provide extra time to load the legs and impart more spin to create a better angle. However, some players prefer the attack point of contact, which relies less on the legs and core and more on the arms and hands to create the angle. Using this contact point is helpful when not enough time exists to get set up behind the ball.

Variation: For an angled shot off of a down-the-line shot, the coach or partner feeds balls down the line flat or with topspin so that they land midway between the service line and baseline and produce a low ball that bounces back toward the baseline. To generate angle, the player takes the ball on the rise and, with a rally point of contact, hits the angle crosscourt.

Solo variation: The angled shot produces a short ball that bounces or deflects short in the court in the opposite direction of the player, so sustaining a rally can be difficult. The player picks a side and stands 6 to 8 feet (1.8 to 2.4 m) from the backboard. The player hits the ball flat or slightly higher down the line. Once the ball bounces off the backboard, the player hits the angle shot. The player runs over and, off the bounce, hits a defensive block shot straight forward or down the line, has it bounce straight in front of the body, and repeats the process. This approach combines practicing the shot and defensive skills.

Target practice: To provide a more sharply angled target, the player places the pole farther right or left from the target for the crosscourt shot. The player starts with the cone on top of the pole. The player performs the technique practice but aims to hit the cone. The coach or partner feeds balls from the center of the service line about midway toward the alley. After practicing this scenario, the player adds a court cone to practice a range of ending locations on or within 1 to 3 feet (0.3 to 0.9 m) of the sideline, varying from inside the service line to midway between the service line and baseline.

CRITICAL CUE:

The player should swing faster with more topspin and angle when hitting shorter angles.

INSIDE-OUT FOREHAND

Purpose: To develop the technique to move around the ball and redirect it with a powerful forehand to the ad-court (backhand side if the opponent is a right hander).

Technique practice: A coach or partner feeds balls diagonally with topspin or slice that bounce just past the service line and to a midway point between the center hash mark and the alley. Closer to the center is an easier shot, while closer to the alley is a more challenging shot. Using an open stance, the player contacts the shot at the attack point of contact for a drive shot and the rally contact point for a high heavy shot, emphasizing an outward push of the arm and wrist snap with upward acceleration. The shot should clear the net by 1 to 2 feet (0.3 to 0.6 m) and land 2 to 3 feet (0.6 to 0.9 m) from the baseline and the alley for a deep shot or near the service line for the angled shot. For the latter version, a player needs to snap the racket head more upward and outward. Between shots, the player recovers back to the middle and split steps to prepare for the next shot.

Solo variation: When combined with other shots, the inside-out forehand can be drilled on the backboard. One possible sequence is to hit down the line so that the ball deflects directly back, followed by an inside-out forehand, then a high and heavy crosscourt shot, followed by another inside-out forehand; then the sequence is repeated. Other options include alternating inside-out forehands with down-the-line shots or following crosscourt shots with down-the-line backhand shots.

Variation: If a player wishes to practice the inside-in forehand on the backboard, one sequence is to hit down the line so that the ball deflects directly back, followed by an inside-in forehand back to the same spot, then a high and heavy crosscourt shot followed by a forehand crosscourt shot; then the sequence is repeated.

Target practice: Set up the pole 7 to 12 holes from the net strap and 1 to 5 holes below the top strap. Then, move the cone to various locations on the sideline, ranging from inside the service line to midway between the service line and baseline as targets for the shot.

SLICE

CRITICAL CUE:

In the preparation, the racket arm extends in a high-to-low chop or sweep, but on the follow-through it needs to go out toward the desired target. The wrist should release through the contact point to give the shot more bite.

Purpose: To develop the technique to hit a shot that will stay low over the net and is used to break up the rhythm of an opponent.

Technique practice: A coach or partner feeds balls diagonally with topspin or underspin to a point between the service line and baseline (but closer to the baseline) that is midway between the center hash mark and the alley. The player moves to a closed stance, prepares the racket head slightly behind the shoulders and slightly above the line of the oncoming ball, and contacts the ball in the attack contact point for an aggressive slice and in the rally to defensive contact points for a less aggressive slice. The shot should clear the net by 1 to 2 feet (0.3 to 0.6 m) and land as close as possible to the baseline. Between shots, the player recovers back to the middle and split steps to prepare for the next shot.

Solo variation: The player picks a side to drill and stands to that side. The player stands 3 to 4 feet (0.9 to 1.3 m) from the board to work on slices hit on the rise and 6 to 8 feet (1.8 to 2.4 m) back for deep slices. The player starts with a straight-ahead rally of just slices, moving up and back to practice the range of slice shots. The player can sustain a slice rally against the wall by concentrating on extending the arm toward the wall on the follow-through. Then, the player can add crosscourt shots to reset the point and practice the slice from other locations, working on the forehand and backhand slice.

Target practice: The coach or partner feeds a deep ball. Cones can also be placed in the court to highlight the exact location for a deeper slice (2 to 3 feet, or 0.6 to 0.9 m, from the baseline and alley) as well as the exact location for a shorter slice (low and near the service line for the crosscourt and down the line).

LIVE BALL DRILLS

Live ball drills simulate match play while providing the opportunity to continue to work on technique and placement for the various groundstrokes. Live ball drills require players to make adjustments to react to the ball that an opponent hits at them. The following drills range from practicing one stroke at a time to practicing a range of strokes. The drills also vary in terms of court coverage and target area.

ONE SHOT

Purpose: To hone technique and target accuracy while practicing a specific shot in a live ball situation. This drill can be used with the crosscourt, down-the-line, high and heavy, angled, inside-out forehand, inside-in forehand, and slice shots.

Procedure: Two players pick a shot to drill and assume appropriate court positioning at a point midway between the center hash mark and the alley. For crosscourt and deep-angle shots, they are diagonally across from one another on the baseline. For down-the-line shots, they should be straight across from one another on the baseline. For short-angle shots, they should be diagonally across from one another on the service line. The players decide on a target area for the shot that is big enough so they can hit it consistently over a competitive rally. A smaller area can be used for more of a challenge.

Before starting the point, each player completes three controlled hits to the target. For the controlled shots, the partner provides easy feeds for the designated shot and target area. After the controlled hits, the players play aggressively to the target, trying to win the point by forcing the other player into an error—a miss or any shot other than the specific drill shot. Cones can also be set as specific targets so that points are earned for hitting a cone. Games can be played to 10, 20, or 30 points.

FOREHAND OR BACKHAND ONLY

Purpose: To practice full-court coverage using only a forehand or backhand. Players can use this drill to practice the crosscourt, down-the-line, high and heavy, angled, inside-out forehand, inside-in forehand, and slice shots.

Procedure: Player 1 stands in one corner, deuce or ad side, and player 2 covers the whole court. Player 2 must hit either a forehand or backhand on every shot back to player 1. Player 1 can hit any shot to anywhere on the court in reply. Games should be played to 5 points, winning by 1 point if they should tie at 4-all. Players switch sides or roles after each completed game.

Variation: The players pick a specific forehand or backhand to hit every time, such as the inside-out forehand, or force more variety by making the rule that the same shot cannot be hit back-to-back or more often than a designated number of shots, such as a maximum of three.

DONUT HOLE

Purpose: To work on shot recognition and emphasize the time for executing specific shots.

Procedure: Two players stand opposite each other centered behind the baseline. Two cones are placed on each side of the court about 4.5 feet (1.3 m) from each singles sideline and 3 feet (0.9 m) from the baseline to form a box, or donut hole, in the midcourt (see figure 3.5). Any ball that the opponent hits into the hole is considered a *go for it* ball. Players can play games to 7 or 11 points.

Variation: Before they start, the players can agree on what type of shots they will hit (for example, drop shots or runaround forehand shots) when a ball is hit in the donut hole.

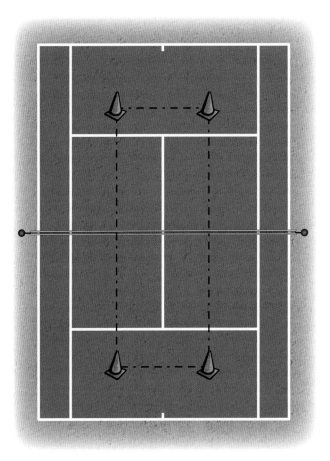

Figure 3.5   Cone setup.

CROSSCOURT VERSUS ANGLED SHOT

Purpose: To practice crosscourt and angled shots in a live ball situation and to gain experience with shot recognition for executing angled shots.

Procedure: On both sides of the court, the coach or player sets up two cones (see figure 3.6). One cone goes about 2 feet (0.6 m) from the alley and midway between the service line and the net to designate a target area for the short-angle shot. The other should be placed 4 feet (1.3 m) from the baseline and alley to form a target area for the crosscourt groundstroke or deep-angle shot. Both players start on their respective center hash mark. They rally with crosscourt shots to the designated area until one player hits a ball that lands outside of the crosscourt target area. When this happens, the point is played out crosscourt trying to hit balls into the short-angle target area. The player who hits the first seven short angles to the target area wins.

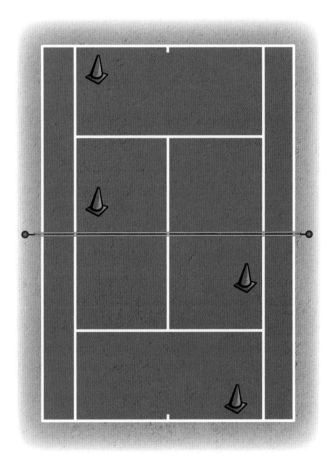

Figure 3.6 Cone setup.

DOWN THE LINE VERSUS HIGH AND HEAVY

Purpose: To practice the down-the-line and high, heavy shots in live ball situations and to gain experience with shot recognition.

Procedure: Two players face each other on opposite sides of the court in the crosscourt position (on the baseline, midway between the center and alley). One player feeds a ball to the other, and players rally with normal groundstrokes. When one player hits a short (or attackable) ball, the other player yells, *Go!* and then hits aggressively down the line. On the *Go!* signal, the player who hit the short ball must run over and hit a high, heavy ball as a recovery tool for the down-the-line shot. After the high and heavy ball, the players use the whole court to finish the point. Points are played to 11, 15, or 21.

Variation: A slice hit on the run can also be practiced after the *Go!* ball is called out.

CHAPTER 4

SERVE SKILLS

The serve is one of the most important shots in tennis. The main goal in serving is to use power, swing, and placement to create a tennis weapon. This weapon can help the player take control of the point by intimidating the opponent and keeping the opponent on the defensive. The player has more control of the serve than any other shot, so it makes sense to learn how to execute powerful and perfectly placed serves at opportune moments.

Although a good serve requires good technique, this shot is also a mental challenge. A mentally strong person can block out distractions and focus on delivering a strong serve to dominate a set or a match. This puts a lot of pressure on the opponent, making service games of greater importance. The opponent knows that holding serve can mean the difference between staying in the match and losing it. It is valuable for the player to gain confidence from standing on the baseline, looking over at the opponent, picking the correct location, and executing a successful serve.

Some of the best servers of the game are Andy Roddick, Roger Federer, Rafael Nadal, Maria Sharapova, Justine Henin, Serena Williams, Venus Williams, Pete Sampras, Stefan Edberg, Boris Becker, Martina Navratilova, and John McEnroe. All these players have or had great serves, but for different reasons. Players are usually characterized as having serves with power, accuracy, spin, consistency, and variety. However, a player who can hit a big serve in a hotly contested match situation is set apart from the rest.

No matter the player's level, the serve is the first and best indicator of whether the player is making an impact on an opponent. This chapter addresses the different types of serves and serve styles and how to maximize their effectiveness. It also addresses the technique needed to hit a great serve. Finally, the chapter covers the intangible and necessary ingredients needed to take the serve to the highest level.

DEVELOPING THE SERVE

The four types of tennis serves are the flat serve, the slice serve, the topspin serve, and the kick serve. Each serve has a different technique and performs a different function. It is important for every player to know how to hit and use all of these serves to add variety to the service game. The player should develop a serve that can lead to free points or to a return that allows the player to continue to dictate play.

All four types of serves can be used on first or second serves and for every serving style. Usually, a flat first serve is followed by a topspin or a slice second serve. The slice serve can be used on both first and second serves. However, sometimes variations in the pattern can be very effective, such as when a player attempts to fool, confuse, and surprise an opponent.

The best serve style for the player depends on the individual's overall game style. Whatever serve style the player chooses, the following list of thoughts demonstrates the proper mindset for any good server.

- I will get my opponent playing from behind in the game.
- I will mix up the different locations I serve to and use my variety of serves to keep my opponent on the defensive.
- I will find ways to win free points.
- I will serve mainly to my opponent's weakness.
- I will keep a running mental chart of where my opponent returns and what types of returns are used so that when I get into a crucial situation I can make an effective choice.

The three main styles of serves are defined here:

- **Big serve.** With this serve, the player mainly uses power to win free points.
- **Serve-and-volley serve.** With this serve, the player attacks the net and uses finesse and athleticism to win points.
- **Serve-and-stay-back serve.** For this serve, the player uses spin, location, and a variety of serves to keep opponents on their heels.

The following is a breakdown of the attitude and thought process of players who use each style of serve.

Big Serve Style

The clutch power servers—such as Pete Sampras, Boris Becker, Roger Federer, Andy Roddick, Serena Williams, and Venus Williams—hit the big power serve to turn the momentum their way. The goal of using the big serve is to overpower the opponent with serves that are hit to the body or hit hard past the opponent. It is preferable for a big server to be tall in order to more easily hit down on the serve, but plenty of smaller players have big serves, too. The big server needs good strength and motion to maximize power. More often than not, this server also has very good technique. Big servers have good location and a proper mix of serves. This type of server likes to use body serves as well as balls hit to the corners. The big server has a variety of serves, such as the slice or topspin serve, that are equally as effective as the flat serve.

The following list presents the mental attitude and thought process of a player who chooses the big serve.

- I have a big serve, and I am going to blow this serve by my opponent.
- My opponent will not break my serve.
- If my opponent breaks my serve, I will make this game the toughest he has ever won.
- Even if I am down, I will dig myself out of the hole.
- I will get a great start in every game to keep my opponent frustrated and feeling as if she cannot come back.

Serve-and-Volley Style Serve

The serve-and-volley style serve is meant to keep the pressure on the returner just enough to hit a good volley or overhead. Serve-and-volley servers such as Martina Navratilova, Stefan Edberg, Patrick Rafter, John McEnroe, and Taylor Dent, are considered great servers because of their ability to combine all the traits of a good server—consistency, power, accuracy, spin, variety, and location—to transition to the net effectively and often.

The serve-and-volley style server is very accurate. The player using this serve uses power and spin to hit precise spots at crucial times during a match. The successful serve-and-volley server understands the angles of the court, moves effectively, and has great vision. This server likes to be at the net, has good reach, has good technique, and knows what volley to hit in what situation in order to keep the opponent on the defensive. A player who chooses the serve-and-volley approach should be a good athlete who likes to bring the action to the opponent.

The following list presents the mental attitude and thought process of a player who chooses the serve-and-volley style serve.

- I will attack my opponent, and my opponent will get tired of passing me.
- My net game will beat my opponent's groundstroke game.
- My style is different from my opponent's; that difference is my strength.

- My serving and volleying force my opponent to deal with passing shots and shorter points instead of long, drawn-out rallies.

- I don't mind if my opponent passes me. In fact, from every pass, I learn where to move in a crucial situation.

Serve-and-Stay-Back Style Serve

Justine Henin, Rafael Nadal, and Andre Agassi have used location and spin to start a rally with a shot that is strategically beneficial to them. The location of Nadal's serves gives him the best opportunity to hit his forehand weapon on every first ball. Players who use the serve-and-stay-back style serve can use placement and disguise to keep their opponents guessing. These servers confuse their opponents by mixing up their serves and frequently changing location, speed, and spin.

The following list presents the thought processes of the player who chooses the serve-and-stay-back style serve.

- I will hit serves to locations that return balls to my strengths from the beginning.

- I have to focus on and execute the right strategies so I can take control of this point.

- I have to maximize my first-serve percentage.

SERVE AND STYLES OF PLAY

The serve is a vital part of the player's game style. Because the player's favorite shots dictate game style, on-court demeanor, and weapons, the serve becomes an integral part of how those traits are displayed. Consistently delivering a big serve in a tight match allows the player some mental breathing room, which could be the difference between winning and losing the match.

Specific serves correlate to each style of play, and they enhance the effectiveness of that style. In service games, a player can be effective in different ways. The player can use power, spin (both slice and topspin), variety (placement in different spots and use of different types of serves), consistency (ability to hit in crucial situations), and accuracy (precise location and timing) to get the preferred game style off to a good start. The following section examines how the serve plays into each of the styles of play.

- **Aggressive baseline play.** For this style, the main goal for the server is to hit a serve that gives the player free points and allows opportunities to hit an aggressive shot. The aggressive baseline style is the offensive version of the serve-and-stay back style serve.

- **Serve-and-volley style.** The main goal for this player is to hit precise serves that allow effective transitions to the net. The serve-and-volley style dictates an aggressive nature and a desire to constantly attack the net against an opponent.

- **All-court play.** This player's main goal is to combine the goals of aggressive baseline and serve-and-volley style into a blended style that uses variety when serving.

- **Rallying baseline play.** This player's serve is effective, but not as effective as the other, more aggressive game styles. This player starts rallies to get the point started in a more neutral fashion (at times offensive and at times defensive).

- **Defensive baseline play.** This server's main goal is to start a rally by serving to the opponent's weaker side to start the point. Usually, the serve of the defensive player breaks down in crucial situations, or the player gives an opponent an aggressive return. This style is the defensive version of the serve-and-stay-back style.

GRIPS

Regardless of serve or play style, technique is the cornerstone to a great service motion, and technique begins with the grip. Most professional tennis players choose to hit their serves using the Continental grip. This grip allows players to hit all the serves—flat, slice, and topspin.

The Eastern backhand grip also works to hit all the serves, especially a topspin serve. This grip closes the racket face slightly more than the Continental does, so it makes a topspin serve easier to hit. The Eastern backhand grip makes hitting a slice serve slightly more difficult. Less advanced players tend to use the Eastern grip and eventually move their grip toward the Continental grip as their technique improves.

FOOT PLACEMENT

The player's goal for foot placement is to establish a stance that allows good serve technique in order to optimize control of the ball. When setting the feet for a serve, the player must think about what style of serve and play to use and how to maximize the stance to allow for the intended movement on the serve.

The most common stance for linear movement is closed (one foot in front of the other). Linear movement (see figure 4.1) keeps the body's momentum more in a straight or slightly diagonal line and does not incorporate a great deal of trunk rotation and angular momentum. Angular movement (see figure 4.2) incorporates more use of shoulder and trunk rotation and requires that the feet be more closed. The different types of movement are related to the type of serve the player hits. The power serve, which includes the flat and strong slice serves, is a blend of linear and angular movements. Topspin serves rely more on the angular movement of rotation with the forearm, shoulders, and hips.

Even before the player serves, the foot placement sends a message as to what kind of server the player is. How close or how far away the player stands to the center hash mark says a lot about how the player will serve. A player who stands close to the hash mark shows a sense of control of the court and an ability to serve to all locations in the serving box without the angle created by standing farther away from the center. Also, this player

Figure 4.1   Feet position for linear movement.

Figure 4.2   Feet position for angular movement.

may be planning to quickly run around a particular shot, such as the backhand, and standing closer to the center better allows this opportunity. A player who stands farther away from the center uses the greater angle to pull an opponent off the court and may prefer the location of the return from the opponent. For example, on the ad side if a right-handed server hits a strong flat or slice serve wide and the opponent catches it late, the return will be down the line and right into the server's forehand, which is the server's weapon.

TOSS

Although tennis players may have a variety of motions, knee bends, takebacks, and contact points, the toss is essential for making a serve work. The toss on the service motion can determine whether a player's serve is a great success or a source of frustration. A player needs a toss that is reliable, perfectly timed, and in the right location. The toss should be rhythmically timed with the serve arm moving backward to start the motion. For toss technique for specific serves, see Technique for Specific Serves on page 89.

The first move of the toss arm is important to the service motion. The direction to which the toss arm travels upward dictates the type of serve to be hit. One of the best ways to extend the arm upward is called the V (also known as J) toss. When the arm hits the low point on the downward move and then heads out toward the direction of the inside of the thigh, it creates a big V (or possibly a J) shape. The exact shape doesn't matter, but it is essential to determine the location along that V path that will give the server the best trunk rotation and contact point. The V can be made smaller to suit a service motion or it can be eliminated.

For any toss, the player's goal is to move the arm upward, slowly and deliberately, while providing balance for the ball so that the ball has little or no rotation. The smooth motion of the toss arm going upward (see figure 4.3), called the *carry,* is important because it allows the hand to release the ball in a fluid motion. It also allows the player to feel a stretch in the toss arm and upper back muscles to create the optimal reach for the serve. The V toss stretches the upper back muscles as the arm reaches up. This toss is the perfect way for servers to create and use proper angular momentum and rotation in their motion.

The toss itself should be high enough for the racket head to reach up and contact the ball with the arm fully extended. Problems can arise if the toss is too high or too low in relation to the body. If a toss is too high, the server must wait and time the contact point correctly. While the server waits for the ball to come down, the elbow and the body succumb to gravity and often start to shrink down, creating a less effective serve because the player's technique does not

Figure 4.3 **The toss.**

COACHING POINTS

A server who uses linear movement (pointing more toward the court) would probably use a straighter toss or a slightly abbreviated V toss. That type of toss would drop in front and then extend back up in the same direction and would be extended more in front of the body. The player should use the linear toss only with a quicker motion because the toss reduces the amount of time available to execute the serve.

hold up. Sometimes the player ends up hitting a lower contact point, which causes the head to come down too quickly or the player's shoulders to rotate too soon, driving the ball to go down into the net.

A lower toss is fine if the motion is quick and fluid and the technique is efficient, but a breakdown in the technique can cause the server to reach more forward to compensate for the low toss. A low toss that is farther out in front is not recommended but can be effective enough for some servers to get the serve in. Over time, this player will create a new contact point that is potentially too low to be a power serve.

A toss that is too far from or too close to the body can also cause problems. A toss that is too close to the body causes the server to lean back awkwardly before going through the motion. This movement can lead to improper balance throughout the motion and a subsequent lack of power. A toss that is too far away causes the server to alter the motion such that the power zone is lost. The *power zone* is the feeling the server has when proper technique has provided a contact point designed for maximum power.

Although toss location depends on the type of serve, it should be consistent. An inconsistent ball toss can contribute to bad serving habits and create problems for servers. Some coaches like to see a tossed ball in the 12 o'clock location for all serves; other coaches prefer a 1 o'clock toss for a slice serve, a 12 o'clock toss for the flat serve, and an 11 o'clock serve for the topspin serve. (These examples are for a right-handed player; just the opposite is true for a left-handed player.) As long as the location is consistent, the server can maximize the disguise of the serve.

KINETIC CHAIN

When building a world-class serve, the kinetic chain and its effect on the service motion are an important area of focus. The components of the kinetic chain follow, and the components are discussed in detail in the upcoming sections.

1. Stance
2. Knee bend
3. Hip rotation
4. Trunk rotation
5. Arm rotation
6. Elbow extension and forearm pronation
7. Wrist movement
8. Follow-through and landing

1. Stance

Good balance and a comfortable stance provide a solid foundation that allows the player to reach up properly for the ball. Choosing the right stance is important to maintaining good balance and rhythm throughout the motion. The two main stances used to hit a serve are the platform stance and the pinpoint stance. The technique the player uses should not be affected by these two stances.

The platform stance positions the legs in the same location throughout the entire serve. Foot placement should be about shoulder width apart for a comfortable, balanced feel (see figure 4.4). This stance favors a server who uses more angular movement, has great timing, and can go straight up to hit the serve without bringing the back foot up to meet the front foot.

The pinpoint stance starts out as a platform stance, but during the motion the player brings the back foot up to meet the front foot (see figure 4.5). This stance can result in a little more momentum moving forward and upward and may help the player more easily reach up for the serve.

Both stances are effective and should be tested to check the player's power on the serve. To test the pinpoint stance, the player stands on the baseline and simply tries to hit a ball into either the deuce or ad service box without using the legs. Then, the player uses the pinpoint stance and looks for any drastic change in power. A lack of power may signify that the player is losing power when moving the legs up, that the player needs to alter the position of the feet in the stance, or that the swing itself is technically incorrect. Players often bring up the back leg incorrectly. Usually they do not step all the way up to the other foot, which can cause instability in the motion. In such cases, players should make technical adjustments and try again. A lack of power may also be a signal to try the platform stance.

To test the platform stance, the player simply goes up and hits the serve without going across the baseline. Next, the player incorporates a little more angular momentum through trunk rotation to see if it improves.

Figure 4.4   Platform stance.

Figure 4.5   Pinpoint stance.

In the platform stance the weight starts on both feet and then transfers upward and into the court as the player reaches up to hit the serve. The pinpoint stance has a more distinct weight transfer. Some players like to start on the front foot and then rock back onto the back foot before moving back forward and upward to the serve. Other players like to start on the back foot and transfer the weight forward and upward. Experimenting with both stances helps players determine the best stance for the serve.

2. Knee Bend

The position and motion of the knees are essential to a good serve. The knees can help provide flexion in the beginning of the serve motion, but mainly they are used to extend and lift the body up to hit the ball. As the player reaches back and is about to get the elbow in its set position, the knees flex forward to start the loading process of the legs (see figure 4.6). The knee bend should be comfortable and allow for enough power as the knees extend and move upward. A proper knee bend dictates how high the player can reach up for a good contact point, which depends on the player's size and the type of serve. The optimum contact point is the position at which the serving arm is fully extended and the knees have provided an upward and slightly forward reach.

3. Hip Rotation

The next part of the chain is the motion of the hips. From a position where the racket head is either stationary or, in some cases, slightly swaying, the hips make a slight rocking motion forward and gain momentum before rotating backward to put weight on the back leg. As the ball is tossed for a topspin, flat, or slice serve, the player rotates forward and tries to position the hip closest to the net over the baseline (see figure 4.7). For a beginner to intermediate level player, the uncoiling motion of the hips occurs with a pivot of the front foot; for more advanced players, it occurs in the air. On the topspin serve, the body angles into the court similar to the slice or flat serve but the racquet

Figure 4.6 Knee bend with hip angulation on the serve.

Figure 4.7 Hip position for a flat serve.

Figure 4.8 Hip position for the kick serve.

brushes upward on the ball to give it topspin so that it bounce into the opponent. The toss is at 12 or 1 o'clock. The hip action for the kick serve is different. For this serve, both hips push forward and to the side fence, allowing the server to reach back and brush up on the toss at 11 o'clock (for a right-handed player) to impart the kicking topspin, which causes the serve to move away from the opponent (see figure 4.8).

Just before the beginning of the upward reach for the ball, each player has a distinct motion. For a smoother swing, the player should get the racket hand to rock slightly forward in conjunction with the hip. This rocking forward drives the shoulder up and starts the process of getting the racket in the power zone prior to contact.

4. Trunk Rotation

As the hips rotate backward and the toss arm makes the V to begin the carry, the trunk naturally begins to rotate backward, causing the shoulders to make a half turn. Because the toss arm is carrying the ball up, the front shoulder is higher than the back shoulder and elbow. The elbow rotates backward so that it is in a position past the center of the back at about the same height as the rib cage on that side.

5. Arm Rotation

The traditional takeback starts with a downward movement of both arms at the same time (see figure 4.9). The toss arm moves toward the thigh of the front leg, and the serve arm moves down and backward, reaching back with the palm down to a comfortable position. How far the serve arm moves backward depends on the speed of the motion. The serve arm finishes with the setting of the elbow and arm in a *power zone,* meaning that the shoulders are balanced but tilting upward toward the toss arm.

After reaching back the arm lifts to set the shoulders. This movement should be fluid, not jerky. As it lifts the racket head up, the serve arm should keep a little bend in it. The image of keeping the palm down throughout is useful because it prohibits a bad flaw that can develop in the wrist set just before contact. An open palm can limit the server's power. At the same time the serve arm moves backward, the toss arm carries the ball up to release.

COACHING POINTS

Poor foot stance can have a negative effect on trunk rotation. For example, if the stance is too closed (the back leg too far behind and to the back), the hips could be hampered from adequately rotating forward, causing their position to be too closed to produce power on the serve. Overrotation of the trunk and shoulders can have a negative effect on the serve as well. If the trunk and elbow rotate too far back, they need a split second longer to rotate forward. Because the serve is a precision stroke, this extra time could cause the toss to travel too far down, thus creating a low contact point.

The racket head then reaches up and back toward the shoulders, creating a set position of the elbow (see figure 4.10). The serve arm bends to make an L shape (90-degree angle), but the front shoulder is tilted upward. This position is also known as the trophy pose. Where the elbow sets depends on the service motion, but it should be slightly below shoulder level and slightly rotated backward. The player must be careful not to overrotate, which could result in loss of power. From this power position, the serve arm reaches up to strike the ball. When the arm is at the bottom of the backswing behind the back, it is externally rotated at the shoulder.

Figure 4.9 For the arm rotation, the arms move sequentially.

Figure 4.10 As the arms move up, the serve arm reaches the set position, or trophy pose.

COACHING POINTS

The abbreviated (or sequential) serve is becoming popular today because of players such as Andy Roddick who use it effectively and with power. The abbreviated takeback is perfect for someone who prefers to get set faster and use less arm movement. It also works for players who lose power in the arms or legs or who struggle to produce a fluid motion with the full takeback swing.

In the abbreviated motion, the toss arm starts as the player angles the hip into the court. The toss is delivered a little faster, and it is usually done with the player loading the legs followed by the serve arm coming up quickly. The serve arm starts the movement after the toss arm. Instead of using the simultaneous motion of down together up together to set the elbow, the player takes the serve arm straight back and in a higher path than the usual motion. The path should be in line with the shoulders or, in some cases, slightly lower and downward. The goal is to move the serve arm into position more quickly than for a standard serve.

6. Elbow Extension and Forearm Pronation

The goal of elbow extension is for the player to be able to hit the ball as high as possible and near the height of the tossed ball. This is the power contact point. As previously noted, the elbow sets slightly lower than shoulder level and at a 90-degree angle. The elbow is comfortably to the side and, once set, it should not dip downward. Then, the player extends the elbow upward and slightly outward to create a power loop and gets ready to strike the ball (see figure 4.11). On the upward swing, the serve arm internally rotates at a very high speed and creates the acceleration needed to hit the serve forcefully.

As the serve arm starts moving forward and the elbow extends outward, the forearm pronates (rotates inward; see figure 4.12) and provides the wrist a good angle for striking the ball. It is similar to giving the ball a high five with the racquet face. The goal for the toss arm is to keep it extended as long as possible until the serve arm rotates forward. As the serve arm moves, the toss arm should naturally fall down and across the body.

On a slice serve, the pronation of the serve arm is a glancing movement on the outside of the ball. On a topspin serve, it is a little more exaggerated as the racket face heads away from the body and toward the sideline. At this point in the kinetic chain, the kick serve also adds arching of the back (see Topspin and Kick Serve on page 90) to load underneath the ball in order to go up.

7. Wrist Movement

On the takeback of the arm, the wrist is slightly hyperextended as the hand bends back at the wrist. As the wrist accelerates toward striking the ball, the wrist straightens and then continues to flex as part of the follow-through. This action is called *snapping of the wrist*. Many coaches look for this action when they help students create a flat serve. A key area of focus is to make sure to keep the palm down in preparing to strike the ball. Opening the palm limits the player's ability to hit a great serve.

Figure 4.11 The elbow extends.

Figure 4.12 The forearm pronates.

8. Follow-Through and Landing

The completion of the serve begins with the weight transfer from one leg to the other and then the racket moving through the contact point. After the ball has been struck, the arm begins to decelerate and the body begins to recover and prepare for the return (see figure 4.13). Which foot lands first depends on the server's preference.

TECHNIQUE FOR SPECIFIC SERVES

A player has three areas of focus for developing the serve: power, spin, and placement. For the flat serve the player must focus on power, while slice and topspin serves require a focus on using a variety of spins to wreak havoc on the opponent. All four types of serves require developing the quality of placement. The following are some scenarios for the different serves and the specific techniques for executing them. Combining the technique for the flat serve, the slice serve, the topspin serve, and the kick serve with variations in location, spins, and tactics, can give the player many options for constructing and winning the point.

Figure 4.13   Follow-through and landing.

Flat Serve

The flat serve is the most powerful serve of the four types. The ball hit off this serve has little or no spin. The player should hit it to the lines or corners when trying to get a ball by the opponent, hit it at the body to stop an opponent, or move the opponent out of the way. When hit correctly and at the right time, pace, and location, this serve is very effective.

Preparation

This phase of the flat serve is explained in the Kinetic Chain section. The body prepares for a smooth and fluid service motion that includes effective use of the legs. On a flat serve, the toss should go up in the air approximately 2 feet (0.6 m) from the proper extension of the arm (arm fully extended, fingers pointing up with the palm open) in front and about 1 foot (0.3 m) to the right for a right-handed player or to the left for a left-handed player.

Forward Swing and Contact

The elbow rotates backward to a position where the server can look backward and see the elbow bent and slightly rotated past a straight-back position. As the arm extends from the elbow position, the toss goes up, and the body gains momentum upward toward the ball; the shoulders turn forward. The serve arm then starts to come up, and the forearm pronates as the elbow extends upward and slightly outward; the inside of the forearm faces slightly outward, similar to the position for throwing a baseball or football. As the server reaches to hit the ball, the legs extend at the point of contact, and then the wrist snaps down on the ball.

Follow-Through

After contact, the racket head continues downward and eventually follows through on the opposite side of the player's body.

Figure 4.14 Slice serve preparation.

Figure 4.15 Slice serve contact.

Slice Serve

The slice serve is very effective because of its sidespin. The optimal locations include a serve that slices away from the opponent and a serve that slices into the opponent. One of the server's goals is to keep the opponent from getting a good read on the ball and increase the likelihood of a weak return. The slice is a great serve for variety, which helps keep opponents guessing, and it is very effective if used in combination with the flat and the topspin serves.

Preparation

The preparation is similar to that for the flat serve, but on a slice serve the upper body turns more sideways while leaning slightly farther back in the load position. Overrotation is apparent when the body moves uncomfortably backward. The rotation should tilt slightly backward, but not too exaggerated to avoid coming from farther back to get in the proper position. On a slice serve, the toss arm goes out about one ball length farther toward the left of the left-handed player or to the right of a right handed player, making a bigger V shape and allowing for more trunk rotation through contact (see figure 4.14).

Forward Swing and Contact

The arm continues upward, the elbow extends, and the forearm pronates so that the inside of the forearm moves outward and the wrist snaps toward the outside of the ball. This creates a glancing blow that imparts sidespin on the ball. If the arm does not pronate when extending, then the arm travels too closely to the body, creating a cramped motion that hampers fluidity.

The front shoulder and toss arm are more rotated in order to create the extra angular momentum needed for the slice. The angle of the body and front shoulder stay slightly more closed as the body uncoils. The position of the front shoulder creates the angle that the racket must travel to make the contact that produces the slice. Because the toss for the slice serve should be more to the outside, the contact point (see figure 4.15) for the slice serve is about one ball farther out (to the right for right-handed players, left for left-handed players) than the flat serve.

Follow-Through

The follow-through takes a little longer because the wrist was heading around the ball. The racket head eventually settles at around waist level.

Topspin and Kick Serves

The topspin serve is very effective on clay courts or hard courts because of the bounce that is created by the service motion and the safety of its height when it goes over the net. This serve can really cause problems for returners who don't like to or can't handle higher-bouncing balls or balls that bounce out of their strike zone. A good topspin serve usually bounces into an opponent and a good kick serve usually bounces away from an opponent, depending on the location of the serve and spin. A topspin serve that bounces directly into an opponent should land about a foot (0.3 m) in front of the opponent and bounce into the body. A kick serve with the goal of bouncing away from the opponent is hit out wide.

Preparation

For the topspin or kick serve the back arches as it rotates back so that the hips push forward, parallel to the baseline, and the shoulders angle backward. The racket head and shoulders tilt backward while the body settles and holds the arched-back position (see figure 4.16). The back needs to be strong enough to hold the position for a split second before the abdominal muscles contract. The shoulders stay turned until the serve is hit and then rotate forward to the direction of the serve. Because of the arch in the back, the knees load slightly more than in other types of serves.

On the toss, the arm goes back from the V shape to the side. It is thrown back in a straight line, in conjunction with the arching of the back, and heads comfortably back. Then the body moves forward and the ball is struck. The kick serve is usually tossed above or slightly behind the head of the server; it goes over the left shoulder for a right-handed player and the right shoulder for a left-handed player. The toss for the topspin serve is lower and more in front than the toss for the kick serve.

Forward Swing and Contact

For the kick serve the body remains facing the side fence until the ball is off the racket. The racket trajectory is upward and across the ball or left to right from 7 o'clock to 2 o'clock. During this phase, the player should focus on the hips moving upward to facilitate moving up and then out. Once the arched back extends, the forearm and racket naturally pronate, so the inside of the forearm faces slightly outward and upward. As the legs drive upward, the racket head is at an angle that, if the player drives upward with the legs properly, can cause the racket head to brush up on the ball producing the kick serve. Topspin is created from the extension of the knees upward and toward the target combined with the racket head driving up and out toward the sideline (see figure 4.17).

The difference between the wrist snap for the kick serve and the topspin serve is that the serve arm hits the ball at different angles. For the topspin serve, the ball is tossed lower and in front of the player and brushed from six to twelve o-clock, or bottom to top of the ball, creating a forward topspin serve. On the kick serve the ball is struck from 7 to 2 o'clock (5 to 11 o'clock for left-handed servers), or diagonally upward, which imparts an oblique spin, causing the ball to jump or kick.

Figure 4.16   Hip position for the topspin serve.

Figure 4.17   Topspin serve contact.

Follow-Through

On a kick serve, the wrist snaps out farther away from the body and therefore takes a route of snapping out first and then bringing the racket head around, heading toward slightly above the waist on the opposite side of the body. The topspin serve has a less pronounced swing path outward but more up and over motion.

MAXIMIZING THE EFFECTIVENESS OF THE SERVE

The player can maximize the effectiveness of the serve in four ways: hitting with power, adding a variety of serves, using disguise, and serving for location. Hitting with power is obviously something all players want; combined with the other three options, it can create an air of invincibility.

- **Hitting with power.** Hitting with power is an effective strategy for intimidating an opponent. It is used to get a free point or to get a weak reply from the opponent. The player uses power mainly on the flat serve, and hits to the corners or through an opponent. Hitting with power on every serve has its drawbacks: The opponent can get used to expecting a certain serve or pace, and the player can experience greater fatigue from hitting hard all the time.

- **Adding variety.** It is important that all players use variety in their serves. A proper mix of serves does not mean always serving hard to different locations; it means adding variations such as sometimes using a second serve as a first serve, or perhaps hitting different types of serves. A good server keeps track of what serves are effective against the opponent and when best to use them. At the start of a match, the player should hit serves to the opponent's strengths as well as weakness. This helps the player gauge just how strong the opponent's strength is. This information helps the player know what to expect on the return and devise strategies for winning the point.

- **Using disguise.** A good disguise starts with a ball toss that is in the same location regardless of whether it is a first serve or a second serve and whether the serve is a slice, flat, or topspin serve. (The toss behind the head on the kick serve does not allow for disguise.) The returner should not be able to guess what type of serve will be hit. Most good returners can read the hips and motion of the servers to know what serve is coming. They also may focus on the ball when the server is bouncing it or preparing to start the motion. So, the more consistent the server's early movements are, the greater chance of a successful disguise. To prevent the returner from getting a good read on the ball, the server can try to hide the ball in the hand as long as possible. Rotating the trunk may hide the ball from the returner's view. Another way to disguise the serve is with a quick toss or a toss that is hidden by a longer reach of the arm. The returner doesn't usually see these types of disguises, so they can be surprising as well.

- **Serving for location.** It is vital to serve to a variety of locations. Players should use variations of the out-wide, body, and T serve hit to specific locations, for example, the body forehand, body backhand, a serve that starts to the body and kicks out wide or vice versa, or a slice serve that starts to one location and moves to another. Many times players get stuck going for big serves to the lines and neglect the body serve. The server should use the butterfly method when serving—mixing up the location from the corners to the body and from the body to the corners. To visualize the butterfly method, imagine the shape of a butterfly on the court. The wings go out for a serve hit wide, and then they come back in for a serve hit to the body. Some players are very good at returning when they are stretched out, so the body serve is necessary.

CREATING AN AURA

Once a player begins to maximize the effectiveness of the serve, holding serve becomes easier. Great servers have an aura surrounding their serve, which means their opponents fear their serve or at least think it is hard to break. Following are some tips and thoughts for players to create an aura surrounding their serve.

- **Establishing a routine.** Routines in general are very important in tennis, but for a serve, routine is essential. All great servers have a routine before they serve. For example, Maria Sharapova's routine includes pulling back her hair and taking a little hop, signifying her preparation for the serve. A consistent routine can calm a player in match play situations. The pre-serve routine should include how the player steps up to the line, the way the player gets in a balanced position for the stance, the number of times the player bounces the ball, and how the player begins the motion. How to perform this pre-serve routine is up to the player, but the goal is to be consistent.

- **Taking command of the court.** A strong look to the other side, an energy hop, or pumping up can help a player take command. The player should stand up tall and develop a plan for the point before stepping up to the line, keeping in mind that the serve can control the flow of play.

COACHING POINTS

The serve is the one shot over which players have the most control, and yet amazingly players frequently lose their service game. Although the return game has improved, the problem of holding serve derives mostly from the psychological battle players face as well as the effectiveness of their serves. Holding serve, especially for a player who has just broken serve or who is in a pressure situation, is a real test. For many players, the pressure leads to shorter breathing, the legs feeling shaky and weak, and the mind becoming unclear about the best location for the serve. Other players may start to think about winning instead of about executing a good serve.

The best way to approach serving in these situations is for a player to focus on the serve location based on strategy or on the opponent's strengths and weaknesses. Another option that can help a player hold serve is to focus on a component of the serve. For example, after retrieving a ball from the back or side fence, the player should stand behind the baseline and practice the toss or maybe a flex of the knees to trigger the mind to focus on that component of the serve. It helps to step up to the line after using this trigger, go through the routine, and deliver the intended serve. The player can think of this trigger as a way to get the point started in the way the player wants to. This trigger is helpful when the player feels nervous or is struggling to get in a first serve.

- **Using a consistent ball bounce.** The ball bounce varies for each individual. Whatever the player chooses, it is important to stay consistent and make it part of the pre-serve preparation.

- **Being mindful.** Good servers usually look as though they are always thinking—and they are. They give themselves constant reminders of what they need to do to hit a good serve; they are plotting their strategy.

- **Embracing the challenge.** Good servers like the challenge of getting out of trouble with a big serve, fooling an opponent, or, if they do lose their serve, making it the hardest game that returner has ever played. Embracing the challenge means delivering in big situations and delighting in an escape from a near break.

PUTTING IT ALL TOGETHER

The serve can be the difference in the tennis player's ultimate level. A simple progression to develop a player's serve is as follows: First, the player must analyze the type of role the serve will have in the game style. Then, the player can learn and perfect the proper technique needed to hit all the serves and maximize effectiveness; develop the ability to hit for power, variety, location, and disguise; and create an aura surrounding the serve to show that the serve is reliable and doesn't break down under pressure.

Improving the serve takes attention to detail and a lot of practice. The best way to understand and practice the serve is with a bucket of balls on a tennis court. This is where the player can experiment with different ways of serving, work on skills, establish a good rhythm, and develop the serve into a shot that matches playing style. Chapter 6 provides drills to work on learning the different serves, practicing rhythm, and maximizing the effectiveness of the serve.

CHAPTER 5

RETURN SKILLS

The serve return is the player's first line of defense against the opponent's serve. An effective serve return is the best and quickest way to get opponents to doubt their ability to beat the player. The server has all the advantages, so an effective return is not easy. A successful return is part vision, part technique, and part good decision making. For vision, the player needs training to see the ball well. Proper technique increases the effectiveness of the return. Good decision making means that the player needs to hit the correct return at opportune moments.

The basic goal of the return is to get the ball back in the court. The difference between good returners and great returners is whether the ball is merely returned or returned with a strategy in mind. For a great return, the ultimate goal is to take the opponent's first strike and establish the returner's first strike. A first strike is a ball that gets a player on offense. The psychological boost that comes from returning a great serve is invaluable. Whether the player uses a well-placed return to back up an opponent in the court or makes the opponent hit one more ball, the ability to return effectively gives the player confidence in a match. The following characteristics are important for successful returns:

- **Consistency.** A consistent return is less offensive. The goal of the consistent return is to neutralize the opponent every time. This returner tries to put pressure on the server by not missing any returns and consistently coming up with effective ones.

- **Variety.** A good mix of returns is a valuable tool to have, especially when the player makes smart decisions about when to use which return. A returner who smells the opportunity to hit it hard, knows when to get it back higher and deeper, or decides to use a slice at an opportune moment is a force to be reckoned with.

- **Accuracy.** A successful returner can place serves to a favorable location. The player who has the ability to hit it deep in the court, down the line, or at a crosscourt angle and properly places the returns, puts an opponent on the defensive and gains a great advantage.

- **Power.** Returning for power can be equated to high risk and high reward. This all-or-nothing approach is definitely offensive. The returner can hit certain shots, such as a forehand, with power when it is a weapon. This type of returner can also hit for power by taking the return early and using the power of the serve to direct the return. The risk is missing the return and giving free points to the server.

The return was a cornerstone of great champions such as Jimmy Connors, Andre Agassi, Chris Evert, Björn Borg, and Mats Wilander. They were able to keep pressure on an opponent with their ability to take a strong serve and return it effectively. They made an opponent's strong serve seem like a weakness. Their returns revolutionized the way tennis was played.

Today, many players want to have a good serve and try to get good enough to start a point, but they rarely work on their return. As a result, the return becomes the natural time for most tennis players to not try as hard. Today's ultimate returner is Rafael Nadal—not because his return is stronger than everyone else's, but because he never lets up. He tries his hardest on each point. Kim Clijsters is a top returner, too. She uses her return to take control of the point immediately. Her aggressive style puts her in an offensive position from the beginning.

Executing a successful return can be a challenge. The player's reactions and the technique of the shot need to be sharp in order to react to an opponent's serve. Servers have the upper hand, so finding a measure of success on the return can help a player influence the outcome of the situation. Obviously, a player won't always be able to hit effective returns, but establishing a return that works against a particular serve style is important. Against a big serve, an effective return may simply be a neutralizing return that keeps the server from getting into the first strike immediately. Against a weak serve, it may mean hitting an aggressive return that puts the returner on the offensive.

This chapter discusses the different types of returns, the techniques to hit them properly, and the thought process associated with returning the serve. Chapter 6 provides drills to hone a player's skills in order to become a great returner.

DEVELOPING THE RETURN

The optimal return style depends on a player's overall game style as well as the opponent's serve. The three main styles of returns are offensive, defensive, and neutralizing. The offensive return can also be considered the first-strike return because it is an aggressive strategy to establish a first strike on the return. The defensive return is used to get the ball back in the court somehow, someway, with a blocking shot or a slice. The neutralizing return is used to try and create a fair starting point for the rally with any shot.

The following is a breakdown of each type of return. Although a player may prefer one type of return, a great returner must be able to play all three types to react effectively to the opponent's serve.

Offensive Return

Offensive returns are hit aggressively and usually on weak first serves or on second serves. If the player's goal is to use the return to take control of the point, an offensive return is needed. A player can hit an effective offensive return in three ways. One way is to be very aggressive on any serve the player can read well. Another way is to transition to the net to put pressure on an opponent. The third way is to hit the ball hard or at a medium pace to an opponent's weakness or deep in the court. Each of these offensive return styles can be hit hard with a flat, topspin, or slice shot. More importantly, they all give a player a greater chance of getting an easier shot on the next ball.

When hitting an offensive return, the player can hold position in the court (usually near the baseline), then step in and take the serve on the rise or move backward. The player's offensive style depends on the player's preference, success rate, and overall game style.

Defensive and Counterattacking Return

All players would like to hit offensive returns every time, but it is not always possible, so they have to be flexible in their service return goals. The returner's mindset must be adjusted based on the server's strengths. If an opponent has an overpowering serve, then simply making the return becomes an effective tool, especially if the server is used to getting a lot of free points on that serve. Through the course of a match the returner can wear out the server mentally because they have to work so hard to achieve their goal of establishing a first strike. This type of return can lead to the server feeling as though the returner is a scrappy defender, and a player that gets everything back in the court.

A defensive or counterattacking return is blocked back with a flat shot or slice that may provide the player with ample time to recover back in the court. This return is used in a variety of situations: when an opponent has hit a good serve that is powerful or tricky, when the server has served to the returner's weakness, when a ball bounces or spins out of the returner's optimal strike zone, or even when the returner simply doesn't like to hit a return. Regardless of the reason for using the defensive return, the player must always remember that the goal is to get the ball back in the court. Of course, it is beneficial to do a little more than simply return the ball, so as to prevent the opponent from starting out the point with a winner.

Sometimes the player's positioning in the court or a weakness in executing a certain type of return can dictate a defensive return. It may also mean the player has misfired on a return and hit it poorly, resulting in a short or weak return. This means the player is likely to be in the defensive phase at the beginning of the point. The positioning associated with a defensive return is one where the player is compromised in the court and can't execute the shot well enough to push the server back in the court.

Neutralizing Return

Players use the neutralizing return to initially minimize the opponent's strengths and even out the playing field to make the next shot easier to handle. The degree to which a returner can neutralize a serve depends on the strength of the server. Whenever possible, the neutralizing return should be elevated to an offensive return, especially on second-serve returns or returns where the server is becoming easier to read.

The court position for the neutralizing return can vary. In general, stepping inside the baseline to take a ball early can enhance the returner's ability to neutralize a serve. Another possible position is staying near the baseline in order to get the player out of their pattern of establishing a first strike. Being too far back in the court or in a defensive position makes neutralizing an opponent's serve more difficult because the returner must hit a bigger return.

RETURN AND STYLES OF PLAY

As discussed in chapters 1 and 2, it is important to play within a particular style of play. The five styles of play are also relevant to the return. The return should become an extension of the player's game style. The strategy for returns is different for each style of play.

- **Aggressive baseline play.** This game style is aggressive and focused on a first-strike ball. The aggressive baseline player wants to dictate play with groundstrokes, so it makes sense to try to do so immediately. This style uses offensive powerful topspin and flat returns. A player using this style should learn how to hit a swinging volley. The aggressive baseline player is smart to balance the return game by sprinkling in some neutralizing returns with offensive returns. This strategy is essential when the player is fooled on a serve or when the opponent has a good serve and the best the player can do is get it back.

- **All-court play.** This style combines finesse and power in a variety of ways to return in an offensive or neutralizing fashion. This type of returner can hit aggressive topspin or flat shots, a good slice that stays low, a good blocked shot hit for depth, or a delicate drop shot.

- **Serve-and-volley style.** The player who uses this style wants to maintain an aggressive nature, even on the return. It is possible for this returner to use groundstrokes to return, but it is also possible to try to take the shot early and transition to the net. This offensive style generally lends itself to transitions to the net, slice approach shots, and drop shots. The serve-and-volley attacking style is hard to develop on the return because the player needs to develop attacking shots as well as defensive shots in order to have a plan B. Players using this game style usually start to shine toward the pre-college years. Balancing this style of play with ability to play parts of other styles can be very productive in college. Playing on the professional tour takes an attacking style, with weapons.

- **Rallying baseline play.** This style is especially used for returning in an effort to neutralize the server. The player who adopts this style does not like to be as aggressive as players using the other styles and prefers playing a more conservative return. This player may be able to hit more aggressively, but not consistently, and ultimately tries not to be on defense after the return. This player hits effective, but not overpowering, flat and topspin groundstroke returns as well as slices. Most players start out with the rallying baseline style of return. As players develop the return, they should adopt a more aggressive style.

- **Defensive baseline play.** Returners who play this style do so because they have a technical flaw (such as poor vision or movement) that prohibits improvement, their court positioning is far back, and their return is weak and lacking depth. The player who adopts this style hits flat and topspin shots and slices, but is not able to hit them consistently or very effectively. This player tries to hit neutralizing returns but ends up hitting mainly defensive returns and begins most rallies after the return on defense. Defensive returners may use poor location on returns.

RETURNS AND SERVING STYLES

Chapter 4 examined the attitudes and thought processes of the player who uses each type of serve. The returner needs to find the right frame of mind and attitude to combat each type of serve. They are discussed next.

The following list represents the mental attitude and thought process of a returner who is up against a big serve.

- I will break my opponent's serve to undermine his confidence.
- I will hit every return back into the court and never give my opponent a free point.
- I will get my opponent down in the game (e.g., 0-15 or 15-30) so that she starts to put extra pressure on the serve.
- I will put pressure on the server's second serve so that he will try to overhit, which may result in a decrease of his first-serve percentage.
- I will confuse my opponent by standing in different locations and never giving her the same looks.
- I will mentally fatigue my opponent by making him work hard to hold the serve.

The following list presents the mental attitude and thought process of a player who is returning a serve-and-volley style serve.

- My returns are better than her attacking style.
- I will use the two-shot passing strategy (see chapter 8) and make him play the first volley at his feet forcing him to hit the ball up and allowing me to pass on the next shot.
- I will make all my returns and make my opponent beat me with the volley.

The following list presents the mental attitude and thought process of a player who is returning to a serve-and-stay-back server.

- Since my opponent is not serving and volleying, I will try to be more aggressive on my returns.
- I will focus on depth on my returns because doing so gives me a chance to push my opponent back and take control of the point. If needed, I will position myself farther back in the court and take a bigger swing on the return.

GRIPS

The grips for the return don't change much from the normal groundstroke, unless the player is stretched out and has to use a Continental grip (used for a block shot) just to get it back. One of the most important considerations for the grip is not which grip to use but which grip to hold while anticipating the return.

Two schools of thought exist on this issue: holding the grip of the player's strength and holding the grip of the player's weakness. Most players, especially those who use the two-handed backhand, hold the grip of their forehand and, as the serve comes to the backhand, use the nondominant hand to quickly turn the grip to the backhand grip. For players with a big disparity between their forehand and backhand, holding the grip of their weakness can be helpful. For example, a player whose one-handed backhand is not strong on the return may want to use the backhand grip expecting the server to predominantly serve to that weakness. This conserves time when preparing for the weaker shot. It is usually easier for players to switch a grip to their strength than switch to their weakness.

Another consideration in holding the grip is where to hold the racket while waiting for the serve. Returners can hold the racket slightly to the side of their strength, their weakness, or establish a neutral hold that can be switched easily to either the forehand or backhand grip. One point everyone can agree on is to hold the racket in front of the body. It should be comfortably placed in front using the grip of preference. Where it is placed in front of the body also is a consideration. The racket head can be held up or facing the other player. Players should experiment with all these grip considerations and establish a way of returning that results in the most consistent return possible.

STANCE AND LOCATION

Figure 5.1 Return stance.

The stance is very important to the success of the return because it provides a solid base of support for the player's movement. The player's goal is to establish a stance that allows for the quickest movements to the oncoming serve. The stance also gives the player the best opportunity to properly load the legs and arms to retrieve the serve. The player must choose a stance that is comfortable and that facilitates hitting the types of returns that are within the player's game style.

Generally, most players are in the ready position and facing the server across the court (see figure 5.1). The stance should be neutral and not slanted one way or another to give away any clues to the server, unless slanting to one side gives the player an advantage or the player is trying to get the server to go to a particular location. Players can slant to a weakness, knowing that it is easier to adjust to their strength. The stance should be low or based on a lower core, meaning that the sight line should be a little lower to track the serve. A lower stance also facilitates getting into a loaded position.

Players can experiment with different types of stances to suit their style. Court location also says a great deal about style; for example, it can indicate whether the player is an aggressive or defensive returner. Three locations on the court can be equally effective: behind the baseline, on the baseline, or inside the baseline. The main consideration for the player is what location gives the best opportunity to hit an effective return.

Behind the Baseline

This position favors all three baseline styles. The aggressive baseline player wants extra time to hit a big return, the rallying baseline player wants to neutralize the serve, and the defensive baseline player wants to hide a weakness or needs more time to get in good position. The clay court specialist also favors this position because it gives more time for the high-bouncing serve to come into the strike zone. This return positioning favors the returner who likes to set up and hit the return similar to a groundstroke; being farther back in the court allows the extra time to do so.

This location is farther back in the court, so the main disadvantage is that if the player is not able to hit a strong return from this position, the server has a distinct offensive position in the ensuing rally. The returner is susceptible to a drop shot or drop volley. When the returner stands far back in the court, the server has an easier time transitioning to the net because the server has more time to react to the return. Consistently returning from behind the baseline can lead to easy hold games for the server, which in turn leads to the opponent being more focused and fresher for the returner's serve game.

On the Baseline

The aggressive styles, including the aggressive baseline style, all-court style, and serve-and-volley style, favor this position because it puts them in a better position to be offensive. This court position gives the player more options than the other two locations. The returner is in a central location and should be versatile enough to handle it. When attacking the serve, the player can move in and take a weaker serve on the rise and catch the opponent by surprise. If the serve is hard to read, then the returner can play defense from a favorable position.

The main disadvantage of this location on the court is that it relies on the strength of the player's technique. Playing from this position requires the returner to have clean and efficient technique. A returner who stands in this location is challenged to be offensive and neutralizing, so poor technique causes the returner to be inconsistent or not as effective, which can give the server a distinct advantage.

Inside the Baseline

The three more offensive styles (aggressive baseline play, all-court play, and serve-and-volley style) favor this return. The type of player who wants to be in this position is effective at taking the ball on the rise or is able to time the return and uses this court position to take time away from the server. This returner also has a way of unnerving the server, especially if the returner is effective. Players such as Robby Ginepri can read the server's motions and see the ball well from this position.

The main disadvantage of this return location is that it is a low-percentage return. Every ball hit from this location is early or on the rise (unless the server has a very weak serve), so a player who cannot hit consistently early or on the rise, takes a big risk. Success from this location relies on excellent technique and great vision on the return. This return is susceptible to errors because normal serves that might not be too difficult to return from a deeper location, now become a challenge. The logic of a player who chooses this location will stem from one of the following strategies.

- **The need to be offensive.** I am going to be offensive no matter what because that is my style.

- **The need to be practical.** I need to take advantage of the server from the beginning because he has better groundstrokes than I do, and if I move back, I will really give him an advantage.

- **The need to take advantage of variety.** I have a variety of shots from this area and will try to break up the server's rhythm.

The player's location on the baseline can also vary based on preference as well as strengths and weaknesses, but the goal is to not give away too much court. Standing too close toward the center can give an opponent too much room to angle a wide serve toward the alley, and standing in the alley should only be used when a server continually exploits that area or has strength there. In that situation, the returner takes away the server's strength.

Another goal for stance and location is to make the server think about what type of shot the returner is going to hit or where the returner will stand. To this end, the location on the return can alter during a match with the goal of not giving away too much. When the server has to think about what the returner is doing, the server's attention turns to making adjustments, which may give the returner an edge.

TRACKING THE BALL

Tracking the ball is essential to a good return, and it requires instinct and intelligence. It takes instinct to react quickly to a ball and intelligence to get a sense of what serve is coming. Good technique and good vision are also vital to tracking the ball. Returners should study and analyze the server's routines, including ball bounces, tosses, service motion, and windup and delivery, to see if a player gives away any serves.

When tracking a ball hit from the server, the returner must get an early read on what is coming. The returner needs to try to see the ball in the server's hand and visualize it going through the potential routine and the motion; this is called *early tracking*. Early tracking enhances a returner's ability to see the path of the serve after contact (late tracking) because the returner tracks the ball from the server's racket rather than just as the ball crosses the net. Most beginners track the ball as it crosses the net. This timing is too late for a player who wants to be offensive.

Effective tracking takes several steps. First, the returner begins to watch the ball as the server holds it and steps up to the line. The returner should mentally run through these questions: Is the opponent hiding the ball or is it easy to see? Where is the hand with the ball placed? Is the ball on the racket or near the racket? What does the opponent do with the ball after bouncing it? Keeping track of all these details can provide key information. The following observations about how a server sets up for the serve do not always hold true. However, they can offer a look into how an alert returner can pay attention to key details.

- If the opponent is hiding the ball, he may have a well-disguised serve, and the upcoming toss may be equally disguised, so the returner must pay close attention to the body movement.

- If the ball is easy to see, then the returner should be able to see the toss and the motion clearly.

- A ball placed on the racket may signify a clean motion, which means the returner won't be able to pick up a lot of variations in the opponent's swing. (Usually, a server who starts with a ball set on the racket has a good start and a good finish.)

- If the opponent's toss arm is not set on the racket, it usually means the server has an unusual or different toss arm delivery or service motion.

- A server who has a solid serving routine tends to be an effective server.

Next, the returner follows the server's routine for the ball tosses. The returner should ask these questions: Does the server bounce the ball fast, slow, or rhythmically? How many times does the server bounce the ball? How quick off the ball bounce does the server get into the service motion? Again, though not fool-proof, the following observations provide insights into a server's action.

- A fast-bouncing ball may signify a quick motion or that the server is in a hurry, which indicates nervousness.

- If the server bounces the ball slowly, she may have a slow serving style that requires the returner to be patient in preparing to return the serve.

- A rhythmic bounce usually leads to a rhythmic motion.

- A returner should count the number of bounces a server uses for preparation. If the number is the same every time, the server is well practiced. If the number varies, the returner should pay attention to the bounce count and the serve that comes after it to see if any patterns exist.

Third, the returner watches the server's toss arm go up and sees the position of the server's body. The returner should ask these questions: Does the arm carry the ball up, or throw it up? Does the body make any turns in relation to the ball going up? If a server tosses the ball differently for different serves, the body motion for each serve is likely to be different, too. The following cues can provide the returner with an initial idea about the location of a serve.

- A toss outside at about the 2 o'clock position for right-handed players (10 o'clock for left-handed players) could indicate a slice.

- A low or high toss at 12 o'clock is usually a flat serve (unless it is tossed low and out, which is a low slice).

- A toss to the 12 o'clock position followed by a player brushing up on the ball would indicate a top spin serve.

- A toss behind going from 11 o'clock to 2 o'clock for the right-handed player (2 o'clock to 11 o'clock for left-handed players) with arching of the back means a kick serve.

- A body serve is difficult to identify because this serve can be hit from any position. However, most servers use one particular serve to hit to the body unless they are really smart servers and can use a variety of serves.

Finally, the returner pays attention to the server's body angle, the movement of the legs, and the general feel of the server's motion. The returner should observe how the server looks when making contact with the ball. The returner must also use good vision when observing the server's body positions on the first or second serve. Paying close attention to the ball can help the returner see the nuances of the server's body as they prepare to serve. The player's ability to be offensive or neutralize an opponent's serves with the return is very intimidating to a server, especially a good one.

Other factors can contribute to good tracking skills. The racket can provide a source of tracking, too. The returner holds it in front and in a position to point the tip of the racket head toward the direction of the ball. The front arm can also provide tracking. Off the stance, the returner takes a step with the outside leg to get behind the ball, and at the same time the front arm reaches out to get in its abbreviated takeback position. The front arm, especially if it is balanced and somewhat in front, can help in tracking the serve up to contact. Stance and movement greatly affect tracking skills. Excessive jumping up and down or side to side require constant adjusting and readjusting. Standing too tall and not being at the sight line of the serve can also throw off tracking skills.

After establishing a routine and a way of tracking a server from the beginning of the serve, the returner is better equipped to track a serve after contact. To improve tracking after contact, the returner can study the server's tendencies (e.g., for big points, he likes to hit here), know how different serves affect the ball (e.g., a kick serve produces a high bounce), and use the eyes to dictate movement. Oftentimes, returners move too much or guess where the serve is going instead of just watching the ball. Doing so can cause the returner to become off balance, and it could alter the plan for the return.

MOVEMENT

An essential part of the return is the timing of the split step and subsequent movement to the serve. The two main methods are the split step and moving forward to the ball or the split step and moving backward away from the ball. Another method is to not move at all, but stand still when returning the serve.

Figure 5.2 Split step for the moving forward method.

- **Split step and moving forward.** This method is generally initiated by a split step as the ball lands in the service box, shifting the weight to a slightly forward position (see figure 5.2). The main consideration in this method is how big to make the forward split step. This method can be very effective when the returner gets a good read on the opponent's oncoming ball because the body's momentum is moving forward to meet the ball.

    If the returner does not have well-developed tracking skills, this return has limitations. As stated earlier, too much movement can hamper tracking skills. Another potential problem is that if the serve is powerful, the returner could be moving too far forward to meet an oncoming power serve and not allowing enough time to prepare properly.

- **Split step and moving backward.** This method is similar to the moving forward method but it uses backward movement instead. This return can be very useful on slow hard courts or clay courts. This method is used when the player likes to run around a weakness or get in better position to hit a more aggressive shot. It has two potential negative consequences: Backward movement requires the returner to hit a better shot from a deeper position, and if the server sees the returner backing up, the returner could give up valuable ground on the ensuing rally and get aced out wide. A high-bouncing serve requires the backward method because of the opportunity to move backward and hit a shot in the returner's strike zone that is similar to a normal groundstroke.

- **Staying still.** This method is used if this is the player's choice of stance or when the opponent's serve is hard to read. It is a good method to get the returner's eyes more focused on the ball and to establish good contact on the return. Instead of taking a big, hopping split step forward, the player simply stays in place and tries to stay still as the server is in motion. This helps the returner track more effectively. At the server's contact with the ball, the returner takes a small split step forward with a quick shoulder turn to the ball, allowing the returner to come into the power strike zone. This way of returning minimizes movement and helps to get a better read on the serve.

A tip for the player using this method is to flex the abdominal muscles, stick out the posterior as in a squat, get the hands low, and focus on taking a quicker swing. The feet would be balanced, but feel a little forward momentum. The amount of movement would depend on the speed of the serve.

RETURN TECHNIQUE

The following description of the offensive and defensive return takes a close look at the actions that make up the parts of the return: preparation and backswing, forward swing and contact, and follow-through. Each return type has specific movements and techniques that distinguish whether the return will be offensive or defensive. As noted at the beginning of the chapter, another style of return is the neutralizing return. The technique for this style is the same as for the offensive or defensive returns; the difference is one of intent. A player uses a neutralizing return when attempting to minimize the effect the server has on the next shot. Neutralizing returns are hit to the middle of the court.

Offensive Return Technique

Offensive technique is dictated by moving forward and taking the ball early. The player decides whether and how to be more aggressive with the return as well as how to go for the shot. This is the toughest part of the offensive return—knowing when to be more aggressive and knowing when to get it in.

Preparation and Backswing

The player uses the usual grip for each side (see figure 5.3). The semi-Western and Eastern grips or somewhere in between are recommended; they are the most popular grips played today. The backswing is similar to the groundstroke but likely needs to be executed with a smaller, quicker loop in the backswing. The size and speed of the loop depends on the pace of the serve. A player can use the normal groundstroke loop if the shot is weak and there is ample time to take a bigger swing. If possible, the player should move diagonally forward to cut off the angle of the serve and reduce the response time of the server. However, when the serve is strong, a player may need to alter the movement.

Figure 5.3 **Preparation for an offensive return.**

Figure 5.4 Contact for an offensive return.

Figure 5.5 Follow-through for an offensive return.

Forward Swing and Contact

The forward swing is similar to groundstrokes, but it is more compact and is hit in a low-to-high fashion. It can have a straighter follow-through when just reacting to a serve. The impact zone (see figure 5.4) could be higher, lower, more forward, or more backward, depending on the upcoming serve and the returner's movement to the ball. The returner tries to move forward, getting the body weight behind the return.

Follow-Through

The follow-through for an offensive return (see figure 5.5) can be similar to the groundstroke, unless the player is deciding to come to net, in which case the player would take a shorter swing, placing the ball or hitting a slice shot that allows time to transition. The follow-through should be done in balance and with forward momentum to give the offensive returner a more penetrating shot.

Defensive Return Technique

Defensive return technique usually starts with poor court position, or poor technique. Usually this is seen as a poorly executed slice, a weaker or poorly executed normal groundstroke, or a block return when the returner is just trying to place the return deep in the court. The technique discussed here is for the blocked return.

Preparation and Backswing

When hitting a defensive return, the returner attempts to use the normal grip but may be caught in another grip, especially when there is no time to react to the upcoming ball and even more so when the returner has poor technique. This is a ball hit back over the net by any means possible. The returner needs to get the racket head behind the ball or at least in a position to square the racket face so that the ball will go back over the net and deep to the opponent's corner of the court.

Forward Swing and Contact

On a defensive return every possible effort should be made to swing the racket forward. The attack point of contact is used for angled serves that need to be cut off at an angle, and the rally or defensive point of contact is used for balls hit to the body or balls the returner got a late read on. Players should try to contact the ball with a compact swing and a firm grip to add pace to the shot.

Follow-Through

The follow-through for the defensive return is whatever is possible for the player in the situation, depending on the power of the serve and the player's court positioning. In this situation, the player usually tries to keep the ball in play and recover as soon as possible for the next shot.

PLAYING THE RETURN

The three main styles of returns are offensive, defensive, and neutralizing. The four types of return shots are the flat drive shot, the topspin shot, the slice shot, and the block shot. The aggressive flat or topspin, and, in some cases, the slice return are considered offensive. The blocked shot return is considered defensive, but the slice and the moving backward return versions can be either offensive or defensive depending on their effectiveness. At some point in every match, all players are likely to play all these returns, so it is important to know how to hit all of them.

Aggressive

The aggressive flat or topspin is one of the most offensive returns possible. A player who can hit either one of these shots on the return is doing pretty well because this type of return is something all players strive to develop. With the right amount of depth, power, and spin, an aggressive return can put the server on the defensive. Serena Williams has one of the most offensive returns on the women's tour. Her goal is to put her opponent on the defensive from the beginning, and give herself a great opportunity to stay on the offensive throughout the point.

How   The player should always be focusing on clean technique, which in this case is an early read on the serve, a proper split step, an efficient and immediate takeback, a good first-step movement, good balance, and follow-through. The returner should have in mind an idea of the optimal location, the intended way to hit it (flat or topspin), and how aggressive the shot will be.

Where   The returner can hit the aggressive flat or topspin returns from any of the locations on the court, but it is more effective when it is closer to or near the baseline. The player can still hit an aggressive return from a defensive position behind the baseline, but this position gives the server a split second longer to prepare for the return. This return is usually hit deep (2 to 3 feet, or 0.6 to 0.9 m, from the baseline and alley) in the court or at a sharp angle (near the service line) and is hit for power. The player should hit aggressively to a particular target and maintain control while doing it. Going for too much or losing control of a shot can lead to errors and may backfire as a strategy, giving the server the advantage.

When   The returner should hit this type of return when the serve is weak, when the returner is feeling confident, or when the returner wants to take a chance. A player should try to do this when up in games (e.g., 15-40, 0-30, 15-30) to maximize low-percentage return chances.

Block Shot

This shot can be offensive or defensive. The offensive version is hit when the player is looking to transition to the net off the serve, and the defensive version occurs if the returner is not in a good enough position to be aggressive. Novak Djokovic uses his athletic build and great hands to block the return effectively, especially when he is out of position while executing the return. He can also use this shot to surprise the server by coming to the net and putting pressure on the opponent, or he can simply block it deep to recover and reset his position.

How   The returner gets the racket head on the pathway of the oncoming serve and makes a quarter turn of the body while bringing the racket back about head level. The player pushes out in a gradual high-to-low fashion similar to a high volley. However, instead of the lofty ball of the volley, the player has a fast-paced ball approaching. On the offensive block, the player moves forward with momentum toward the net. The defensive version would try to recover back to the middle in time for the next shot. For proper execution, both styles require relatively good balance.

Where This return can be played from any location, but the more offensive locations near or inside the baseline are preferred. Because this shot is usually used for placement and not as much power, hitting a block shot from a defensive position behind the baseline could keep the returner in a defensive position. The goal is to hit this ball deep in the court with a bit of loft or, if the returner is really good at it, at a lower trajectory. This shot can be hit crosscourt or down the line based on preference and execution. The logical choice would be down the line because if the player is transitioning to net, it provides better court position. However, the player could use a crosscourt shot if the server has poor movement or a weakness to the crosscourt side. In other words, whatever works best, is best.

When This shot is hit when the returner is trying to get to the net as soon as possible. It is mostly effective on a second serve or a weak first serve. The returner usually takes the ball on the rise or close to it when hitting the offensive version. The defensive version is used when the serve was good and the best response is to block it back because the returner got a late read on the serve or was off balance.

Slice

This return is offensive or defensive. Roger Federer uses the slice backhand return almost exclusively. He is very effective at keeping the ball low and not allowing the server to gain much of an advantage once the rally has begun. The offensive version is hit when the player can move forward and see the potential for transitioning to the net. The defensive version stays low to make it harder for the server to get an easier next shot. This is a very effective shot and especially effective when mixed in with more aggressive drive returns.

How This shot is hit similar to the block shot, but the slice has more undespin or more of a high-to-low follow-through. The slice also uses the carioca step (see page 43–44) during the hit, which keeps the shoulders turned through the shot.

Where The best location for executing the offensive slice is on the baseline or inside it, and the defensive slice is usually hit behind (but not too far behind) the baseline. The slice should be hit to a position deep in the court (approximately 2 to 3 feet, or 0.6 to 0.9 m, from the baseline and alley), either down the line or crosscourt, and should stay at a low trajectory. As with the block shot, the slice can be hit crosscourt or down the line. Down the line gives better court position, but crosscourt can be effective if the server has poor movement or a weakness to the crosscourt side.

When The player can hit this return offensively when stepping into the court and in good position in the court. It is most effective when the serve is weak or becoming predictable and allowing the player to be more aggressive. The goal of the best slice shot is a ball that lands deep in the court or low to the ground and is tough for the opponent to hit. This return is hit defensively when the returner is stretched out and it is the only way to get the ball back in the court, or if the returner is in a defensive position when hitting it.

Moving Backward

Moving backward on the return originated on clay courts because the speed and bounce of the serve on clay courts allow extra time to run around and hit the return on the strong side. This return can be offensive because the player is moving backward to gain a better chance to hit with a weapon. The return can also be defensive if a player misjudges the ball, doesn't hit an effective shot, or gets off balance. Rafael Nadal uses this type of return very effectively on a variety of surfaces and prefers the extra time to prepare for his return.

How   Moving backward on the return should be done quickly, as soon as the opponent tosses the ball up in the air. The easiest way to back up is to backpedal and then split step as the opponent strikes the ball. This quick movement allows the returner to execute a powerful shot from a defensive position.

Where   The returner can stand on or near the baseline and then move backward or can be farther back (1 to 3 feet, or 0.3 to 0.9 m) and then move backward. When moving back from a deeper position, the player needs to hit a great shot with depth to consider it offensive. The moving backward return should be hit deep (approximately 2 to 3 feet, or 0.6 to 0.9 m, from the baseline or alley) either down the line, crosscourt, or hit to a location that may neutralize the opponent.

When   This return should be played when the returner has a real strength in a shot or is trying to hide a weakness. The player can apply the strategy of using the strongest shot to get to the opponent's weakest shot. Moving backward can be an option when the player needs extra room to run around a well-hit serve. If a player is having trouble adjusting to the pace of the serve, moving backward provides another option. This style of return should not be used against an effective serve-and-volley style server, unless the effectiveness of the returner outmatches the effectiveness of the server. The serve-and-volley style player uses the split second of more time to close even tighter on the net, which can make for easier volleys. Moving backward is most effective on a weak or kick serve.

CHARACTERISTICS OF A GOOD RETURN

The following is a summary of the characteristics of a good return. As players establish proper return technique and learn the different returns, they should incorporate these characteristics into their play.

- **Good vision and tracking.** A good returner sees the ball early and can track it through contact. This vision sets in motion technique that allows the returner to be more offensive and to have more options. It can dictate the type of shots the player hits. For example, a player who sees the ball well gets there a split second earlier and can execute a topspin shot instead of a more defensive shot. Poor vision and tracking skills can make the returning process less reliable and can cause inconsistencies and technical errors.

- **Great balance.** Aggressive returns require a great deal of balance for the player to get the best possible ball strike every time. Balanced returners can get themselves in position no matter what serve is hit, and they can have the balance to execute the shot they want to hit, even from a stretched-out position. Good balance also aids the player's recovery back in the court for the next shot. Good vision, proper stance, and movement to the ball affect the player's balance.

- **Good shot selection.** Knowing what type of shots to hit in the right situation requires vision, balance, and great instinct. The best players can see an oncoming serve and assess in a split second how to attack it. A good return is measured by the winner hit, the well-placed shot, or the ball that allows the returner to come to the net. It can also be a shot returned that the server thought was an ace. The goal of good shot selection is understanding when to go for a winning shot and when to just get the ball back. It is the true test of the returner. A great returner can blend offensive shots with defensive shots and be consistent. Poor shot selection can lead to loose errors or easier, weaker shots the opponent can use to stay on the offensive.

- **Bravado.** A returner needs a certain bravado that says, I'm not going to back down, and I will get that serve back. As discussed earlier, Rafael Nadal takes this a step farther by showing that he will fight for every point to maximize his game. A player who has such bravado on the return and the serve can give the opponent the feeling of being pressured all the time.

It is great to try to incorporate all the characteristics of a good return, but the player should never lose sight of the fact that the primary goal of the return is to just get it in. Starting off with this mentality may sound defensive in nature, but every player must start here and build off it, knowing that getting it in at least keeps the rally going. Where it goes is up to the player.

MAXIMIZING THE EFFECTIVENESS OF RETURNS

The following tips can help a player stay sharp and focused when returning serve.

- **Focusing on the big serve coming.** For an opponent who has a big serve, it helps to always expect the biggest serve when the opponent is down in a game. Armed with this expectation, the player is mentally prepared to handle the big serve that inevitably will come. Returners often relax when they get a break point. They wait for the server to miss or are not as aggressive as they should be when returning in this situation. A player with this attitude can be reminded to focus by thinking *and* saying aloud that the server's best serve is coming.

- **Making the opponent play.** This mentality is similar to the scrappy defender mentality; the ultimate goal is to apply pressure on the server. Sometimes, this can be done with an aggressive return, but many times it can be done by just thinking, I will make the server play no matter what the server's serve is like. This trick is beneficial when an opponent is tired and prone to miss easy shots, or when the opponent has played a lot of tough points in a row and thinks he hit a great serve only to see it come back and have to hit another ball.

The following tips can help to break up the server's rhythm by using different stances and varying returns.

- **Using different stances.** There are no rules as to where to stand when returning serve. If a player is having trouble returning serve, trying to hide a weakness, or needs to break up a server's rhythm, then trying different stances is an option. The player can stand close in or way back when returning a big serve or a serve-and-volley style serve. Another option, especially if hiding a weakness, is to give the opponent the open court of the player's favorite shot. This strategy can sometimes make the opponent go for more than usual on the serve, potentially throwing off the rhythm.

- **Varying types of returns.** Varying the types of returns can also break up an opponent's rhythm, because the opponent gets used to seeing the same type of return coming back and starts to expect it. By hitting aggressive, neutralizing, and defensive returns to different locations, the player can confuse the opponent and cause a change in rhythm enhanced by indecision.

CHAPTER 6

SERVE
AND RETURN
DRILLS

The serve and return are the two most important parts of the tennis game. How a player starts points says a great deal about that player's overall game style and projected level of success. The ability to start a point in an advantageous position gives the player confidence and helps the player grow and develop. An effective serve or return makes an immediate statement about the player's strength, accuracy, variety, and consistency.

A successful serve and return allow players to start a point on offense, allowing them to focus on what shots they should use to keep an opponent on defense. As a result, players are likely to develop a variety of groundstrokes to use to their advantage. Conversely, when players start points in a defensive position, their initial reaction is to play defense first. As a result, their opponents dictate their shots, and the players have to work hard in each point to get back into an offensive position. A successful serve and return gives players the freedom to explore offensive strategies, making the game more interesting and fun.

SERVE DRILLS

The drills in this section will ultimately provide an advantage when the player begins to play points. This section presents the following types of drills, which are designed to help players improve their game. The drills are presented in a progressive fashion, thus maximizing a player's serving effectiveness.

1. Grooving drills to work on fundamental techniques and warm up the player's service motion

2. Power technique drills to add power to the player's fundamental techniques and overall service game

3. Specific serve and location drills to work on variety, disguise, and location for the player's service game.

Grooving Drills

The goal of these grooving drills is to help the player practice the techniques and rhythm of the serve and to prepare the player for more complex and intense practice or match play. All serves are made up of a series of precise movements that combine rhythmically to produce a successful service motion. Performing grooving drills is one way to really focus on development and consistent execution of these phases of movement.

Overall, these drills are designed to help the player simplify the service motion. They focus on the specific phases and on using specific cues when practicing the serve. Effective for the flat serve, the slice serve, and the topspin or kick serve, these drills progress from noncontact drills to contact drills on the baseline. The player can perform the noncontact drills anywhere on the court or even away from the court for extra grooving practice. All of these grooving drills should be a daily part of the warm-up routine before doing the power drills or practicing specific serves and locations.

TOSS CONSISTENCY

Purpose: To establish the optimum extension and location for the toss and develop consistency.

Procedure: Standing on the service line, the player goes through the service motion without hitting the ball. The player tosses the ball and freezes at the top of the release. The ball should come back down and land back in the outstretched hand. The player should focus dually on the toss arm extension and the end location of the toss—the two main factors that lead to a consistent toss. Players do 2 sets of 10 repetitions. A high number of catches for every 10 repetitions would be 7 or 8 out of 10.

Coaching points: A toss that doesn't land back in the player's hand may indicate a lack of arm extension or too much wrist usage. The toss arm should always feel as though it is carrying the ball upward toward the release point, ensuring good extension of the arm. When the toss arm isn't extended properly, the wrist has a tendency to flick the ball up into the air, causing an inconsistent toss. The player's goal is to open all the fingers at once at the top of the toss arm extension so that the toss has little or no spin.

> **CRITICAL CUE:**
> This drill can be used as a diagnostic in practice on a day when a player's serving is erratic. The drill quickly determines whether the player's toss is the culprit.

RELEASE AND FREEZE

Purpose: To check the rhythm and positioning of all moving parts during the toss and takeback and to be sure the leg work, takeback, and toss all work together to set up the serve. Seeing the relationship of the arm, the legs, and the ball being tossed can quickly clean up rhythm issues and hitches (stops and starts in technique) that develop in the swing.

Procedure: The player stands on the service line, executes the service motion, and freezes at the moment the toss is released. The player looks back to see where the elbow and feet are positioned. The shoulders should have a forward and upward tilt, the elbow is at a 90-degree angle upward and outward from the body, and the palm is facing downward. The feet are together, and the legs are loaded in the pinpoint stance or balanced comfortably and loaded in the platform stance. The player should focus on the trophy position so that the upper body loads backward and the front hip points outward toward the net. The player should be looking up at the toss arm. The player repeats this drill 5 to 10 times to establish consistency in the position of all moving parts at the time when the ball is tossed.

Coaching points: Characteristics of good motion include the elbow being close to the set position, upright, and not dipping toward the body when the ball is tossed. If the arm and racket head are in a low position at the toss, a late contact point results. If the arm is not set at the toss, the player needs to speed up the arm movement. If the feet are not in a location that allows the body to explode upward, the player needs to work to coordinate the foot movement with the toss.

THROWING

Purpose: To work on the position and movement of the serving shoulder and arm throughout the service motion. The takeback directly affects the acceleration and resulting power generated on the serve. Throwing for distance mimics the techniques of the service motion.

(continued)

Throwing *(continued)*

Procedure: The player and a partner or coach stand about 10 feet (3 m) apart and warm up by throwing a tennis ball back and forth. The two players gradually increase the distance between them and add more loft to the throws. After warming up, they proceed to the baseline. The player goes through the serve motion and throws 10 balls to the deuce side and then 10 balls to the ad side and then repeats. On the first 10 balls to each side, the player should verify a full takeback so that when serving, the player achieves maximum acceleration toward the ball and a full extension of the serve arm. On the second set of 10 balls to each side, the player should assess the extension of the arm before and after release. The arm should extend toward the target, and the hips should rotate forward. The player should see the arm extend and finish in front of the body. The entire rhythm of the server should be one fluid motion from the takeback to the release.

Coaching points: A quick release or an upward or downward release signify poor extension and can be fixed by throwing more balls and making this drill part of the daily serving routine.

EXTEND AND TRAP

Purpose: To work on coordinating toss height and achieving full arm extension for optimal contact on the serve.

Procedure: The player stands with the front foot against a tall wall or fence and assumes the service stance. The player takes an abbreviated swing and tosses the ball up so that it travels up the wall or fence, aiming for a height equivalent to the fully extended hitting arm. When the ball reaches its peak and optimum contact point, the player reaches up with the racket and traps the ball against the wall or fence and holds the position. While maintaining good balance, the player then checks for maximum extension of the hitting arm. Holding and pressing the ball against the fence also practices applying the push or power needed to finish the stroke. The player should repeat this action until contact consistently occurs with a full extension. Then, the player takes this feeling to the service line and practices serving with a focus on this new extension and contact point.

Coaching points: When the focus on extension at the contact point learned in this drill is transferred to actual serving at the baseline, the player is likely to hit the first few balls way past the service box. This means the drill worked. The player then needs to use more wrist snap and greater leg power to get the ball in the court.

WRIST SNAP EXECUTION

Purpose: To develop a concise contact and to learn the feeling of properly snapping the wrist to get the ball in the court for different types of serves.

Procedure: The player stands on the service line and hits 5 to 10 serves into the deuce or ad box using normal service motion. The focus is on extending the racket up and snapping the wrist down to get the ball in the court. The player practices the wrist snaps needed for the different serves and then practices serving to different locations for each type of serve. After hitting the first 5 to 10 serves, the player moves back to a position halfway between the service line and the baseline and serves again. After another 5 to 10 serves from this spot, the player moves back again.

Coaching points: For each location, the player must adjust the wrist snap and arm extension to successfully get the ball in the service box.

WRIST SNAP DISGUISE

Purpose: To practice proper wrist snap with disguise by delaying the adjustment for a particular serve.

Procedure: The player stands at the baseline and practices serving. As the player releases each toss, a coach or partner shouts out a location, such as wide, body, or T. The player adjusts accordingly to perform the indicated serve. The player should attempt 5 to 10 serves to each service box. This drill should be repeated in training until the player can consistently execute the proper wrist snap for each particular serve. Initially, servers may find this drill difficult because they are not used to adjusting for a type of serve while the ball is in air. Realistically, the ability to execute the serves in this drill consistently may take a few practices.

Power Technique Drills

To hit with power, a player needs a technically sound serve, which players can accomplish using the preceding grooving drills. To add power, players must focus primarily on leg work and the wrist snap. The strength and explosiveness of the back leg is the main contributing factor to maximizing power. The next five drills combine to work on adding leg strength, maximizing upper and lower body rhythm, placing the toss in the power zone, and adding power to the wrist snap.

BACK LEG STRENGTH

Purpose: To develop back leg strength and establish good use of the legs to explode up to hit the ball. This drill teaches body position: loaded back and ready to thrust upward and forward.

Procedure: The player stands on the baseline with a racket but no ball. The player takes a ready position as if to serve and then transfer the body weight onto the back leg. The player holds this position for 1 or 2 seconds and then explodes upward, going through the service motion. The explosion upward should be slightly exaggerated and slightly higher than usual. The player focuses on driving the back leg up and rotating the front hip forward. After making one imaginary swing, the player resumes the serve stance and repeats the movement. The server performs the drill up to five more times, moving toward the net on each serve. The player should focus on feeling the weight distribution from the back leg to the front while maintaining the good body position needed for a strong serve. This is a great shadow exercise that can be done with or without a tennis court.

Variation: The player can use a tennis ball and incorporate the toss into this exercise. With the toss, the player checks to see if the racket arm position is in a good location. If the arm or the racket head is not ready to swing when the ball leaves the hand, it could highlight a need for a quicker takeback.

CRITICAL CUE:
As weight shifts from the back foot to both feet, the player pushes off as if jumping off a diving board. Both feet should come off the ground 1 to 4 inches (about 2.5 to 10 cm).

NO LEGS

Purpose: To practice optimal coordination of the upper and lower body, which will help get maximal results from using the legs for power.

Procedure: The player practices 8 to 10 serves without using the legs at all but otherwise using a normal service motion. Doing so demonstrates how restricted a player's power is on the serve when not using the legs. The player hits 8 to 10 more

(continued)

No Legs *(continued)*

serves, this time adding the lower body movement. The player notes the difference in power when using the legs versus not using the legs. If the player does not notice much difference or if the serve is actually better without the lower body movement, the player should experiment with the stance or rhythm of the serve. This drill can help identify disconnections between lower body and upper body rhythm.

POWER ZONE TOSS

Purpose: To identify the power zone for toss placement and to highlight the feeling of keeping the weight back, which is necessary on all power serves.

Procedure: The player stands on the baseline with a ball but no racket. The player goes through the motion of serving but lets the toss drop to the ground. the player, coach, or partner marks this spot with a cone. If the toss lands close to a foot in front of the baseline, it is too far forward. Another cone is then added to highlight a goal location closer to the baseline. The toss and drop is repeated until the toss is consistently landing near the goal cone, which is in the power zone. The player then picks up the racket and incorporates the full serve to determine whether the new toss works with the full service motion. The goal cone may need to be adjusted, based on the feel of the serve and power generated, but the key is to have the toss in a position that doesn't cause a collapse in body position or result in reaching too far forward.

Coaching points: Most servers like the toss slightly in front of the baseline because it helps them move forward through the serve and hit with more power. However, this can lead to servers developing a toss location that is too far in front of the body, hindering their ability to create power on the serve. If the server continually tosses the ball too far forward (approximately 1 foot, or 0.3 m, in front of the baseline), then the server may be losing power on the motion.

CRITICAL CUE:

The player should think about the body staying behind the baseline and using a contact point slightly in front of the baseline. The general location for the power zone toss is twelve o'clock, above and forward from the body. This cue develops the feeling of going up higher for the contact and hitting up past the point of contact.

WRIST SNAP POWER

Purpose: To isolate the wrist snap at contact and help develop wrist strength.

Procedure: The player practices serves using a full motion but with just a platform stance and no leg movement forward. The serve is accomplished through upper body action, while focusing just on the wrist snap to generate power. If the serve goes into the net, a slight upward movement of the legs can be added to the motion, but just enough to get the needed height to clear the net. The player repeats this procedure 10 times. Then, the player practices another 10 or more serves while including the normal leg movement, but this time with a focus or movement that is straight up and not out, relying on the wrist snap for power and placement.

SERVING FIVES

Purpose: To practice power techniques from the previous four drills using repetition while progressively increasing power on the serve. When players are warmed up and hitting balls as hard as possible, they can identify the actual level of power they are capable of, enhancing their ability to tap into this power when needed.

Procedure: The server hits serves to both service boxes in sets of five and follows a progression of power, starting at 75 percent of maximum power for the first set of five, then 85 percent for the next set, and 95 percent for the next set. Then, the player hits two sets at 100 percent. Finally, the player hits a set of five of each serve type to each of the three basic locations, focusing on 90 to 100 percent power. The total number of serves practiced in this drill should not exceed 60. When repeating the drill at subsequent practices, the server should start at a lower power zone for any serve and location for which technique was inconsistent. The server should work to maintain technique and gain consistency and then advance to the next power zone.

Coaching points: Serving too many balls in practice, serving too hard for long periods of time, or serving with poor or worn equipment can be harmful to players' arms.

Specific Serve and Location Drills

When addressing the different types of serves (flat, slice, and topspin or kick) and the different locations (out wide, body, and T), players need to follow a progression. Players first need to drill the technique of hitting a particular serve to a general location, such as the service box.

When players are comfortable with their technique, they can introduce cone targets to drills to further pinpoint specific location and enhance accuracy. The cone for the T serve should be placed in the T corner of the service box (1 foot, or 0.3 m, from the midline and service line). The cone for the body serve should be placed approximately midway from the midline dissecting the service box in two and 2 to 3 feet (0.6 to 0.9 m) inside the service line. The out wide cone should be placed approximately 2 feet (0.6 m) from the singles sideline and 2 feet (0.6 m) inside the service line.

Players can make target practice more enjoyable by trying different variations of games, such as trying to hit a certain number of serves (5, 10, or 15) to a certain location. Players should practice their first serve and second serve, varying the locations. Players can work for accuracy, consistency, variety, or whatever helps them focus and keeps practice interesting and fun.

FLAT SERVE (POWER)

Purpose: To develop the flat, power serve.

Technique practice: Refer to page 89 for a review of serving technique. For most power serves, the visual cue for the toss is twelve o'clock, but this may vary slightly from player to player. At the end position of the service motion, players need to check that the wrist snaps down and the fingers point directly downward in front. The player practices serve technique until the motion feels fluid and the serve arm is sufficiently warmed up. Then, the player continues the drill by progressing to target practice.

Target practice: The server starts on the service line and attempts to serve the ball in the box and have it hit the back fence. With each successful attempt, the server takes one step back until reaching the baseline. Once on the baseline the server attempts to hit a powerful flat serve that lands in the box and bounces once before hitting the back fence as high as possible.

(continued)

Flat Serve (Power) *(continued)*

Coaching points: Some players lean their bodies toward or away from the serve location. Neither is ideal. Leaning in either direction can alter the swing path, which makes hitting the location more difficult. Players should focus on maintaining a straight posture, contacting the ball in the same location each time, and they should use the wrist to direct the serve to the desired location. Players' height can affect their ability to hit out wide. Taller players may need to use less outward wrist snap, needing only to change the body angle. Shorter players must contact the ball higher, and they must have strong upward body movement.

SLICE SERVE

Purpose: To develop the slice serve.

Technique practice: Refer to page 90 for a review of the technique. The player's wrist snap should bring the palm down with the fingers pointing in the direction of the body. The player practices the serve technique until it feels fluid and rhythmic and the player has properly warmed up the arm. Then the player moves on to target practice.

Target practice: The player, coach, or partner sets a cone in the deuce and ad service boxes (2 feet [0.6 m] from the service line and 6 inches [15.2 cm] from the singles line). Practice hitting 10 serves wide toward the cones so that the ball lands in the box and goes over the singles and doubles sidelines. Try to hit the ball so that it bounces into the side fence or netting.

TOPSPIN OR KICK SERVE

Purpose: To develop a high-bouncing serve similar to a high-bouncing topspin groundstroke.

Technique practice: Refer to page 90 to review the serve technique. The player should pay attention to the outward wrist snap; it should look and feel like throwing a dart to the side. As the wrist snaps outward, the fingers settle outward in the general direction of the shot. The player practices the serve technique until the motion is fluid and the player has properly warmed up the arm. Then, the player continues the drill by progressing to target practice.

Target practice: The player, coach, or partner sets 2 cones on the backhand corner of the service boxes. On the deuce side the cone is placed 6 inches (15.2 cm) from the service line and center line. On the ad side, the cone is set 3 feet (0.9 m) from the service line and 6 inches (15.2 cm) from the singles line. The server practices hitting topspin or kick serves to a partner that bounce higher than the partner's shoulder. Instead of hitting a return, the partner should catch the ball to show the server how effective the serve is.

SERVE LOCATION SCORING

Purpose: To develop the ability to hit serves to different spots through a progression of targets. This drill can be performed using any of the serves.

Procedure: The player aims at three locations (out wide, middle, and service T) in each service box. The locations may be marked in the service box by using additional tennis balls or targets. The player starts serving to one location on the deuce side and plays an entire standard scoring game serving to that target. If the player misses the first serve to the desired target, the player must use a second serve to the same location. If either serve makes it in the target area, the player goes up 15-love in the game. If the player double-faults or doesn't hit the target area, then the player goes down love-15. The player should follow this pattern of trying to hit in the same location for a game, then move to the next target on the deuce side and then the next, until the player is ready to serve on the ad side.

Variation: The player can add realism and pressure to this drill by playing against an opponent. Servers alternate for every point. If the server hits the target area, the server gets the point and goes up 15-0. If the server misses both serves, the other player gets the point, and the server is down 0-15. After one player goes up or down in the game, the second server repeats the same process; if they make one of their serves, they will either go up 30-0 if the first player missed their serves or 15-all if the first server was successful. When one player wins this game, the players play the next game to the next target area. Players can play a set in this fashion. This drill is useful for coaches needing to drill a group of players because it can accommodate four players (two on one side and two on the other) and be part of a rotation.

SERVING A GAME OF PIG

Purpose: To practice serves under pressure. This drill works on all types of serves and placement.

Procedure: Two players use cones or balls to divide each service box into three quadrants. The players spin a racket to determine who serves first. The server calls out the type of serve and its location in the service box (such as wide slice serve). If the server hits the spot called with the type of serve called, then the second player must duplicate the serve. If the server does not serve the designated serve or does not serve to the designated spot, the serve goes to the other player. On the first miss, servers earn the letter P. On the next miss, they get an I and on another miss they get a G. The first player to spell P-I-G is out.

RETURN DRILLS

The following progression of drills works through the characteristics identified for a great return. These drills start from basic and progress to advanced drills. First the drills work on vision or tracking the ball, then answering with power, and finally progressing into drills to learn and fine tune the different returns. For players to be their best, they must learn and practice all of the following return techniques and scenarios through drilling:

1. Vision drills to tune into tracking cues and preparatory techniques

2. Power drills to work on movement and acceleration for setting up and hitting through the zone for increased power and depth

3. Specific return drills to work on consistency, accuracy, and variety

4. Live ball drills to develop and test players' return skills in pressure situations

Vision Drills

A returner's vision drives the body and hand out to the ball. A player's ability to see the oncoming ball and ability to read the server's motion both contribute to good, strong contact with the ball. If the player can get an early read on the server's serve or target, then the player can begin to take the advantage away from the server. The following drills are designed to help the player develop and improve vision and ball tracking skills. If a player can track a serve early enough, then the player has a greater ability to be aggressive. Before performing these drills, the player should review the tracking technique information in chapter 5.

BILLY BALL

Purpose: To develop tracking skills and movement to the ball.

Procedure: The player and a coach or partner set up in any location on the court that allows enough space for the coach or partner to be about 3 feet (0.9 m) away from the player in a diagonal location. The positioning should simulate the position of a server and a returner set up in the normal return position. The coach or partner holds out a ball at various angles in the direction of the returner, simulating the starting path of different serves. Zeroing in on the ball's movement, the player split steps and moves to the ball, focusing on quick and precise movement. After each ball, the player moves back to the starting position and prepares for the next move.

Variation: The coach or partner can toss the ball in different directions instead of holding it. The player can catch the ball or make easy contact with a racket.

SHORT COURT TO BACKCOURT

Purpose: To work on tracking skills over increasing distances. This drill also aids the tracking of overheads because the shots also come from the service line.

Procedure: A coach or partner serves balls lightly crosscourt from the service line to the opposite service box. The player stands on the service line and returns the balls crosscourt. The player should focus on tracking the ball and moving to the ball's path as quickly as possible, then soundly execute the shot. After returning 8 to 10 balls, the player moves back 3 to 5 (0.9 to 1.5 m) feet and takes another 8 to 10 balls. This pattern continues until the player reaches the baseline. With each new location, longer focus is needed to track the ball and attune to the differences in trajectories and spins on deeper balls. The drill is repeated with the player returning down the line.

Variation: The coach or partner can hit harder serves to simulate the pace of a real serve. The returner can then focus on the tracking and technical skills needed for increasing amounts of acceleration on the ball.

Power Drills

The ability to create a power return depends on three factors: movement to the ball, stroke preparation, and acceleration at contact. A strong move with the outside leg is the primary step in a successful return. The number of steps needed after the primary step depends on a player's movement skills as a returner and the speed of the serve. The goal of any movement on any return is for the returner to maintain balance and prepare for the serve with the eyes and the body. The loading step drills in chapter 3 and the drills that follow are essential for developing the desired movement and loading for the return.

COMPACT MOVEMENT

Purpose: To practice the forward movement or flow needed when returning for power.

Procedure: The player takes position for completing returns from the baseline and then sets up three cones in a triangle: one cone 3 feet (0.9 m) directly in front of the player and two cones slightly to either side and 2 feet (0.6 m) in front of the player. The front cone marks the player's movement forward to execute the return shot, and the side cones mark the player's outside leg movement to either the forehand or the backhand side. The player assumes the ready position. A coach or partner serves different serves (flat, slice, and topspin or kick) in sets of 5 to 10 from the service line on the opposite side of the court. Within each set, the coach or partner serves to each of the three locations (out wide, body, and T). The player returns the serves to the target location specified by the coach or partner. The player focuses on the cones for a visual target of the direction for desired forward flow and the compact feel of the movement. The types of serves and the return locations should be specified before the drill begins. When the player has mastered this version, additional sets should randomize the serves and return locations to give the returner more realistic practice.

Coaching points: Compact movement keeps the body loaded and balanced, creating more power on the return. The compact feel comes from maintaining a good athletic stance.

TAKEBACK AND LOOK

Purpose: To coordinate preparation and body movement with the bouncing of the ball off the serve so the returner is positioned for an aggressive and powerful return.

Procedure: The player gets in the ready position to return serves from the baseline. A coach or partner serves balls in sets of 10 from the baseline. As soon as the server hits the ball, the player takes the racket back and prepares the body to contact the oncoming ball. When the ball bounces, the player stops all movement (as best as possible) and quickly checks body and racket positioning. The returner specifically checks that the racket preparation is set and the body is in balance and poised for a return. The server varies the location of the serves and uses different types of serves, allowing the returner to recover between serves to get ready for the next serve. After practicing this drill for 3 to 5 minutes, the returner can then begin to execute returns for an additional 3 to 5 minutes.

Variation: To increase the difficulty, the server can move to the service line. The server needs to slow down the pace of the serve initially to allow the returner to adjust. Then, then the pace can gradually increase. In this version, the faster pace makes the player prepare earlier and more quickly.

RETURN AND RELEASE TECHNIQUE

Purpose: To develop the arm extension used on the return.

Procedure: The player gets in the ready position to return serves from the baseline. A coach or partner stands at the service line and serves different types of serves (flat, slice, and topspin or kick) to the three different locations (out wide,

(continued)

Return and Release Technique *(continued)*

body, T). On each return, after making contact with the ball, the player practices the follow-through by releasing the racket immediately into the other hand at the end of the extension. (Refer to the Release Technique drill on page 59.) On the forehand side, the nondominant arm catches the racket in front of the body with the butt cap facing toward the net and the coach. The racket head should be flat. For the two-handed backhand return, the player should extend through contact and then hold the extension position at the follow-through. The racket position should point toward the server. Although the normal follow-through is out and across the opposite shoulder, holding the extension position emphasizes the use of the arms.

Coaching points: The position of the server on the service line tests the returner's ability to use a quicker or abbreviated takeback and release from a ball hit with more pace. The arm extension greatly enhances depth on returns and provides a platform where acceleration and wrist snap can be added for an aggressive strike on the ball that results in a powerful return.

RETURN ACCELERATION AND WRIST SNAP

Purpose: To develop the acceleration of the wrist snap that adds speed and topspin so that return shots bounce irregularly or out of an opponent's strike zone.

Procedure: The player stands on the service line and receives serves from a coach or partner who is positioned on the opposite service line. The coach or partner serves balls to the returner at a medium pace. The player hits 10 returns to a predetermined location. Then, the player moves back 3 steps and returns another 10 serves. Finally, the player moves back to the baseline and returns another 10 serves.

Coaching points: The returns from the service line require a quicker takeback and greater acceleration through the ball with extra emphasis on the wrist snap to finish the shot. The deeper location returns need the same quickness of preparation, but they require normal depth on the takeback to generate more power. While moving back, the player should continue to focus on maintaining the acceleration that was needed to return balls at the service line.

Specific Return Drills

The strength of the aggressive flat or topspin return, the slice, and block returns from the three return locations (inside baseline, on baseline, and behind the baseline) determines whether the return is considered offensive, neutralizing, or defensive. Specific return drills give the player the opportunity to zero in and improve on a particular return. The ability to execute a variety of returns is vital to the player's overall game. If used properly, it can make the player a tough opponent.

Because the technique for the return can be similar to that for a groundstroke, especially on a slow-paced serve, players should master the techniques and targets with their groundstrokes (using the drills in chapter 3) to create a foundation for adapting these shots for the return. For faster-paced serves, players should use an abbreviated preparation. Returning serves requires a change in timing and some tweaks to technique and positioning to deal with the increased pace and different trajectories and angles of a serve (coming from full extension above the server's head).

Where the player hits the return determines what ball the player faces next. To keep a server from getting into a rhythm, it's important to have a variety of returns to keep the server guessing as to what shot is coming back. Players should aim to hit their returns so that they can hit their weapon next or so that they are able to use a tactic they like to gain strength in the point. Each type of return has a specific location that works best, but the realistic goal is to hit a return that pushes the opponent back or off the court and allows the player to start the point off on a positive note. Crosscourt returns are mainly hit flat or with topspin; topspin, flat, and slice returns are mainly hit through the middle; and drives and slices are mainly hit down the line.

1. **Offensive returns.** The two popular offensive returns used in today's game are the aggressive flat return and the aggressive topspin return. The goal of both returns is the same: to push an opponent back in the court or pull a player off the court. These returns should be hit for depth and with power, and they are most effective when played from in front of the baseline. They can be hit crosscourt, down the line, or down the middle, but the optimal ending location is crosscourt because of the larger area to execute the shot.

2. **Neutralizing returns.** These returns are not quite offensive but not quite defensive. A player hits a neutralizing return to stay even off the return or to not give a server an easy next ball. This return is usually played as a slice shot, but can also be played with topspin from the baseline or slightly behind it. The player focuses on forward movement, but doesn't have the same go-for-it mentality used on the offensive returns. The optimum location for the neutralizing return is down the middle to make it hard for the opponent to create any sort of angle with pace off the shot.

3. **Defensive returns.** These returns are used to get the ball back in the court to a location that will not give the server an easy put away. The shots a player can hit are the block return, which has little or no spin, and the slice for when a player is slightly out of position and reaching. This return should be used primarily to hit down the middle and down the line to create less angle and options for the server's next shot. The returner can maximize this return if able to hit it to the server's weakness. This return is usually hit from just behind the baseline or even farther back behind the baseline.

The following drills can help players work on each of the different return options. These are working drills, or *no-frills* drills, because the player works on a part of the game. If any of the players struggle with poor execution, they should continue working on that return until they feel comfortable and before the coach or partner moves on to another serve. Players should drill all of the returns using the forehand and backhand.

AGGRESSIVE FLAT OR TOPSPIN RETURN

Purpose: To develop a penetrating aggressive return to any location.

Technique practice: The returner stands on the baseline in the normal return position, and the coach or partner stands on the service line on the opposite side of the court. The coach hits a few warm-up serves to the returner, and then the pace increases as the drill progresses. The coach or partner starts with flat serves hit toward the returner's forehand and backhand. After the returner has established

(continued)

CRITICAL CUE:
The player should first focus on hitting aggressive returns that would push an opponent back. Then, the player should focus on being more precise with the return location.

Aggressive Flat or Topspin Return (*continued*)

a rhythm, the server serves slice and kick serves to their locations (out wide and T). For the aggressive flat return, the returner focuses on forward movement to meet the ball and on hitting it flat or with a little topspin, low over the net, and deep toward the baseline. The server serves 5 to 10 repetitions for each serve and location, altering slightly if the returner has trouble with a particular serve or location.

Coaching points: The amount of power a player can generate on the return is key to hitting successful aggressive flat or topspin returns. As a result, a player's preparation is vital. In this drill with the server at the service line, the player develops a faster preparation because the serve arrives quickly. When moving back to the baseline, the returner should maintain the faster preparation, allowing for focus on adding more power. The power on this return is generated in part by the pace on the serve, so the returner must time the return to maintain the pace of the shot. To help with timing, players should master this shot (flat or topspin) in their groundstrokes before trying to establish it on the return.

Target practice: Players place the target cones and have the coach or partner serve from the baseline. For each location, the wrist snap and arm extension needs to accelerate and finish toward the target. For crosscourt, the player should focus on making contact early (before the front foot) and hitting around or over the outside of the ball. For down the middle, the player should hit with a slightly later contact point that is closer to the front foot. For down the line, the player should hit with a later contact point and with a more open racket to create a higher trajectory to clear the higher net down the line.

NEUTRALIZING RETURN DRILL

Purpose: To develop a consistent return that neutralizes the opponent by depth or placement.

Technique practice: The player stands on the baseline positioned for a return. A coach or partner serves balls from the service line. The pace of the serves starts out moderate and increases as the drill progresses. The server should vary the type of serve and location. The player practices moving up to the baseline to make the return, focusing on a longer takeback for a weaker serve and a shorter take back for a faster serve. The player should work on greater extension of the arm and a more pronounced wrist snap. For the neutralizing topspin return, the returner focuses on forward movement, aiming to hit a little higher over the net, and hitting deep in the court. For the neutralizing slice return, the returner should focus on keeping the ball low over the net and deep in the court.

Coaching points: The power that is generated from this return is a combination of the speed of the serve and good technical movement from the returner. For the topspin return, the key characteristic is the deep landing location (near the baseline). The key characteristic for the slice return is its low trajectory over the net and through the court that results in a low bounce (without a lot of pace) that forces the opponent to hit up.

Target practice: The player places the target cones and has the coach or partner serve from the baseline. For each location, the wrist snap and arm extension need to accelerate and finish toward the target. For crosscourt returns, the player should focus on making contact early (before the front foot) and hitting around or over the outside of the ball. For down the middle returns, the player should hit with a slightly later contact point (closer to the front foot). For the neutralizing topspin return, the player should focus on depth and height, and for the slice, the player should focus on depth to keep the server behind the baseline. For down the line returns, the player should hit with a later contact point and with a more open racket to create a higher trajectory to clear the higher net down the line.

BLOCK RETURN

Purpose: To develop a defensive return to use when an aggressive serve, due to the pace, placement, or angle and height of the bounce, cannot be returned neutrally or aggressively.

Technique practice: The returner is positioned behind the baseline to provide more time and space to react to a fast-paced serve. The coach or partner starts serving hard from the baseline and moves up a few feet at a time toward the service line to force faster and faster reactions to the serve. The partner should vary the serve types and serve locations, serving 5 to 10 times before moving up in the court. The returner prepares for the shot by getting the racket head behind the level of the oncoming ball and moving forward if possible. The shot is blocked back, and the arm extends similar to a volley. The trajectory is 4 to 5 feet (1.3 to 1.5 m) over the net, and the returner should try to place the ball deep in the court. The player should practice making the return from the baseline (optimal location), focusing on a shorter takeback, greater extension of the arm, and a firmer wrist.

Coaching points: Some players prefer to hit aggressively on every return, but this type of return should be used when a player did not get a good read on the serve or when the serve is effective. Placing a conservative return back in the court is better than executing an aggressive shot from a defensive position that results in an error. Returning from behind the baseline, the player has space for a great deal of movement, enough sometimes to run around a shot, take a longer backswing and swing (normal groundstroke swing), and use maximum wrist snap. The pace on this return is generated mostly by movement and the normal groundstroke swing (rather than the pace of the ball).

Target practice: The player places the target cones on the court. The angle and lack of pace of the crosscourt location gives the opponent many options, so unless the crosscourt location is the server's weakness, it is not used. For down the line, the player hits with a later contact point (more over the front foot) and with a more open racket face to create a higher trajectory to clear the higher net down the line. The follow-through is similar to an extended volley technique.

Coaching points: As the server moves up, placing the return becomes difficult and the blocking aspect of the drill becomes more prevalent. However, players should strive to continue the goal of trying to place the block because doing so provides a better chance to stay in the point.

RETURN LOCATION

Purpose: To learn to recognize when to hit each type of return based on serve-receive location.

Procedure: The coach or partner hits serves from the normal serving position on the baseline to the player standing in the normal return position. The server hits a variety of serves (flat, slice, and topspin or kick serves). After 5 to 10 returns

(continued)

Return Location *(continued)*

at the normal position, the player moves behind the baseline, on the baseline, or inside the baseline as dictated by the players success rate on each type of serve. The server serves 5 balls each to the T, the body, and the out wide locations. The returner focuses on hitting returns from the different locations near the baseline: offensive from in front of the baseline, neutralizing from on the baseline, and defensive from behind the baseline. The player receives 1 point for each ball returned from the correct court position. The server can help judge the position of the return to determine each point. Players practice to 10 points.

Coaching points: **This drill helps returners understand the potential benefits of each return location. For example, a kick serve may be easier to return from a defensive position to avoid the high bounce. Plus, a player may have greater success returning inside the baseline and may want to adopt a more offensive return.**

CRICKET

Purpose: To develop consistency in returning to a specific location, regardless of whether the return is defensive, neutralizing, or offensive.

Procedure: The coach or partner hits serves from the normal serving position on the baseline to the returner, who stands in the normal return position. The server hits serves using a variety of serves (flat, slice, and topspin or kick serves). The returner must make a return to each location (crosscourt, down the middle, and down the line) from each possible return position (in front of the baseline, on the baseline, and behind the base line).

LIVE BALL DRILLING

The next progression in drilling is to pit server versus returner. This live ball setup will further develop players' skills by testing them in different pressure situations. In a match setting, the server wants to be confident in the effectiveness of the serve and ability to hold serve. On the other hand, the returner wants to be aggressive or at least neutralizing in the location and type of return with a goal of breaking serve. The following drills help the player continue to practice the techniques and targets from the different serves and returns with the added advantage of an opponent, who acts as a barometer for the player's progress in these areas.

TARGET

Purpose: The server develops a serve that disrupts a returner's game plan. The returner practices executing the return to the desired location, regardless of the type of serve.

Procedure: The returner and server designate one or more locations for the returner to hit regardless of the serve. The returner sets up cones in the target area or areas. The server and returner then play games in which the server hits a variety of serves to different locations. If the returner makes the return to the target area, the returner receives a score of 15-0; if the server forces the returner to miss the intended location, the server gets a score of 15-0. Only the serve and return are played in this game; the point is not played out. Players can play a set in this fashion or play points to 11 or 15.

VARIETY

Purpose: The server improves accuracy while determining the possible return options. The returner adds variety to the return game.

Procedure: Two players play points, consisting of only a serve and return, in which the server hits to only one location: out wide, into the body, or down the T. The players determine the most likely return location or percentage play (see page 188 in chapter 10 for help) and then agree on acceptable alternative returns or locations. Off the serve, the returner tries to hit an agreed upon return to a predetermined location. The server gets a point if the returner produces an error (hits the return out wide or into the net). The returner gets a point if an alternative return is played. No point is earned if the returner produces a shot to the expected location. The first player to 7 wins.

Coaching points: The server's goal is to maintain accuracy, consistency, and effective technique while mentally cataloguing the types of returns coming back off that serve. The returner's goal is to maintain consistency while mixing up the return game just enough to score points and keep the server from winning.

SECOND SERVE GAME

Purpose: The server practices the second-serve situation and learns to win points without the big first serve. The returner practices focusing on aggressively attacking a second serve.

Procedure: Two players play a game to 11; the server can only use one serve. When playing this game the server can use any serve desired, but it is better to focus on a particular location each time. The returner practices hitting aggressive attacking returns off a variety of different types of second serves.

Coaching points: The main point of emphasis here is the fact that the server has one serve. The server's tendency will be to hit the one serve to a comfortable location. However, to learn to rely on different serves in crucial situations, the server should try to develop different serves and hit them to different locations.

FIRST- AND SECOND-SERVE PLUS-MINUS GAME

Purpose: The server practices making effective first and second serves. The returner practices hitting effective returns off both the first and second servers.

Procedure: The server hits a first serve and a second serve to the same box (deuce, ad). Each serve is considered a point. If the server wins both the first and second serve to the same side, then the server receives a plus 1 score. If the returner wins 1 of the 2 points, the score does not change. If the server loses both points, the server receives a score of minus 1. The server tries to get plus 5, and the returner tries to get the server to minus 5. When the returner plays this game, the goal is to neutralize the first serve without overhitting and put as much pressure as possible on the server's second serve.

Coaching points: With two evenly matched players, this drill can be challenging. While performing this drill, the returner will quickly highlight a couple of key points for the server: The server can't win this game without a high first-serve percentage or with a weak second serve.

BREAK, NO BREAK GAME

Purpose: To focus the server's ability to hold serve and the returner's ability to break serve in pressure situations.

Procedure: One player serves, and the other returns. Players flip a coin or spin a racket to see which player serves first. Using normal scoring, up to three full games are played. The goal of the server is to hold serve, in order to focus on breaking the next game. The goal of the returner is to break serve. A win is awarded when a player holds serve after breaking an opponent. If both players continue to win their service games or there is no hold after a break, then the competition can keep going as is or it can switch to a tiebreaker format, in which a break, no break format is used for points instead of games.

Coaching points: This drill highlights the mental ebbs and flows of the server and returner. The mental shift needed from trying to break an opponent to holding serve can be challenging. The tendency for many players is to relax after breaking their opponent's serve and then not pay proper attention to their own serve. Also, good tennis players adjust when they are down; the idea that a player may go down a break is threatening.

GOALIE GAME

Purpose: To learn to return serves from every part of the court.

Procedure: The returner starts deep behind the baseline. The coach or partner serves from the service line on the other side of the net. The game is played to 5 points. The server is trying to score with an ace or service winner. The goalie, or the service returner, is trying to make five saves, or returns. For every return made, the returner steps forward and attempts to make a save from the new spot.

Coaching points: The returner should work to measure the returns with shorter and shorter backswings when stepping closer toward the net.

CHAPTER 7

NET SKILLS

Some people think all it takes to be a good tennis player is a good serve, return, forehand, and backhand. However, an all-court player needs a good net game, too. *Net play* means the ability to finish the point at the net. The ability to transition to the net effectively, hit a beautiful volley down the line to set up an easier volley, or hit a drop volley adds another challenge yet also another dimension to the player's game. Effectively playing and controlling the net takes a great deal of nuance and athletic ability. Learning the net game requires instinct, positioning, and confidence.

Successfully coming to the net requires the player to want to be at the net, to like the excitement of hitting at a quicker pace, and to enjoy the thrill of putting a volley away. Although developing net play gives players many more options to win points and adds a great deal of variety to their game, it encompasses a part of the court that can be intimidating in the beginning. Improving in this area takes trial and error; players need a thick skin and should not worry about getting passed. Players should think about the shots associated with net play and envision how to use them in the overall vision for their game.

Modern professional tennis does not have many serve-and-volley style players anymore. It is an excellent strategy for finishing off points, but transitioning to the net after a serve has become more difficult in today's game. Tennis is based mainly on groundstrokes, and modern technology has provided more powerful rackets, which means more powerful swings and more powerful returns.

This chapter introduces the shots associated with transitioning to the net, the different types of volleys and overhead shots, the techniques for hitting those shots correctly, and the strategies in which they are used. Chapter 9 provides the drills for maximizing performance and establishing a complete player.

DEVELOPING THE NET GAME

Imagine having only one way to win points and how much harder a player would have to work a point in order to win it. When in a groundstroke rally, a basic goal for the player is to try to get the opponent to hit a short ball. What a player decides to do once getting a short ball or a weak shot, and how well that player plays the net, dictate that player's overall success. Most tennis players of a similar playing level can trade groundstrokes with an opponent, so the ability to transition effectively to the net and put away a volley can set them apart. The net play shots that a player needs to develop for a well-rounded game are the approach shots (including the swinging volley), the standard volleys, and the overheads.

No matter how often a player transitions to the net, an effective net game can make a big difference in the success of the player's game style. When developing a net game, a player should first understand his or her strengths in net play (e.g., a good approach shot, volley, or overhead) and consider his or her overall on-court personality (on the continuum of ultra-aggressive to aggressive to not very aggressive). Then, the player can decide what role the net can play in strategies for success.

Players should first learn the net play shots specific to their style of play. The aggressive baseline style uses the following shots: normal aggressive groundstroke approaches; sometimes the backhand slice, swinging volley, and standard volleys that are put away; and powerful, well-placed overheads. The all-court and serve-and-volley styles share a repertoire that includes aggressive groundstroke approach shots, slices, on-the-rise approach shots, volleys, and the overhead hit for placement. The defensive and rallying baseline styles use normal groundstroke approach shots, the slice, the standard volley, and, depending on the shot, the placement overhead or power overhead.

Players should improve or develop the shots for their style of play to make their game more complete. After those shots are developed, players should then look to add new net play shots that could enhance or change the game style. For example, an aggressive baseline player who has perfected his shots may want to incorporate volleying off the serve. If he is successful, this aggressive baseline player may become more of an all-court player.

NET PLAY AND STYLES OF PLAY

Each game style uses the net game differently. The rallying baseline player and the defensive player generally come to the net only when the opponent has hit a short ball. As a result, their use of net play is infrequent, and so these styles are not discussed in detail here.

- **Aggressive baseline style.** This game style is built on power groundstrokes and trying to finish off the point with a groundstroke. The aggressive baseline player's net play consists of the player moving in the court and hitting a swinging volley or running to the net to hit a volley or overhead into the open court. It is strategic, but it is not strategic volleying. In other words, this style does not focus on a succession of potential volleys that need to be placed strategically. Instead, it focuses on finishing off a point.

  Although he is a net rusher, Rafael Nadal makes the most of every trip he takes to the net. Nadal's net play usually happens when he has exhausted an opponent in a long, punishing rally, and he finally gets the attackable short ball. He knows where and how to play his volley. His volleys are not spectacular, but he places them in locations that give him the best chance to win. Nadal occasionally hits swinging volleys, but most of his approach shots are on punishing groundstrokes, where his first volley makes a major impact. Kim Clijsters also makes sporadic trips to the net, but when she transitions forward, she hits a winner. Her swinging volley, which is strong on both the forehand and backhand, is an extension of her groundstrokes just inside the baseline. She moves in fast after recognizing that an opponent is in trouble. She may play one volley to set up a second volley that she can more effectively put away.

- **All-court play.** Players using this style use strategic volleying and net play to round out their game. The all-court player may develop different strategies or plays that she consistently uses to come to the net. This player gets a feel throughout the match as to whether she needs to transition to the net more or less depending on the success of the groundstrokes. Roger Federer uses his net play to show off the classic all-court play style. He can serve and volley, he can use approach shots, and he takes chances. His athleticism gives him the ability to play all types of volleys effectively and complements his great groundstroke game. Federer epitomizes the all-court play style by consistently making his volleys, by accurately placing his volleys, and by being able to hit a variety of volleys.

- **Serve-and-volley style.** With the exception of Taylor Dent, the traditional serve-and-volley play on every serve is no longer used on the professional circuit. However, the serve-and-volley approach is useful as a surprise tactic for breaking an opponent's rhythm or as a tactic of variety. The player hits a serve and sneaks in for the volley. This strategy works very well when a player is not known to be a serve-and-volley style player. It is a great way to gain momentum.

  The serve-and-volley style player who uses this tactic more frequently gets accustomed to being at the net and needs to be a strategic server. The approach is usually set up after a couple of rallies back and forth, so the player approaching uses groundstrokes to transition. The volley off the serve depends on the strength of the serve. If the player comes in occasionally, one of the best ways to serve and volley effectively is to hit a serve out wide and come to the net. Players often use the kick serve to the backhand as a successful serve-and-volley tactic to open up the court for the volley or the serve to the T to maximize power and create less angle on the return.

APPROACH SHOTS

The main shot a player uses to transition to the net is the midcourt approach shot. The goal of using the approach shot is to put the player in the best possible position either to win the point with the approach itself or to hit a good volley or overhead, depending on the opponent's reply. A good approach shot keeps the opponent in a defensive position by surprising the opponent with shot selection or the location of the approach. An approach shot is usually played deep in the court with a low shot or higher, heavier ball, but it can also be played short or off the court to break up an opponent's rhythm or to expose a weakness. The shot a player chooses depends on that player's favorite approach, the location of the opponent, and the opponent's movement.

The approach shots are played as variations of the baseline forehand or backhand, using a range of no spin to extreme topspin. The forehand approach shots are usually hit flat or with topspin. At times, the slice can be used. The one-handed backhand approach can be hit with any of the three spins: flat, slice, or topspin. The two-handed backhand approach is hit flat or with topspin. However, it is advisable to develop a one-handed approach for more variety. The approach shots also use a shortened, measured backswing that adjusts to the location, height, and speed of the incoming ball.

Grips, Stance, and Movement

Players should use the Eastern or semi-Western grip to hit the forehand approach shots and their preferred backhand grip for the flat and topspin backhand approach shots. For the slice approach shot, they should use the Continental or Eastern backhand grip.

For the topspin approach shot, players can use an open, closed, or neutral stance (front leg in line with back leg; see figure 7.1) if they are close to the approach shot or a more open stance if they are farther away from the ball or if that is their preference. For a swinging volley approach, the stance would be open and in some cases closed if that is preferred. This approach is taken out of the air, so good timing and technique are required. The stance for the slice approach is mainly closed but it can be open if the player is a little out of position.

A player's movement to the ball is an integral part of the technical success of transitioning to the net. The player's movement allows for getting in the best possible position for the next shot and hitting it with the best possible technique. Poor movement to the ball can create a breakdown in the stance or prohibit the player from achieving a stance at all, which can greatly limit the success of the shot.

From the baseline, the player should push off the split step using the outside leg and try to move as quickly as possible. The

Figure 7.1 Neutral stance.

first steps should be big and explosive so that the player has time to adjust with little steps at the end of the movement to be balanced for the shot. As the player runs forward, the player picks out an area about 3 feet (0.9 m) in front of the approximate location of the contact point and quickly turns the hips to shuffle forward and make the necessary adjustment steps to get into the stance and hit the shot. The goal is to get into position so that the feet and body are positioned approximately sideways or perpendicular to the net.

An approach shot that requires more movement may prohibit the player from getting the full hip turn. In that case, the player should try to get some measure of a hip turn to help adjust the legs for the shot. An approach shot hit on a dead run may prevent any hip turn. In this situation, the player should try to use good hands and any measure of adjustment for balance in the legs to hit the shot.

Stroke Technique

The approach shot can be hit either on the forehand or backhand side with topspin, as a slice, or as a flat shot. This shot is usually hit from anywhere inside the baseline. To execute a successful transition shot, the player should visually split the court into thirds while aiming the shot. Most approach shots are hit to the outer thirds, particularly down the line, which gives the player optimum positioning, but the middle third can also be used as a tactic on the approach shot. The player should minimize the angle of the passing shot.

Preparation and Backswing

To be consistently effective, the transition shot needs good leg loading. The legs move forward with small adjusting steps and begin to load just before the player strikes the ball. The player loads by getting underneath the ball according to the type of approach shot to be hit. The player is a little lower if balanced for a topspin approach (to provide more spin) and slightly less so if hitting a flatter ball. At the same time, the shoulders and trunk turn sideways to the net (see figure 7.2).

The backswing is a normal groundstroke, but if the player is slightly out of balance or the ball has a lot of topspin, the player should shorten the swing. On the slice approach, it is advisable to get the racket behind the level of the oncoming ball and hit it similar to a normal groundstroke, or shorten the swing if the ball is difficult to handle.

Forward Swing and Contact

The body drives upward for the topspin shot but stays more coiled and maintains a lower balance throughout the execution for the slice. For the flat shot, the body starts low and maintains this position with a balanced movement more out toward the location of the shot.

For the topspin stroke the racket head is accelerated (low to high). For the slice, the player could either block it deep (flat ball) or cut in a high-to-low fashion. The contact zone for the approach is a touch farther away from the body than for the groundstroke. The topspin approach is contacted a bit in front of the normal groundstroke. The contact for the slice is slightly behind the front knee.

Figure 7.2 Proper preparation for an approach shot.

Just before the contact for the backhand slice, the back foot starts to go behind the front leg to create the carioca step. The racket head is above the wrist and slightly opens for the slice. At impact for a topspin shot, the racket head is low and the racket face is slightly closed (see figure 7.3).

Follow-Through

For the topspin transition shot, the normal groundstroke motion is used with a slightly abbreviated motion on the swing and a shorter backswing. The speed of the racket head should increase as the player directs the ball toward the target (see figure 7.4). On the backhand transition shot, if a player chooses to hit a slice, the player should accelerate the racket head speed with a goal to knife the ball with underspin, causing it to skid and stay low. The swing path for both shots follows a high-to-low, down and across movement (see figure 7.4).

Using Approach Shots

It is important that the player develop a variety of shots, using both the forehand and backhand and a variety of spins and locations. (For more on spins and locations, see chapter 1.)

Block Approach

The block approach can be used as a forehand or backhand, although less effectively as a two-handed backhand. The approach is similar to the slice approach, but without the slice imparted on the ball. This shot is a good shot for seniors and players learning how to approach, but it is used more out of necessity today when the player is late getting to the ball.

Figure 7.3 Body position just prior to contact.

Figure 7.4 Topspin transition shot.

How   The player takes the racket back with a quarter turn and sets up similar to the slice, trying to get the racket head level with the oncoming ball. The player pushes the ball flat and deep into the court in a straightforward fashion. The shot goes to the deep portion of the court with a slightly higher trajectory than the slice. The shot uses the attack point of contact and the midlevel strike zone.

Where   This shot is hit from inside the baseline, either midway between service line and baseline or closer in toward the service line. This shot is hit deep in the court (behind midway between the service line and baseline down the line). This shot can also be placed shorter in the court to draw an opponent toward the net. Location is important with this shot because this ball has little spin and may be easier for an opponent to hit.

When   This approach is mainly used when a player doesn't have enough time to get set up for a topspin or slice approach, but the player still feels as though it is advantageous to transition to the net. This shot can also be hit as a block shot when the player gets out of position while transitioning to the net and wants to keep approaching by using this shot.

Aggressive Approach

The aggressive version of the approach shot is hit with the preferred groundstroke grip. An abbreviated takeback version could be hit with greater acceleration using the normal grip or a grip more toward the Eastern forehand grip. Francesca Schiavone is effective in using an all-court style of play that is comfortable in the backcourt and also in the midcourt. She is not afraid to transition to the net and use an aggressive midcourt approach to take time away from an opponent and safely get into the net.

How   This shot is most effective when it is played in the attack point of contact and in the midlevel strike zone. The aggressive approach shot is hit as a hard-hit groundstroke, but the player has moved inside the baseline to do it. The player's goal on this approach shot is to make contact on the rise with an abbreviated swing and take adjustment steps to time the shot. So, the movement needed for this shot is usually a quick move forward, then some adjustment steps to help time the ball and the approach shot.

Where   This shot is usually hit from around the service line. The ball generally comes from a crosscourt shot, so the player can hit the aggressive approach shot down the line to the open court and then advance forward. A player should hit this shot deep in the court, allowing enough time to get in the optimal volley position, which is two to three steps toward the net in the direction the player's shot was just hit. In some cases, the midcourt approach shot can be hit crosscourt, but this depends on the path of the opponent's shot and where the ball is going to land. For example, a ball hit from an opponent that is more angled may give the player an opportunity to go back behind the opponent on the midcourt approach shot. The player should be careful here because the midcourt approach that is not hit crosscourt well enough can lead to bad court positioning, which allows for an easy passing shot for the opponent (more court to pass the player on) down the line.

When   A player usually hits this shot when the opponent is off the court or has hit a short or weak ball. This scenario provides an opportunity to hit a midcourt shot that allows the player to transition to the net more effectively. The player should hit this shot before the opponent has time to recover from the previous shot. This shot can be very effective in wrong-footing an opponent and giving the player a head start to the net. The most aggressive two-handed backhand is the down-the-line approach shot, mainly off a crosscourt backhand or inside-out forehand that lands far enough toward the middle of the court to make this shot in front of the baseline. (See Down-the-Line Backhand Approach for more information on page 138.)

Swinging Volley

Robin Söderling and Venus Williams both use this stroke to their advantage. Söderling has a very powerful game with lethal groundstrokes. When he decides to transition to the net off a powerful groundstroke, oftentimes he gets to about halfway between the service line and baseline because of the effort he puts in his shot. In order to maintain his offense, not letting the ball drop and the opponent reset his position, Söderling comes forward and hits a swinging volley similar to his groundstrokes. Venus Williams moves up in the court so well that she can take a relatively well-hit ball from an opponent and hit a swinging volley to the open court or behind her opponent. This shot keeps her on offense and gives her an easier shot to transition to the net.

How   This shot is played as a normal groundstroke with the player's usual grip, except the player takes the ball out of the air. If properly prepared and enough time exists to execute the shot, the player can take a full swing. Or, if the player prefers, an abbreviated swing is possible, too. The abbreviated swing can be used to speed up the process of transitioning to the net when playing an opponent who moves and recovers well. If the player is slightly out of position but still wants to hit the shot, the player needs to use an abbreviated swing that is used off of a quarter turn of the shoulders. The contact point is a rally to attack contact point in the upper middle to high-level strike zone.

Two-Handed Shot   The two-handed shot (see figure 7.5a) is very popular today because it is similar to a groundstroke, except it is taken out of the air. The player must move forward with good balance and extend the arms to accelerate in a manner that is similar to that for a groundstroke.

One-Handed Shot   This shot is tougher for a one-handed player (figure 7.5b) and it requires great timing, skill, and shoulder strength. It is hit like a normal groundstroke but out of the air. The player must maintain balance and extend the arm upward and outward with a wrist snap that is out and across the ball. To do this effectively, players should use the mid- to lower-level strike zones with a rally or defensive point of contact. The preferred

Figure 7.5   The *(a)* two-handed backhand and *(b)* the one-handed forehand versions of the swinging volley.

stance is slightly closed to neutral, or it may be open if the player is comfortable hitting in an open stance with a full upper body shoulder turn. This shot can also be played as a high volley for a one-handed player who doesn't have a heavy topspin shot.

Where The swinging volley is usually hit from inside the baseline in the area known as *no man's land:* midway between the center hash mark and the alley and between the service line and baseline. Once seeing the opportunity, the player can step up and hit a ball to the open court (preferred location) or back behind the opponent to wrong-foot the opponent. The best location for the swinging volley depends on the path of the oncoming ball, the strength of the opponent's shot, the player's court position, and the best location choice for execution. It can be hit deep in the court or with greater angle. The player should be careful not to leave openings for the opponent's passing shot, which can develop as a result of a poor crosscourt approach.

When This shot can be used when the player is in a rally and recognizes an opportunity to step into the court and dictate play or keep an opponent running. It is really more of a try at a winner. The player sees the opponent in trouble hitting the shot and decides to sneak in and hit a regular or swinging volley out of the air to force the opponent into a mistake or an easier volley that the player can put away.

Slice Approach

The forehand version of this shot isn't used much in today's game, unless the player is late getting to the shot and it is the only option. Roger Federer has a great backhand slice approach that stays low and allows him ample time to come into the net.

How This is a one-handed shot designed to stay low and make an opponent hit upward. Using a Continental or slightly Eastern forehand grip, the slice approach is hit either aggressively on the rise or as a normal approach shot. The slice hit on the rise has many benefits. Taking the shot early catches the opponent off guard and the ball stays low and deep, giving the player extra time to get in better position at the net. The amount of time a player has to move forward dictates how far to take back the racket. For more time, the player can use a full backswing. For less time or if taking the ball on the rise, the player can use a shorter backswing.

The technique for the slice approach shot is similar to that for the normal groundstroke (see page 43). The contact point is slightly in front of where it would be for the normal groundstroke, especially when the player takes it on the rise. For a ball hit on the rise, a player uses the attack point of contact and the low- to midlevel strike zones.

Like the offensive groundstroke, the backhand slice approach uses the carioca step. The player must turn the shoulders to the ball (half turn when in good position and a quarter turn when stretched a little). The racket sets back toward the back leg and is positioned level with the oncoming ball. The shot is hit from high to low and extended outward with the arm. The carioca step gives the arm a longer extension. This shot uses the attack or rally point of contact and the low- to midlevel strike zone.

Where This approach is usually played near the service line and is hit down the line to the open court, either deep in the court or shorter in the court to surprise or wrong-foot an opponent. The player should use this shorter approach version when an opponent doesn't like to move forward.

When The slice backhand is a great shot to use to transition to the net and take time away from the opponent. This shot is hit when a player sees the opportunity to attack. The goal of the shot is to keep it low and give the player extra time to transition to the net. The slice approach can also be used when a player doesn't have enough time to swing on the shot, or is moving too fast through the ball to take the appropriate swing. This type of approach is used against speedy opponents when time is of the essence.

Down-the-Line Backhand Approach

Robin Söderling is aggressive, so his down-the-line approach shot is meant to be hit as a winner. It is important to remember that even when a player hits an aggressive shot down the line and hopes to hit a winner, the player needs to be ready to finish off the point with a possible volley. This can be called a delayed approach shot because in this case the player is transitioning forward, and the likely volley is a swinging volley or a put-away volley. Serena Williams uses the down-the-line approach shot very effectively. She goes for an aggressive shot, but her goal is to follow it in and execute a winning volley.

How   The player's preferred backhand grip is used on this shot. For maximum effect, players should use a more closed stance to get behind the ball. This shot can be hit on the rise if the player wants to take more time away from the opponent. This shot can and should be used as a higher, heavier ball that has a high trajectory to give the transitioning player more time if they are late getting to the ball.

Two-Handed Backhand   This ball can be hit as a normal groundstroke if the player reads the oncoming ball early enough and steps into the court. The rally point of contact is preferred, and it is in the midlevel strike zone. The player should make a half turn if prepared and a quarter turn with an abbreviated takeback if the body is stretched out wide. The player must time the movement forward to connect with the ball on the bounce. The player can hit a flat drive if in proper position or with topspin if a split second longer is needed to transition to the correct court position. This shot is hit from midway between the service line and baseline and usually midway between the center and the alley and to the outer thirds of the court.

One-Handed Backhand   The player takes an abbreviated swing on the takeback and tries to catch it on the rise in the low- to midlevel strike zone and at the attack point of contact. Players using the one-handed version often lose control when the ball is in the upper level strike zone. The one-handed player can drive the ball if in great position or use topspin to give a split second longer preparation for the volley. This player also has a little more range on balls hit out wide.

Where   An approach is usually hit from between the service line and baseline and midway between the center hash mark and the alley. It should be hit deep in the court to allow for transition or short in the court to an opponent who doesn't move well from back to front.

When   The approach shot should be hit when the player gets a short ball and wants to transition to the net or, for a more aggressive approach, to hit a winner. This shot is designed to take time away from an opponent, and it gives the player a better opportunity to finish the point. The player should recognize the oncoming ball as short, anticipate the bounce, and move in aggressively with forward momentum. If the opponent is recovering and not in great position on the court, the player takes the approach as quickly as possible, giving the opponent less time to recover. If the opponent has recovered, the player should be more aggressive and try to hit a winner.

VOLLEYS

After transitioning to the net, the player must be prepared to hit a volley, an overhead (see the Overheads section on page 145), or, if the opponent has a great lob, a desperation shot (see chapter 8). Being able to volley effectively is vital to the player's game. Because volleys are shots taken out of the air, they are designed to lessen the opponent's reaction time and help the player advance toward the net more effectively to finish off a point. All volleys require good technique, balance, and feel. The location and strength of a player's volleys determine whether the player will be on offense or defense on the next shot.

Grips, Stance, and Movement

The Continental grip is the best grip for hitting a forehand volley. For the backhand volley, the player can choose the Continental or Eastern grip. Some players like to build a little underspin into the volley, so they may have a more Eastern backhand grip, which is especially helpful when the players are stretched out on the volley or hitting a low volley. The best movement preparation is the split step, which provides the following advantages:

- It allows movement in every direction.

- It activates the legs, preparing them to move explosively.

- It allows the player to make a quick cut to the ball.

Players jump into a position with the feet shoulder width apart and the body facing the net. More advanced players jump toward the path of the oncoming shot with the outside leg. Players try to get low by bending the knees, not the back, to get on eye level with the oncoming ball. Good volleying posture means the body is loaded lower, the knees are bent, and the chest is upright (see figure 7.6).

The location of the oncoming ball dictates the stance used for a volley. A player should step toward the direction of the shot off the split step, which can be to the side to get behind the ball or at a diagonal to cut off a more angled shot. However, if the volley is closer to the player, the player should move around to the ball for contact.

Figure 7.6   Stepping out for a forehand volley.

Stroke Technique

The standard volley represents the foundational technique for all volley variations. The standard form of the shot is hit in the midlevel strike zone. The shot is hit as a power volley (going for a winner) or for placement to put a player in better position for the next shot. The following sections discuss the swing pattern for a great volley. This technique is applicable for both the forehand and backhand.

It is important to note that the preferred backhand for the standard volley is the one-handed backhand because it gives greater reach, allowing a player to hit more shots effectively. If a player's arm strength isn't adequate, the player should use a two-handed backhand volley and slowly try to build up arm strength. When hitting the two-handed backhand volley, the player should hold the nondominant arm at the throat of the racket to aid the dominant arm in balance through the shot. The technique is otherwise similar, but better adjusting movements with the hands, feet, and torso are required to get behind a shot with a two-handed backhand volley.

Preparation and Backswing

On the one-handed backhand volley, the racket moves backward slightly in the path of the oncoming ball so that this preparatory movement ends to the side of the head or even slightly in front. The player can think of the racket position as framing the ball with the racket head positioned so that the player looks through the racket strings at the volley. By coordinating the head and eyes to be near the racket head (1 to 1.5 feet, or

0.3 to 0.5 m apart), the player can make an easier execution and a sharper volley. The body is open and facing the other side of the court or slightly turned (quarter turn; see figure 7.7). The elbow is comfortably to the side and positioned midway between shoulder height and waist height. The proper posture is balanced; the knees are bent and the chest is upright. The angle of the racket face is slightly open.

The setup for the two-handed backhand volley requires some adjustment to account for the second hand on the racket. One possible setup places the nondominant hand on the throat of the racket and then the nondominant hand releases as the player contacts the volley. Another setup keeps the nondominant hand on the racket and uses it to balance the arms through contact. The nondominant hand can be placed on the grip next to the dominant hand or slightly higher. The two-handed backhand volley is hard to execute on wide shots, so players should develop a one-handed backhand volley to allow for more reach.

Forward Swing and Contact

From a position of balance and off the split step toward the path of the oncoming ball, the front foot steps out diagonally using a semi-open stance. In some cases, a player may turn the hip and hit using a closed stance on the incoming ball (see figure 7.8). Timing and positioning of the front foot depend on a player's distance from the net. A balance step is commonly seen on the first volley; the player steps forward while getting low to meet a ball in the lower-level strike zone. As the player moves closer to the net and has less time to react, a semi-open to open stance is a better choice.

The shoulders rotate forward, and the front elbow extends out to provide tracking and balance. The elbows remain slightly tucked in, but comfortable. The racket face is slightly open and makes contact just in front of and to the side of the player's head. The head and wrist should be about 1.5 feet (0.5 m) apart. To hit a stronger volley, players should not completely extend the hitting elbow. This ensures that they use the hands as well as the body to hit the ball. Balance is important through the preparation and contact.

Figure 7.7 **Forward swing on the forehand volley.**

Figure 7.8 **Point of contact on the forehand volley.**

Follow-Through

The path of the racket moves forward, down, and across the ball. The player should rotate both shoulders forward toward the net when following through on the forehand volley. The backhand volley is just the opposite: The player strikes the ball with the front arm and releases the back arm toward the back fence, keeping the shoulders level and sideways after contact. The player should keep the racket head up above the net band after contact to be ready for the opponent's response and to avoid hitting a sloppy volley.

The court surface and the phase of play influence how players follow through on a volley. On slower surfaces, such as clay, players tend to extend more through volleys. On quicker surfaces, such as quick indoor hard courts, a more abbreviated follow-through works well (see figure 7.9). When playing an attack phase of play on an easy ball, a player might choose to let loose on the follow-through. A better option is to attack the ball with the feet and maintain a shorter follow-through. If a player is on the defensive in a doubles match and an opponent is ripping a ball right at the player, a shorter blocking follow-through would suffice.

Figure 7.9 Follow-through on the forehand volley.

Using Volleys

Developing a variety of volley shots is important. In addition to the standard volley, there are the high volley, lob volley, half volley, low volley, drop volley, and defensive volley. As with the standard volley, each variation can be hit with the forehand or backhand. The type of volley a player uses depends on the player's location on the court, the strength of the opponent's shot, and the offensive or defensive nature of the situation. Of course, the main purpose for any volley is to hit a shot that the opponent can't get to or that gives the opponent less reaction time.

High Volley

Roger Federer uses the high volley well. His balance when moving forward in the court gives him the power and ability to hit to a strategically beneficial location. This shot requires feel and power, and Federer has plenty of both.

How Some players use the Continental grip on this volley while others like to get more of their hand behind the grip, so they choose the Eastern forehand or the Eastern backhand grip. To hit the high volley, a player takes the racket back a little farther so the butt cap of the racket is visible to the opponent. A high volley that goes deeper in the court shows more butt cap. The less the butt cap shows, the closer the shot gets to the net. The forward swing is made with a slight high-to-low movement for a flatter ball, but the goal of this volley is depth. A high volley with underspin is tough to execute and entails a more aggressive high-to-low movement through the ball.

CRITICAL CUE:

On a high one-handed backhand volley, the player should use a carioca step, which helps to generate power on the volley by keeping the shoulders turned while moving forward.

Figure 7.10 Follow-through for the high volley.

The racket face stays a little more open because the racket head needs to be pushed out farther than on a normal volley. The contact point is the rally to defensive points of contact and slightly farther back than the standard volley because it draws off the momentum of the body and the accelerating swing of the racket head. The ball is hit in the upper-level strike zone. The arm continues down across and outward to get as much depth as possible (see figure 7.10). Another version of this shot entails using a shorter backswing and running through the volley using forward momentum to accelerate the ball.

Where This shot is usually hit from the middle of the court between the service line and baseline in the middle third of the court. When deciding where to hit this volley, players should use the same thought process as for the approach shot: mainly to the outer thirds deep in the court or back through the middle to take away the angle of passing shots from the opponent.

When The offensive nature of this shot depends on the player's skill. Players with lower-level skills find it very difficult to put away shots consistently. Players with higher skill levels see it as an opportunity to attack the high floating response and put it away.

Lob Volley

This shot is a combination of a volley and a lob. In doubles play, Bob Bryan and Mike Bryan can execute lob volleys extremely well when both of their opponents are at the net.

How On the lob volley, the racket face is slightly open, which creates the lob effect. This shot is hit flat or with a touch of underspin. This shot is usually deflected with a little backspin because the racket face is slightly open. Trying to add more underspin requires great skill. The shot uses the defensive point of contact and the lower- to midlevel strike zone. The follow-through is short; a low-to-high movement follows the path of the ball. Otherwise, the technique mirrors that of the standard volley.

Where This shot is usually hit from near the service line. The opponent may be moving forward, hoping to put the ball away or get closer for the next volley or may just be caught out of position.

When The lob volley is often executed in the defensive phase of play when the opponent is close to the net and hits a ball right at the player. The player deflects the opponent's pace by opening the racket face and lobbing the ball over the opponent, putting the opponent on the defensive, scrambling to retrieve the lob. The lob volley can also be executed offensively when both the player and opponent are closing on the net quickly but the ball is on the player's racket first. If able to lob volley over the opponent, the point belongs to the player.

Half Volley

The half volley is a shot that uses forward momentum to position the racket so the player can slightly block the shot or deflect it to the desired position. The half volley is unlike other volleys because it is not taken out of the air but off the bounce; as a result, the ball loses speed.

How Generally, the same grips are used for the half volley as for the standard volley. If a player does not have enough time to prepare, the groundstroke grip may be used.

COACHING POINT

This shot is usually uncomfortable for players because they must coordinate the following issues to get the timing right: the racket in the right location, the shorter swing, the ball bouncing with a flat shot or a topspin shot, and a smooth follow-through. The half volley takes finesse and good use of the hands, but it is a great learning tool.

The racket moves back with a shorter backswing (just behind the back on the side of the shot) while the upper body turns. The player turns sideways in a manner similar to that for the standard volley. Then the player hits this shot with a closed stance or, if not in great position, a slightly open stance. The player maintains balance in the legs and stays down through contact.

The racket face is open and moves forward with a sweeping motion of the arm and a quick acceleration of the wrist upward. It is firm and directs the ball to its destination. Players can sometimes take a bigger swing and, if time allows, add topspin to the shot. The shot uses the attack point of contact in the lower-level strike zone, in this case at ankle level, and the body weight transfers forward and slightly upward to keep balance and to direct the shot. Unlike for the standard volley, the follow-through for this shot is a low-to-high movement.

Where   This shot is hit from just behind the service line to the net. The best location to hit the half volley is down the line and deep in the court, which keeps the ball in front of the player in order to be ready for the opponent's passing shot or lob.

When   The half volley is used in two scenarios. One possibility is when a player is approaching the net and the opponent dips a ball down to the player's feet, where the player can't effectively take the ball out of the air. Another possibility is when the player is hitting the ball on the baseline and does not have time to move back in the court or hit a proper groundstroke. In this case, the player can use a half volley to send the ball back over the net.

Low Volley

The low volley is a forehand or backhand volley hit below waist level or that has the player stretched out wide. Great doubles players Max Mirnyi, Daniel Nestor, and Leander Paes use this shot well. All of these players get down and stay down with their volleys until the ball has cleared the net.

How   The player uses the Continental or Eastern backhand grip, although the Eastern backhand grip is preferable because of the natural open face it provides. The low volley uses little to no backswing. The racket is placed in the path of the oncoming shot with an open face (designed for height) and moves from high to low. The shot is hit with the knees bent and the upper body bent over while reaching for the shot (see figure 7.11). The knees hold their position but slowly move forward as the ball is hit.

Figure 7.11   Preparation for the low volley.

The point of contact for the low volley is the attack point of contact about 1.5 feet (0.5 m) in front of the body. For a stretched out low volley the point of contact is about 2 feet (0.6 m) to the side. The shot also uses the lower-level strike zone. Good balance is necessary, and the wrist must be firm. The follow-through is shorter, enabling the wrist to gain a little momentum through the swing with a low-to-high movement, and the body position is maintained to give balance.

Where   The low volley is played primarily from around the service line toward the outer thirds and deep in the court. When hit to this location it allows the player enough time to recover and get set up for the next volley. The low volley is usually played in front of the body or to the side of the body. It is defensive in nature, unless the player has a great low volley, which then is considered more offensive.

When   This volley is played as needed, such as when a player is at the net and the opponent hits to the player's feet, when the ball drops below waist level, or when a player is stretched out wide at the net.

Drop Volley

The drop volley is hit differently than the other volleys because it is used to take the pace off (deflate) an oncoming shot and drop it just over the net level. Austrian player Jürgen Melzer is outstanding at this shot. He has great hands and, as an outstanding doubles player too, he has no problem getting tight into position at the net to execute this shot.

How   Preparation technique is the same as for the standard volley. Then, the racket moves slowly to impact, and the racket face is slightly open just before contact. At contact, the arm slows as it comes forward and stops at contact. The shot uses the attack point of contact in the mid- to lower-level strike zone. The wrist makes a half turn downward on the backhand side and upward on the forehand side, creating more of an open face to give the shot some height (see figure 7.12). This action, combined with a softening of the grip and the stopping of the arm, causes the ball to softly drop over the net. Less turn of the wrist produces a flatter drop volley contact with the ball. The racket face moves slightly downward and backward (a pull back of the racket) for a volley hit in front. For a more advanced player, the racket face can move back and to the side for a drop shot that has a little sidespin.

Where   This shot is usually hit from very near the net, but it can be hit anywhere from just inside the service line. It should be placed to land on the opponent's side directly in front of the player, over the net, and inside the service box, or, if in good position, at an angle inside the service box and just landing over the net. Just as on the drop shot, the player aims to hit the drop volley so that it either bounces three to five times in the opponent's service box or so that it takes one bounce and goes off the side of the court.

When   A player uses the drop volley when the opponent is on the baseline and the player wants to catch the opponent in a vulnerable position. This volley is very effective against any opponent, but especially against players who don't like to move forward, have poor footwork, or lack speed.

Figure 7.12   Preparation for the drop volley.

Defensive Volley

The main reason many players fear playing the net is because they do not want their opponent's best shot coming right at them. The defensive volley, an underpracticed shot, allows players to defend themselves at the net.

How The backhand volley is the best defensive volley. If a player first turns sideways to hit a forehand volley and tries to protect the body from this position, it is extremely difficult. If the player turns to hit a backhand volley and then tries to protect the body, the player is able to block any ball hit toward the head down to the feet. The contact point is the attack or rally contact point, depending on the player's reaction, and the strike zone is in the midlevel.

Where This volley is most commonly hit from inside the service line. Players lacking confidence should move closer to the net because the closer they are to the net, the greater the likelihood that when they block their opponent's ripped shot it will go back over the net successfully for a winner.

When Anytime a ball is hit directly at the body.

OVERHEAD SHOTS

The overhead shot is designed to be a power shot, and players use it to put away a defensive shot or a poorly executed offensive shot. The overhead shot should be strong because the motion is similar to the serve, which gives players plenty of practice with the technique. The overhead is a reflection of a player's bravado on the court; it's the epitome of strong on-court demeanor. Poor movement and a slow read on the ball usually cause a weak overhead shot. Players can hit three types of overheads: the power overhead, the scissor kick overhead, and the backhand smash.

Power Overhead Shot

Andy Roddick uses this shot very effectively. Because his groundstrokes are so powerful, he gets a lot of defensive shots. His game is built on power, and his serve is also good, so he uses his overhead as an extension of a serve in a more favorable position on the court.

Preparation and Backswing

Using a Continental or Eastern forehand grip, the player turns sideways and gets in position for the ball using short adjustment steps. The upper body turns and leans backward, and all of the body weight transfers onto the rear leg (similar to an outfielder catching a pop fly). At the same time, the racket is prepared back and behind the head with technique similar to that for the serve (see figure 7.13). With the takeback, the nondominant hand points at the incoming ball, and the racket is put in the trophy position; the elbow is bent slightly lower than shoulder level. The racket angle is slightly closed from a squared position. The nonplaying arm reaches upward for balance and coordination as the elbow moves backward, bringing the racket face more closed before preparing to accelerate upward. The shot uses the attack point of contact and the upper-level strike zone.

Figure 7.13 **Proper preparation for the overhead.**

A technique and tactical variation occurs on the power overhead when a player lets the ball bounce before hitting it. In this version, the player moves backward, lets the ball bounce, and then uses lateral side shuffles to move toward the ball, transferring body weight into the shot while keeping both feet on the ground. The tactical variation is that if the player decides to let the overhead bounce first because of darkness, sun, wind, or another reason, then it is important to place the overhead if hit from behind the service line and to go for a winner if hit inside the service line.

Forward Swing and Contact

The racket head accelerates upward, and the player reaches up to hit the ball. The body weight transfers forward, similar to an outfielder getting ready to make a throw. The arm extends and the ball is hit with a pronated and extended forearm (the same as for the service action). The racket meets the ball above and in front of the player's head (see figure 7.14). The racket face is squared for contact, but the contact occurs slightly in front so that the racket face is starting to close downward. The nonplaying arm starts a downward movement.

Follow-Through

The playing arm follows through in a manner similar to the follow-through for a serve, and the upper body follows the path of the ball. The nonplaying arm comes down either across the body or to the side (see figure 7.15). The player moves forward, recovering for the next shot.

Figure 7.14   **Contact on the overhead.**

Figure 7.15   **Follow-through on the overhead.**

COACHING POINTS

The power overhead motion is similar to the motion for the serve. If a player hits a better overhead than a serve, the player likely has a breakdown somewhere in the serve base or rhythm, and the power overhead shot can be used to troubleshoot the serve. The only difference between the power overhead shot and the serve is the movement of the feet to the setup. Coaches and players can look at how the player hits the overhead shot and compare it with the serve. If the overhead form is better than that for the serve, the coach and player can evaluate the player's serve stance and any leg movement.

Where The power overhead shot can be hit from anywhere in the court and is designed to be a putaway shot. Generally it is hit to the outer thirds of the court from inside the service boxes or around the service line. The power overhead can also be played to the middle third of the court, but if the opponent is good at anticipating the shot, the player must be prepared for a good defense.

When A player uses the power overhead shot when the opponent hits a high ball, such as a lob or a weak reply, and the player is in good position at the net to put the ball away. The power overhead shot is especially intimidating when an opponent has seemingly hit a good shot such as a lob and the overhead is put away out of the opponent's reach. A variation of the power overhead shot is hit for placement. This variation is used when an opponent has hit an effective lob or when the player is off balance and needs to place the shot. Even if that shot is not a winner, optimum placement puts the player in better position for the next shot.

Scissor Kick Overhead Shot

For this shot, the player uses a vertical jump, creating a scissor kick to get in the right position to execute a powerful shot. If in a good position, the player can hit this overhead shot for power; if the lob is out of reach, then the player can hit it for location. Andy Murray has great leaping ability. So when a lob is hit with a flatter trajectory that is going over his head, he is able to jump up and slightly backward while balanced and still put a great deal of power on his overhead shot. The technique for the scissor kick overhead shot is the same as for the power overhead shot except for a few variations.

Preparation and Backswing

Essentially, the player wants to prepare for a power overhead shot and adjust when the ball goes higher and appears to be going over head (figure 7.16). Once the player has identified this is the case, the player loads the back leg, leans back, scissor kicks the legs, and reaches as high as possible to pull the lob down. Because the body is leaning more backward for this overhead, it takes great balance to execute it well. The shot uses the upper-level strike zone and the rally to defensive points of contact.

Figure 7.16 Preparation for the scissor kick overhead.

Forward Swing and Contact

As the player reaches up to hit the ball, both legs make a counterbalancing scissor kick in the air: The rear leg takes the place of the front leg and vice versa (figure 7.17). The upper body rotates forward, and impact occurs in the air. The contact point on this shot is higher and a little farther back. The player tries to reach up with the hitting arm while uncoiling the hips and shoulders.

Follow-Through

The nonplaying arm moves downward (see figure 7.18). The player lands on the rear foot or front foot, depending on the movement. Then the player pushes off the landing foot to get into position for the next shot.

Where   The scissor kick overhead shot is usually hit from the middle third of the court and hit to the outer thirds, deep in the court or inside the service line.

When   The scissor kick overhead shot is used when a ball is hit slightly behind a player's head or when a player has to jump up to hit the ball effectively.

Figure 7.17   Contact on the scissor kick overhead.

Figure 7.18   Follow-through on the scissor kick.

Backhand Smash Shot

This overhead shot is played on the backhand side and, unless a player has perfected the shot, is often used for location instead of power. The backhand smash shot is rarely used with a scissor kick, but if a very athletic player can execute this shot, it can be very effective. Gaël Monfils is the type of athletic player who makes this shot look easy. The technique is the same as for the power overhead shot except for a few variations.

Preparation and Backswing

For this shot, players use the Eastern backhand or Continental grip. The player turns sideways to get the racket back in position (figure 7.19). The leg movement for this shot depends on how close the player is to the ball. If the ball is hit deeper in the court, the player needs to step back with the back leg while turning the back to the opponent. This movement can be followed by a crossover step and setting the back leg to give power for the momentum upward to the ball. If the shot is closer, the player can shuffle to feel as though the weight is back and ready to move forward with momentum. The racket head stays above the wrist and pulls upward using the guide hand to get it set. The player transfers the weight to the back leg. The player prepares to jump up at a slightly backward angle. The shot uses the attack point of contact and the upper-level strike zone.

Forward Swing and Contact

The player pushes off from the ground, preferably using the rear leg in order to stay in balance, then jumps up and strikes the ball with a downward flick of the wrist (figure 7.20). The playing arm comes down, and the player must stay sideways through the shot. The player contacts the ball above and slightly in front of the body.

Figure 7.19 Preparation for the backhand smash.

Figure 7.20 Point of contact for the backhand smash.

Figure 7.21 Follow-through on the backhand smash.

Follow-Through

After contact, the arm continues to swing in the direction of the shot (figure 7.21), and the player lands onto the rear leg with a balanced finish.

Where This shot is hit from the backhand side to the outer thirds of the court, either crosscourt in the service box for hitting at an angle or deeper down the line to the outer third. The player should predominately use the deep outer third location because this shot is difficult to put away, and this gives the player better positioning for the next shot.

When The backhand smash shot should be an option only when the player does not have enough time to run around and hit a normal overhead shot.

MOVEMENT TO THE NEXT BALL

The goal of net play is to end points quickly, but it isn't always done in one shot. So, the player must be ready for another ball. The player's ready position following a net play determines the success of the next shot. The player should also consider court positioning. Some net players like to get close (within 4 inches, or about 10 cm) to the net, and others like to stay in a position from within 1 to 2 feet (0.3 to 0.6 m) or just inside the service line, where they can be ready to move to the side for a passing shot or backward for an overhead shot.

Wherever the player establishes a base position, preparing for the next shot entails an effective split step after executing the first volley. Now the player is ready to move forward, sideways, or backward to get ready for the next shot from the opponent. The player should remember to track the shot and position the body on the side of the location of that shot. How close the player gets to the net depends on the strength of the shot, the player's current location on the court, the opponent's court positioning, and the likely reply or tendencies (e.g., this opponent prefers to go down the line or crosscourt on her passing shots). These tactical concepts are explored in chapters 10 and 11.

NET PLAY STRATEGIES

Two basic strategies are associated with net play. One strategy is when players are trading groundstrokes and an opponent hits a short ball or a weak shot, allowing the other player to transition to the net. Within this strategy, the player can adopt a mentality of using a delayed approach: After getting the opponent in trouble by hitting a high, heavy topspin shot, the player essentially sneaks to the net to surprise the opponent while the opponent is waiting for the high ball.

A second strategy is for the more aggressive player who likes to win points at the net. This type of player takes chances and uses approach shots, delayed approach shots (sneak attack), balls on the rise, serves, and returns to get to the net. This strategy is based on the serve-and-volley style of play.

The previous two strategies rely on the player controlling or trying to control the situation. The third strategy is not initially in the player's control, but the player tries to establish it immediately. In this strategy, the opponent deliberately hits a shorter ball, such as a drop shot, which forces the player to approach the net.

Transitioning off a Short Ball

When a player serves, returns, or trades groundstrokes with an opponent, the goal is to get a short ball and hit a winner or transition to the net and win the point. The player's level of aggressiveness dictates how short a ball must be in order to decide to come forward. The decision differs from person to person, but if the execution of an attackable ball helps a player win points, it means the decision was successful. For some players, attackable balls include those that land inside the service line, near the service line, or midway between the service line and the baseline. Some players may say that approaching from the baseline is effective for them, but most players would have difficulty achieving consistent success with this strategy.

The following shots are useful when transitioning off a short ball:

- **Deep approach.** This approach can be hit flat and hard or played as a high, heavy shot hit with a higher trajectory and topspin. The player can also accomplish this with a slice approach that stays low, forcing the opponent to hit upward. The player can also move up quickly on a ball and hit a half volley just as it bounces.

- **Shorter angle approach.** The effectiveness of this approach depends on both the player's and the opponent's positioning in the court. If hit correctly, this approach can get the opponent in a defensive position; if hit incorrectly, it can give the opponent an easy shot down the line that may be too tough to cover. This shot is hit in a variety of ways, including with topspin, flat with finesse, or as a swinging volley. The goal is to hit to the open court or back behind an opponent before the opponent has recovered properly.

- **Drop shot approach.** Though difficult, this shot can be a very effective tool for winning points, especially if an opponent does not like to be at the net or doesn't move particularly well. The normal drop shot is played when the player wants to surprise an opponent or the opponent is positioned deep in the court. The drop shot used as an approach shot would be used in the same way, but the difference is that the player would follow it to the net and try to put pressure on any angle the opponent may attempt. This shot, if hit well, puts pressure on the opponent, possibly forcing an error as the opponent tries to retrieve the ball. For instruction on how to hit the drop shot, see chapter 8.

Transitioning off a Groundstroke, Serve, or Return

The success of transitioning off a groundstroke depends on the shots in the player's repertoire, the player's optimal positioning in the court, and any sign of a defensive ball that can create an opportunity. The following transitions can be successful.

- **Swinging volley.** This volley is used when the opponent hits a higher ball that allows time for the player to move up in the court and strike the ball in a manner similar to that for a groundstroke. This shot can be hit into the open court for a possible winner or back behind the opponent to create a defensive opportunity.

- **Serve-and-volley.** The normal serve-and-volley is a style that some players use to win points, but this strategy is different. This strategy is used when the player has hit a good serve and sees that the opponent has hit a defensive return. This gives the player the opportunity to step up in the court for any shot deemed necessary.

- **Return-and-volley.** The return-and-volley is used when the player has good returns and when the player executes a return to a weakness of the opponent.

- **Lob-and-volley.** The lob-and-volley is used when the player has hit a successful short ball to the opponent, who then approaches the net. The player then lobs the opponent's reply over the opponent's head and follows the lob to the net.

- **Sneak-and-volley.** The sneak-and-volley occurs when the player is in a baseline rally. The player hits a heavy, looping ball to the opponent's weakness. While the opponent prepares to hit the reply, the player sneaks to the net for the volley.

An additional transition can occur unintentionally when the player is reacting to a drop shot or a mishit from the opponent and the player is forced to retrieve the short ball. In this scenario, the player's first goal is to try to keep the ball in front of the body, so the player at least has a chance to cut off a poorly hit crosscourt shot from the opponent. The player can return the ball with a drop shot or place the volley deeper in the court. Unless the player has an offensive crosscourt shot, the player should remember to keep the ball in front of the body.

COACHING POINTS

When an opponent intentionally surprises a player with a drop shot or any other trick shot, the opponent will likely know the player's next shot. One of the best ways for the player to turn the tables is to surprise the opponent in return with an unexpected shot. For example, an opponent who hits a drop shot down the line is likely to expect a weak crosscourt reply. The player can surprise the opponent with another drop shot.

CHARACTERISTICS FOR MAXIMIZING NET PLAY

Maximizing net play takes great vision and tracking skills, attitude, proper execution of the volley, discipline of shot selection, and great shot location. All these characteristics give players a greater chance of success. When players go to the net frequently, they learn through trial and error what works and how to finish off a point.

Tracking the Ball

Tracking the ball coming off an opponent's racket is an extremely valuable skill to have when preparing to approach the net and getting ready to hit the next volley. This process starts after the player has hit a successful shot (a shot that moves an opponent back in the court, off the court, or has them on the defensive) and tracks the oncoming ball well enough to get in the best possible position for the shot. Tracking the ball helps the player determine how short a ball will land in the court and whether it is an approachable ball. It also helps to determine the direction of a passing shot from an opponent so the player can make a quick cut to the ball.

When players volley, they must trust their eyes to lead to the path of the oncoming shot. They should pay attention to how quickly the opponent moves, where the opponent makes contact with the shot, the opponent's stance, the strike zone where the ball is being hit, the phase of play they think that they are in, and anything that might provide a hint as to where the ball will go. Tracking a ball takes good instincts and a readiness to move. Tracking a ball correctly means the player sees the ball while holding the split step until just after contact. The player should make sure the legs are balanced in order to explode directly to the ball off the split step. Players often make the mistake of guessing where they think an opponent will hit the next ball only to have the ball go in the location of where they just were.

A few games can help players improve their tracking skills:

- **Hold game.** A player can practice tracking skills by saying "Hold" out loud when a partner is about to hit the ball. This game makes the player stay in position a little longer and helps the player to focus more on the shot that is being hit.

- **Numbers game.** This game uses cones to signify areas (deep, middle, and short) where specific shots are supposed to be hit. One team is at the net while the other team is back. The net players volley to anywhere in the court, but as they do so, they must predict the most likely reply from the opponents. For example, when a player hits a deep volley to the far corner of the court, the most likely response is a lob, so the players would say, "Lob." Eventually, the players should determine three possible responses the opponents will use and rank them in order of likelihood. In the previous example, number 1 is a lob, number 2 is a drive crosscourt or through the middle, and number 3 is down the line (or another low-percentage shot on the court).

Attitude

When tracking a ball and deciding to come to the net, the player needs to have the right aggressive or offensive mindset. The aggressive attitude drives the player to attack with forward movements; the goal is to put pressure on the opponent to come up with a great shot as a response. Generally, the best-case scenario is that the player will only have the opportunity to hit about two or three volleys in a match, so the right attitude is a must. How cavalier the player is in this approach dictates the willingness to take chances and the variety of shots the player uses. It takes trial and error to know what shots will be successful, so the player must not be afraid to get passed in the quest to figure out what works best.

Shot Selection Discipline

Discipline is used on approach shots, volleys, and overhead shots placed for location. On low shots, shots in which the body is stretched out, shots where the player is not in good enough position to hit a winner, or shots in which the player does not have confidence, the player should hit in front of the body or down the line. On balls where an opponent is out of position and the player does have an easy shot, the player can play a crosscourt shot for a winner or an easier next shot. The basis for this discipline relates to the player's offensive and defensive positioning after that shot. By keeping the ball in front of the body and going down the line, the player maintains a better position and doesn't have to recover to the other side of the court because the player is already in good position. A great crosscourt shot when the opponent is on the run allows the player this extra time to recover and possibly put away an easy next ball.

Shot Location

Shot location says a great deal about a player's success at the net. Depending on the opponent's strengths and weaknesses, the player may try different locations for approach shots and volleys. An opponent who is fast and likes to be on the baseline most likely prefers that the player hit a shot back deep in the court because the opponent can recover and hit from the baseline. When playing this type of opponent, the player can hit an approach that lands short in the court to assess whether the opponent likes to move forward as much as hitting from the baseline. This shorter approach can make your opponent change the usual preferred movement and come forward, which allows for the opportunity to use a surprise attack.

Another good location is to hit behind the opponent. Most tennis players try to hit to the open court in an effort to put a ball away. This strategy can still be a good one. However, the natural tendency of a player after hitting a ball is to recover and start heading in the opposite direction of the location of the shot just hit. A shot hit back to that same location can wrong-foot the opponent, possibly giving the player an easier next shot.

SPECIALTY SKILLS

Everyone involved with tennis has at some point watched or played in a match in which someone runs as fast as possible and hits an improbable shot; everyone is stunned and surprised that the player ran for the shot at all, not to mention hit a winner. When players are put into a poor defensive position, it is important to know how to get out of trouble. It takes an awareness of the opponent's position on the court, the right shot to hit, and the balance and movement needed to hit that ball correctly. Whether it is an unbelievable lob, drop shot, or shot hit from the outside of the alley, the specialty shots are nice additions to a player's game. These scenarios don't happen that often, but it is good for players to be ready when the time calls for them.

Specialty shots can boost momentum and mentally wear down an opponent. They can be used to establish a player as someone who can make great shots when in trouble. These shots can also give the player an edge in the third set, by making the opponent try too hard out of worry that the player will come up with a tremendous shot and steal the match away. The following scenarios provide examples of how specialty shots can effectively serve as game changers and swing the momentum in a match:

- A player hits an unbelievable approach shot to the opponent's backhand. The opponent backs up and looks to be in trouble. The player no doubt hopes for an easy ball to volley into the open court. But suddenly, the opponent hits a lob. The player leaps in the air to get it but the shot goes just over the tip of the player's racket and lands inside the baseline.

- A player, who has been trading groundstrokes, out of nowhere executes a perfect drop shot, giving the opponent little or no time to react effectively.

- A player on a dead run executes a miracle shot from outside the alley, showing the opponent he cannot be easily defeated.

- A player runs full speed and hits a winner into the open court off what appears to be an unreturnable shot.

This chapter covers the lob, the drop shot, the passing shot, and desperation shots. The technique to hit these shots and the impact they have on the opponent are also covered. These shots are not usually practiced. Chapter 9 provides the drills to help players practice them.

DEVELOPING SPECIALTY SHOTS

Specialty shots such as the lob, the drop shot, and the passing shot can be used quite a bit during play depending on the opponent's game style. Hit correctly and effectively, the lob and passing shots create doubt in an opponent who is a net player and may force this player to make more errors and go for too much. Therefore, the opponent may think twice about transitioning to the net and may end up playing to the player's style. The ability to hit a drop shot technically correctly also keeps opponents from establishing any rhythm against the player; it keeps them on their toes. Desperation shots are tough to develop in the same way that a player can work on the other specialty shots because of the lack of practice with them. The need for a desperation shot is variable and unpredictable in match play. Still, a player with athletic skills can learn how to use desperation shots as game changers.

The drop shot is used to help a player take control of the point, so it can be considered offensive. The defensive lob, the passing shot, and desperation shots are technically considered defensive because the player is reacting to a shot. If a player has a good topspin lob, passing shot, or desperation shot, it can feel more offensive and may even be considered a weapon. When executing one of these shots, the player's goal is to go for a winner or execute a shot that leads to the player getting back in the point. If a player has particular weaknesses in these strokes, they may always be considered defensive.

SPECIALTY SHOTS AND STYLES OF PLAY

Just as there are different styles of play, there are also variations of specialty shots for each style. As the player continues to develop a style, incorporating certain specialty shots can enhance that player's effectiveness. For example, the aggressive baseline player could improve by learning to hit a drop shot. Players who are effective at specialty shots within their style take their game to a higher level.

- **Aggressive baseline play.** The aggressive baseline player loves to use overpowering groundstrokes to move an opponent around the court and dictate play. The aggressive nature of this style makes for an interesting use of the drop shot. In many ways, this shot takes the player's game to another level. The combination of power groundstrokes and a finesse shot such as the drop shot is lethal and becomes a part of this style's variety. Since the inside-out groundstroke is prevalent in today's game, the inside-out drop shot is becoming a widely used shot to disrupt the rhythm of the opponent. The lob and passing shots used by this style of player are usually aggressive and offensive.

- **All-court play.** Because the all-court player uses variety as a weapon, this player would use specialty shots offensively and defensively, depending on the situation. The all-court player should be adept at hitting penetrating groundstrokes, but this player also has a finesse component to the game. The all-court player is skilled at specialty shots and has the variety of shots to win. The all-court player can execute an inside-out drop shot or a drop shot that lands in front of the player. The all-court player can hit lobs offensively or defensively. This is one of the differences between the all-court player and the aggressive baseline player; the aggressive baseline style is designed for power, not finesse shots. The passing shots are hit offensively, but not necessarily for outright winners—the passing shots are hit to look for the next ball. Finally, the all-court player's desperation shots display a depth of athleticism and an ability to control the ball.

- **Serve-and-volley style.** Specialty shots are an integral part of the game of a serve-and-volley style player because the goal of this player is to get to the net as often as possible and end the point quickly. The serve-and-volley player is adept at specialty shots such as the forehand and backhand drop volleys, lob volleys, and a wide variety of overheads, including the backhand overhead, bounce smash, bicycle smash, hook overhead, between-the-legs shot, and scoop shot. Specialty shots can help distinguish the serve-and-volley style player.

- **Rallying baseline play.** The rallying baseline player would use these shots but as part of defensive play or in keeping the rally going. Specialty shots are just another part of this player's repertoire, which include angles, drop shots, defensive lobs, and differing blends of heights and speeds on the ball. The rallying baseline player uses the drop shot when the opponent appears to be in a defensive position. The lob is hit mainly defensively but is strategically placed, so the net player is not able to hit as offensive an overhead as is desired. Being that rallying baseline players do not have big weapons to accelerate the ball with, they must rely on their foot speed and varying the height of their shots combined with taking pace off their rally balls.

- **Defensive play.** Defensive players like specialty shots such as slice forehands (especially the squash shot and backhands), defensive lobs, and drop shots. They excel at hitting short and deep in the court because it happens frequently to them as a result of their opponents attacking their short balls. Defensive players hit forehand slices including the squash shot and backhand slices because they are stretched out and retrieving the ball. They use the drop shot as a means to end the point quickly because they don't think they can rally well enough or counter an opponent's game. The drop shot becomes a desperation shot for this style. Defensive players often use the lob because they are almost always in a defensive position in the court or in a rally where they are reacting to an opponent's offense. Defensive players are very good at taking pace off shots and making opponents hit additional shots to win a point.

TECHNIQUE FOR SPECIALTY SHOTS

When they learn how to properly execute specialty shots, tennis players can add variety that takes their game to the next level. They can learn to hit a passing shot or lob to defend against a player who comes to the net or learn how to hit a drop shot that throws off an opponent. The best way to learn these shots is to initially think of them as defensive shots. In other words, learn how to hit them in order to combat any style that comes up. Then, for further development, the player can learn how to use the more aggressive versions of these shots to add the element of surprise for the opponent.

Movement on these shots is critical to being able to play them offensively as well as defensively, giving the player more options when the situation presents itself. The techniques of the shots are variations of other shots. For example, the topspin lob is a form of the high, heavy shot. The passing shot is a groundstroke that is hit more on the run or with the added pressure of a player at the net, and the drop shot is a shorter version of the blocked shot approach meant to wrong-foot an opponent. (For a review of the techniques of these strokes, see chapters 1 and 2.)

Lob

The lob can be performed on either the forehand or backhand side and has two purposes: One is to stay in the point by playing defense, and the other is to offensively give the net opponent a shot that is hard to return or will produce a weak or defensive reply.

A defensive lob is usually played when the opponent has hit an offensive shot that has the player on the run and out of position. A player can play a slice lob or a lob hit high in the air with no spin, that allows the player to regroup and get back in the point; if it is played well enough, it may give the opponent a tough shot to put away, so the player can run over and hit a passing shot or another lob. A player who lobs well is very frustrating to play against. When coming to the net, this player creates doubt in an opponent because the opponent must cover not only a possible passing shot but a lob as well.

Players want to be able to hit defensive lobs well enough to break up the opponent's rhythm and also as a way to go on offense. When an opponent isn't consistent at putting away overheads or is inept at transitioning to the net, a player can use short shots to bring the opponent to the net and then lob strategically to have the upper hand when the opponent is at the net or away from a strong position. Note: This strategy is likely to backfire at higher levels of play because the players are too strong.

The topspin lob is considered an offensive lob. It is hit when the opponent approaches the net and the player is in a relatively good position on the court. The offensive lob is hit when the player has time to run over and hit the shot with offensive technique. This is usually accomplished near the singles line on either side and near the baseline. This lob can also be hit closer to the middle of the court and landing deep (near the baseline). The player can play the offensive lob like a normal groundstroke when the ball bounces a little higher, or even if the player is pushed back in the court and is on the back foot.

Another type of offensive lob is the bunt lob, which is hit when the opponent is approaching but hasn't gotten set yet; the player hits a flat ball that catches the opponent moving forward and not expecting the lob. This shot is usually hit as a backhand slice. However, some players perfect the on-the-run forehand slice to the point that they can hit an offensive forehand slice lob, but this is rare.

Bunt Lob

Defensively, the bunt lob is often used when the opponent has hit a deep volley and the player is not in good enough position to hit a topspin lob or passing shot; the only option is to block it or push it back in the court. Offensively, this type of lob is used to catch a player off guard at the net and to hit over the net player's head. It is used when a player doesn't have time to set up for a topspin lob or doesn't want to be defensive. Serve-and-volley style players or all-court players who have good hands (feel for the ball or control of the ball) and instincts usually hit this shot because this shot has similarities in preparation to the volley. This type of lob is also very effective as a return in doubles (see chapter 11).

Preparation and Backswing   For the bunt lob, the player uses a Continental or Eastern forehand grip. The stance can vary from closed if in a more offensive position to more open if on defense. This shot is hit from on or near the baseline. The preparation for this shot is similar to that for the block shot approach but without the forward momentum. The racket is brought back with the racket face open and straight back to a position where the player can then move the arm forward from slightly low to high. For the defensive bunt lob, the backswing is shorter (see figure 8.1), and the technique is similar to a high volley taken from deeper in the court (just inside the baseline to midway between the baseline and service line). The racket goes back, and the ball should have no spin so that it is pushed or blocked outward and upward through contact, and the face of the racket is open.

Figure 8.1   Shortened preparation for the forehand bunt lob.

Figure 8.2 Forward swing for the bunt lob.

Figure 8.3 Follow-through for the bunt lob.

Forward Swing and Contact The racket face is open and moves from a low to a high position. The player swings straight through the shot upward with a flat hit that is firm but controlled (see figure 8.2). The body stays in control and balanced with weight transferring forward when possible. The player is contacting the ball in the rally or attack points of contact and in the lower- or midlevel strike zones.

Follow-Through The racket movement follows the ball's trajectory in a low-to-high fashion or slightly straight through the ball (see figure 8.3). The racket ends up around the shoulders on the opposite side.

Backhand Slice Lob

The slice lob is mainly hit with the backhand. This shot is not hit often, but it can be effective because it gives the player time to recover. The player can use this lob when the opponent is up at the net and hit a volley that has the player way off the court on the backhand side. Any player who has learned to hit a slice can hit this shot.

Preparation and Backswing The player usually stands on the baseline or slightly behind it. The grip for the slice lob is the Continental or Eastern backhand grip, and the stance is more closed. On the backswing, the racket is higher with the racket face in line with the oncoming shot. The player can hit this shot from all stances. Players who are out of position may have difficulty executing this shot. It works best with good balance. Although balance on this shot is ideal, if a player is scrambling to get in position, the preparation could be a slide into the shot or preparing the legs with whatever balance is possible.

Forward Swing and Contact In the forward movement, the player pushes upward from the back leg, the body moves forward, and the racket head moves upward. At contact, the racket face is open, and the wrist is firm. The contact point is the rally or defensive point of contact, and the strike zone is in the lower- and midlevel strike zones.

Follow-Through The follow-through continues upward and finishes above the opposite shoulder. The back arm extends backward to maintain balance.

Offensive Topspin Lob

The offensive topspin lob is another form of a very effective passing shot. When executed well, it is a valuable weapon. Andy Murray is the consummate counterpuncher and has a great topspin lob to keep an opponent guessing as to what his next shot will be. Because he is so effective at counterpunching shots from an opponent, this shot is not seen until it is too late for the net player to react.

Figure 8.4 Preparation for the topspin lob.

Preparation and Backswing   The player should be near the baseline or slightly behind it in a location that is near the alleys or slightly farther back from the middle hash mark. The grip and the preparation are the same as those used for the topspin groundstrokes. The backswing is the same as for the groundstroke, but in some cases it might be a little quicker or shorter, depending on whether or not the player is in place for the shot. This shot is hit from the mid- to lower-level strike zones. To hit this shot effectively, the racket needs to drop under the ball and then accelerate quickly upward. The racket face is turned downward or slightly closed prior to progressing upward. The knees are bent, and the body weight goes backward to maximize the use of spin (see figure 8.4).

Forward Swing and Contact   In the forward movement (see figure 8.5), the player uses the same technique as for a high, heavy topspin shot. This shot has a lot of spin. The contact point can be defensive if the player wants to incorporate more legs on the shot, or rally if the player wants to drive the ball upward and use a stroke with a higher trajectory than the high and heavy topspin shot. The strike zone should be lower-level or midlevel.

Follow-Through   The legs unload on the follow-through, and the racket face continues upward and forward with great acceleration. The finish is higher than normal, and it is above the shoulders (see figure 8.6).

Figure 8.5   Contact on the topspin lob.

Figure 8.6   Offensive topspin lob follow-through.

Drop Shot

The value of the drop shot is its element of surprise. This shot is hit well by players such as Novak Djokovic, who has an aggressive baseline game that mixes power with finesse. Djokovic can use this shot as a way of enhancing his power game. Strategically, the drop shot can be used to bring an opponent to the net who doesn't like to volley or is uncomfortable at the net. The drop shot is used most effectively when the opponent is recovering after a shot and is stuck deep in the court. It is usually hit delicately. The success of the shot depends on the player's execution, the opponent's court position, and speed around the court.

The player can hit this shot in front of the body just over the net, at an angle, and inside out. The inside-out drop shot is derived from players using the inside-out forehand. It can be disguised if the player lines up as if about to hit an inside-out forehand, takes the normal backswing, and instead of hitting it normally, cuts the swing and places a ball inside out just over the net.

Preparation and Backswing   The forehand or backhand drop shot requires either the Eastern or Continental grip. The player should be in front of the baseline when playing this shot. To surprise the opponent, the player's stance should be the same as for the regular groundstroke (figure 8.7). The player takes the racket quickly back, slightly higher than the level of the oncoming ball, with a quarter turn and a shorter backswing, in a manner similar to that for the block shot.

Forward Swing and Contact   The racket face is open and travels down (see figure 8.8) and across the ball for underspin, from low to high for backspin, or from right to left for a right-handed player and left to right for a left-handed player for side spin. Which spin to use depends on what type of drop shot the player is trying to hit. A great drop shot can be played three ways. With underspin, it goes over the net and softly bounces three to five times on the service box. With backspin, it goes over the net, stops or rolls back to the net, or in some cases, bounces on the opponent's side and comes back over the net. With sidespin, it bounces on the opponent's side of the court and goes off the court after that bounce. The contact point needs to be in a position that is comfortable for the player. The drop shot can be hit from all three contact points and strike zones but is best hit from the low- to midlevel strike zone.

Figure 8.7   Preparation for the drop shot.

Figure 8.8   Contact for the drop shot.

Follow-Through The follow-through is short and ends slightly in front of the body. The face of the racket is open at the end of the movement (see figure 8.9). The body is balanced.

Passing Shots

A passing shot is meant to catch the net player out of position or give the net player a shot that is impossible to put away. The technique for a passing shot is the same as for regular groundstrokes. The difference is that the player is facing an opponent in an aggressive position at the net, limiting the space to get a shot by the opponent. Passing shots are usually hit on the run. They require balance and knowing just how much space is available to hit the shot successfully.

A variety of passing shots exist. Three commonly used types include the ripper (which is aggressive), the dipper (which is part one of a two shot pass), and the open-court passing shot. The ripper is usually attempted when the player

Figure 8.9 Drop shot follow-through.

is pulled off the court, and the goal is to hit a winner because it's the only option for winning the point. The ripper may also be hit directly at the opponent with the intention of getting a short ball to attack or forcing an error with the pace. The dipper should be the goal when the player is trying to set up an easier ball on the next shot. The short dipper is usually hit when the player is not in a good enough position to hit an aggressive shot but may be able to hit it at the opponent's feet in hopes of getting another more aggressive passing shot on the second ball. The player uses the open-court passing shot when seeing an opening while the opponent is at the net.

Justine Henin has a great passing shot. Her variety of shots and her quickness to the ball make it difficult for opponents to get in the proper court position in time. Both her backhand and forehand are hit confidently and can be hit as short dippers, rippers, or into the open court.

Preparation and Backswing The open stance is mainly used when hitting passing shots, but it is possible to be in good enough position to hit in a closed stance. The grip and backswing technique depends on the type of stroke (forehand or backhand) and possible spin on the shot (slice or topspin). A flatter drive passing shot is a good choice on the aggressive passing shots. Topspin is better for short dipping shots because the player can dip the ball at the opponent's feet, which makes it difficult to get to the ball. Players usually hit the passing shot and the short dipper from near the baseline or slightly behind it and toward the alleys. The short dipper can be used inside the baseline and at an angle that allows the dip to just drop over the middle of the net and sink down.

If ample time exists, the aggressive and dipper passing shots can be prepared the same way. If the player has less time, the shoulders make more of a quarter turn, and the backswing is shorter. The player should try to prepare early to adapt the length of the backswing to the oncoming ball. The player uses a longer backswing if going for a normal passing shot and a shorter one if planning to use a shorter, more accelerated groundstroke, which requires less backswing and a smaller loop to produce the dipping shot.

Figure 8.10 Contact for a passing shot.

Forward Swing and Contact   The forward swing and contact depends on the speed and spin of the oncoming ball and on the direction of the shot (down the line or crosscourt). The ripper is hit with power and with a blend of topspin and a lower trajectory (see figure 8.10). The forward swing for the short dipper is shorter and is accelerated more upward in a shorter arc going low to high. The swing path of the racket is similar to those of the groundstrokes for the aggressive passing shot but shorter and less extended for the dipper.

When hitting aggressively crosscourt, the contact is in between the attack point of contact for the crosscourt ball and the rally point of contact for hitting down the line. When hitting the short dipper, the player uses the hands more to feel the shot. The dipper is meant to catch a player before getting in a great position.

Follow-Through   The follow-through on passing shots is similar to that for a normal groundstroke, and the follow-through for a short dipper is abbreviated with greater acceleration used. The swing path of the racket during the follow-through is extended on the aggressive passing shot and closer to the body on the short dipper. For the aggressive passing shot, the finish is similar to that for a normal groundstroke; for the short dipper, it is across the body.

Desperation Shots

Desperation shots are notable because they can get a player out of a bad situation. Usually, the opponent has hit a ball that is over the player's head, has the player on a dead run moving backward or forward, and forces the player to come up with a miraculous shot to win the point. A desperation shot that is hit running forward is hit with an incredible angle, as a down-the-line shot out of the opponent's reach, or occasionally as a lob.

The desperation shots hit moving backward are the desperation lob shot, the tweener, and the slap shot. The tweener is hit between the legs, facing away from the net. This shot was made popular first by Yannick Noah, and today is a specialty shot used by many of the top professionals, including Roger Federer. The slap shot is a difficult specialty shot that is played over the back of the head, waist high, and to the side of the body. It is hit with great balance, feel, and can catch the opponent off guard. Following are some key points for players who need to play one of these shots.

On-the-Run Forward

When in this desperate situation, the player should get the racket in front of the body while running. In most cases the player barely gets to the ball, so the shot the player is able to hit depends on the perceived opening. This shot is usually made in the lower- to midlevel strike zones and uses the attack point of contact, just before the ball touches the ground.

The player can hit the desperation shot at an angle, through an opening to the side, or as a lob. This shot should be hit at an angle when the player is on a dead run and feels able to just barely get it up and over the net. This is usually executed with a flick of the wrist. Then the player hopes the shot is executed well enough or that the opponent gets caught out of position enough for the player to win the point. If time allows, the player may want to consider hitting the desperation shot forward or in front. This is the highest-percentage play in this situation, because if and when the player gets it back in the court, it gives the player the best court positioning at the net.

A desperation lob forward must be hit with ample time for some adjustment of the body and the hand. The desperation lob is usually hit when the opponent is already at the net, so preparation and movement are critical. The trajectory of the ball must clear the opponent and still land before the baseline, so it requires great feel.

Desperation Lob

Players must sometimes use the desperation lob because of poor court positioning or because the opponent hit a great shot. The appropriate time for a player to use a desperation lob is on a dead run and with only the time to try to get the ball back up in the air. Desperation lobs are primarily hit in the lower- and midlevel strike zones and in the rally or defensive points of contact.

Tweener

This shot is hit when a ball goes over the player's head at the net. Both players could be at the net already, or this could be a blocked lob that goes over the player's head. The topspin lob, however, is difficult to hit as a tweener because it travels too far away from the player once it lands. As the player turns and runs for the shot and is getting close to the ball, the player decides whether it is possible to get in a good enough position to hit a ball backward between and through the outstretched legs.

To execute this shot, slight adjustment steps are made just before contact to make sure the body position allows the shot. This shot is executed on the baseline or behind the baseline. In the preparation the racket is above the head with an Eastern backhand grip, then it goes downward through the legs. The body is slightly forward to allow a little room for the racket to travel. The player swings downward and flicks the wrist back and through the legs. This ball is contacted close to the ground (about 1 foot, or 0.3 m) in the lower strike zone and between the legs. The follow-through is upward between the legs. The player usually jumps upward and forward at the moment of impact.

Slap Shot

This shot is hit on both the forehand and backhand sides, and it is played when a lob is hit diagonally over the player's head and the tweener is not an option. The player runs back as fast as possible, but this time adjusts the body enough to contact the ball at the side of the body behind the head. The player runs with the racket out and basically slaps or flicks the wrists backward, hoping to get enough of the racket head on the ball. The shot is made in the upper-level strike zone and in the rally point of contact or as close to the body as possible.

For mid- to lower-level balls the racket is prepared in front and at the same level of the head or slightly above, and then it goes downward to the contact point. The player can also hit this shot from the side at knee level or slightly higher for a higher shot. This type of shot is used at the net and requires great feel. When the player is in an outstretched position, this shot is usually used when a lob volley is hit over the player's head but not that deep in the court and subsequently at a lower trajectory. The wrist is flicked backward, but from the side of the body.

USING SPECIALTY SHOTS

How and when to use specialty shots is important to the overall success of the shots. The player can use the drop shot as a tool to get an opponent on the defensive. The inside-out drop shot is used when a player has hit an inside-out forehand, the opponent hits a shorter crosscourt reply, and while the opponent is recovering, the player scoots into the court and hits a drop shot that will wrong-foot the opponent. The drop shot hit behind the opponent is also effective when the player wants to test an opponent's movement forward on the run. Because this shot is hit down the line, the opponent is hitting over the higher part of the net. If the opponent is quick, more options will be available, such as a drop shot back to the player, an angled drop shot, or an easier groundstroke. The one thing to recognize is that the player is using the greater height of the net on this shot, so it is necessary to play it with a little more loft; the player's goal is to get the opponent unbalanced and forced to hit a weak crosscourt shot that the player can put into the open court.

On lob shots, the player can trick the opponent into thinking the next shot is a groundstroke and then push a shot over the opponent's head. Placement and ability to disguise are key to the success of this shot. If the player develops a strong topspin lob, it is possible to disguise the lob so that it looks similar to a groundstroke. In this fashion, the opponent at the net doesn't know if the player is hitting a groundstroke passing shot or a topspin lob until the last second, when it may be too late to adjust.

Passing shots also have a way of making an opponent unsure of how to attack. Finesse type passing shots such as the dipper are meant to be disguised and keep a net player from getting a good strike at the volley or out of position and off balance. If the player's movement is efficient, the player has more options as the opponent approaches. If effective, the more aggressive passing shot can make a net rusher alter the game. Knowing when to go down the line or crosscourt takes on a chesslike game in which two players are trying to figure out each other's next move.

MINDSET FOR SPECIALTY SHOTS

The mindset for the specialty shot game is predicated on ultimate defense and the flare for the fantastic. The thought process for defense is to get one more ball back in the court, to play scrappy defense, and to do anything to win. The more offensive and fantastic side of these shots is being a shot maker, a crowd pleaser, and someone who can come up with great shots. On the practical side it is nice for a player to know that they can come up with the right shot at the right time in addition to hitting an unbelievable shot.

In match play, a player is constantly looking for an edge and a way to get an opponent to give up or get frustrated. Hitting one of these types of shots is a way to effectively get in the mind of the opponent and make the opponent work harder to win a point. In the third set, when a player is looking for whatever edge will lead to a win, the player's effort on these shots may make the difference.

CHAPTER 9

NET AND SPECIALTY DRILLS

Players who can successfully transition to the net can execute volleys and overhead shots that can help them finish a point easily. A player who wants to successfully oppose a net player needs the ability to hit passing shots and lob shots to make the transitioning player apprehensive about coming in and stepping into a defensive role. A net player, who is forced to play defense, may have need for one of the desperation shots from chapter 8. After a desperation shot, the opponent might be tempted to employ a drop shot as the final blow. In this scenario, when one player transitions to the net, the game opens up to a variety of net and specialty skills. To take their games to the highest level, players must be prepared to use all of these skills.

This chapter provides the following drills designed to help the player improve net and specialty shots.

1. Approach shot drills

2. Passing shot and lob drills for possible replies

3. Volley and overhead shot drills for net play

4. Drop shot drills

5. Desperation shot drills

6. Live ball drills

APPROACH SHOT DRILLS

The drills in this section focus on developing each of the specific approach shots played in today's game. Drilling each of these shots can help players add variety to their game and gain the ability to consistently hit approach shots to specified locations as needed. These drills ultimately give players a stronger base of technique and a larger repertoire of shots that will help them develop the strength of their game.

The first five drills in this section (Approach and Catch Movement, Block Approach, Aggressive Groundstroke Approach, Swinging Volley Approach, and Slice Approach) provide the practice needed to execute these shots. When players are comfortable with the technique of each basic approach, they can use the Approach Target drill (page 170) to perfect each approach shot. When players can execute the technique drills so that they can successfully focus on *where* they are hitting the ball and not *how* they are hitting the ball, they are ready to move on to target drilling. Unless otherwise specified in the drill, both the forehand and backhand sides should be practiced. For the following drills, hand feeding is recommended to start. Performing hand feeding drills is one of the best ways to isolate and work on the movement and execution of the approach shot.

APPROACH AND CATCH MOVEMENT

Purpose: To develop quick first steps and balanced adjustment steps for maximal preparation and momentum on the approach.

Procedure: The player stands without a racket on the baseline at the middle hash mark. The coach or partner stands at the middle of the service line on the same side of the court and throws balls about 4 feet (1.3 m) away from the player's body, creating enough room for the player to move forward to shadow the approach shot. The player focuses on pushing off for two aggressive steps, followed by a turn of the shoulders and adjustment steps into a closed stance. The player simulates the forward swing with the arm and catches the ball while moving forward to the net to drop the ball over the net. The player goes back to the starting position to repeat the drill five times.

Coaching points: The next part of the progression would be for the player to hit the ball with a racquet. A common error is that players take too few steps to get into position or they forget the shoulder and hip rotation when getting to the ball.

BLOCK APPROACH

Purpose: To develop a forehand or backhand approach shot with depth and no spin. The player can use this shot when no time remains to prepare to hit an aggressive topspin approach or slice approach.

Procedure: The player stands on the baseline at the middle hash mark. A coach or partner stands at the middle of the service line on the same side of the net and feeds balls softly and with some loft, crosscourt. The feeder begins with easier shots landing midway between the service line and baseline at the edge of the middle third of the court (toward the alley but still technically in the middle). Gradually the feeds can move more toward the service line to practice this shot while on the run, emphasizing the lack of time for a normal setup. Moving toward the ball, the player should prepare with a quarter turn of the shoulders followed by a slightly high-to-low but mainly straight swing through the shot (in other words, flat), making contact just in front of the lead foot. The player focuses on pushing through the ball to execute a shot that clears the net by 6 inches (about 15 cm) to 1 foot (about 30 cm) and lands deep in the court or shortly angled. The player follows the forward movement to the net.

Variation: The player can hit this shot with movement and preparation similar to that for a drop shot. Just before contact, the player changes their intent for the shot to a block approach. The disguised version of the block approach shot is a very effective means for wrong-footing an opponent. The potential for a drop shot usually has the opponent running forward; the block approach can fool the opponent, who gets caught out of position.

> **CRITICAL CUE:**
> The technique is similar to volleying but with a slightly exaggerated takeback and extended follow-through.

AGGRESSIVE GROUNDSTROKE APPROACH

Purpose: To develop a penetrating, offensive forehand or backhand approach shot that is hit to the open court to put the opponent on the defensive.

Procedure: The player stands on the baseline at the middle hash mark. A coach or partner stands at the middle of the service line on the same side of the court and feeds balls at differing speeds and heights crosscourt to land 1 to 3 feet (0.3 to 0.9 m) inside the baseline and midway between the middle of the court and the alley. The player moves forward quickly to take the shot, and hits a hard drive (no spin) or aggressive topspin stroke that lands deep in the court or is shortly angled. The technique is similar to that for a groundstroke, but the amount of forward momentum that is gained from the preparation steps should move the player quickly toward the net. The player's early recognition of an attackable ball and appropriate preparation are key to practicing and executing this shot.

Variation: Players can also hit an aggressive approach off the bounce or on the rise. For this version, the player contacts the ball lower, 1 to 2 feet (0.3 to 0.6 m) off the ground, and before the usual groundstroke contact point. The takeback on this shot is abbreviated and more compact, with a great emphasis on acceleration of the racket head and the body's forward momentum. The body's momentum and the player's ability to stay compact through the shorter contact zone aid in the success of this shot. The player's goal for this shot is to take the ball early to

> **CRITICAL CUE:**
> Hitting the ball out is a common problem with this shot because it's made on the move. The player should aim shorter in the court, such as for the service line.

(continued)

Aggressive Groundstroke Approach (*continued*)

catch the opponent before the opponent has a chance to recover from the last shot. So, at times the player can get away with not hitting a great shot in the perfect location because hurrying the opponent puts the opponent on the defensive, which benefits the player.

SWINGING VOLLEY APPROACH

Purpose: To develop an approach shot with an effect similar to that of the aggressive groundstroke approach. This shot is taken out of the air to take more time away and put the opponent on the defensive.

Procedure: The player stands on the baseline at the middle hash mark. A coach or partner stands at the middle of the service line on the other side of the court and feeds balls using a racket. The feeds should go down the line, landing midway between the service line and baseline in the middle third of the court. The feeds should clear the net by 4 to 5 feet (1.3 to 1.5 m) so that they can be hit out of the air. The player starts to move forward as soon as the ball is hit. The technique is the same as for a groundstroke, except the player hits the ball in the upper- or midlevel strike zone straight out of the air. The player drives the ball flat or with topspin to land deep in the court or at a short angle. The player follows the forward movement to the net. The player should hit 10 forehands, 10 backhands, and 10 alternating.

SLICE APPROACH

Purpose: To develop an approach shot (generally with the backhand) with lots of backspin, which keeps it low over the net. This shot is difficult for the opponent to defend and gives the approaching player extra time to get in good position.

Procedure: The player stands on the baseline at the middle hash mark. A coach or partner stands at the middle of the service line on the other side of the net and feeds a variety of balls (hard, soft, fast, slow, flat, and topspin) down the line to the backhand side. The feeds should start with easy shots that land midway between the service line and baseline at the edge of the middle third of the court (toward the alley but still in the middle). To practice this shot even more on the run, the feeds can gradually move more toward the service line. The player focuses on moving into a closed stance and preparing the racket head slightly behind the shoulders and in the path of the oncoming ball. The player contacts the ball directly in front of the lead foot with an arm extension from high to low, then takes carioca steps to keep the shoulders turned through the shot. The player should focus on making a downward cutting motion (a sweep downward for more slice) and releasing the wrist through the shot to give it more bite; in other words, the ball should stay low and land either deep or at a short angle.

APPROACH TARGET

Purpose: To develop variety in location and consistency in execution of the different targets for the approach shots.

Procedure: The player stands on the baseline at the middle hash mark. A coach or partner feeds a variety of balls (softer or harder, with no spin, topspin, slice, etc.) to different locations, including midway between the service line and baseline to both sides and near or inside the service line to both sides. Each approach shot should be practiced both down the line and crosscourt. The slice is an exception because it is hit primarily down the line. For the crosscourt placement, which is reserved mainly for the strategic short ball, participants set up the squeegee pole 7 to 12 holes to one side of the net strap (right for a right-handed player, left for a left-handed player) and place a cone on top. (See page 68 for more on the setup.) For the down-the-line target, participants place the pole about 2 feet (0.6 m) from the alley toward the net strap, to the right for a right-handed player and to the left for a left-handed player. To adjust for trajectory, they move the pole from 1 to 5 holes below the top strap. The pole should be higher for the block approach shot and lower for the slice or any short-angle approach. The cone on the court should be placed 2 to 3 feet (0.6 to 0.9 m) from the baseline and alley for deep down-the-line placement, 2 to 3 feet (0.6 to 0.9 m) from the baseline and the alley for crosscourt placement, and near the service line for the short-angle approach.

Coaching points: A down-the-line approach is a better shot strategically than a crosscourt approach shot because the volleyer can hit into the open court on a crosscourt pass. A crosscourt approach gives the opponent more options unless the approach is hit well. An important visual cue for the down-the-line shot is to focus on the racket head coming around the ball or hitting the outside of the shot. This visual usually gets players hitting through the ball a little more and can help players gain better control over redirecting the ball.

MULTIPLE APPROACHES

Purpose: To practice the different approach shots in a variety of locations to develop acceleration, the feel for the hands, and the ability to use different contact points.

Procedure: The player stands in the middle of the service line. A coach or partner stands on the other side of the court at the middle of the service line. The coach or partner faces the player and rhythmically hits soft, high, topspin balls. The player drills the on-the-rise variation of the aggressive groundstroke approach or the swinging volley. The player should hit enough balls to get a feel for how to maneuver the wrists and hands to hit the ball from the service line to the various locations. Then, the player moves back to midway between the service line and baseline. In this location, the player continues to work on the previous approach shots, comparing adaptations in execution from the new location while adding the standard aggressive groundstroke approach. Finally, the player moves to the baseline and works on the groundstroke approach shots: block approach shot, aggressive groundstroke approach (standard and the on-the-rise variation), backhand down-the-line approach, and backhand slice approach. For all three locations (service line, midcourt, and baseline), these shots should first be mastered down the line and then crosscourt. At each location, the player hits every shot once, before repeating any. The player moves through these drills after roughly 20 to 30 shots in each location.

PASSING SHOT DRILLS

The passing shot (and the lob; see page 174) is an option for a player facing an opponent who is transitioning to or already is at the net. The execution of the passing shot can vary. One possibility is to hit an outright winner, either crosscourt or down the line, past the opponent. This strategy can be effective when the shot is hit before the net player has had time to set up in a great position. Another option is to hit a hard-to-return shot (usually a penetrating shot at the opponent) in hopes of causing an error or a weak reply that the player can then attack for a winner. This is called the two-shot pass. Another, less aggressive example of the two-shot pass is hitting a shot (could be a short dipper at the opponent's feet) that gives the player a chance to recover in time to hit the next shot as a passing shot. This strategy is usually used when both the player and the opponent are out of position.

The drills in this section are designed to develop each of the specific passing shots played in today's game. Drilling each of these shots will add variety to the player's game and give the player the ability to consistently hit those different passing shots to specified locations as needed. If the shot misses its target and is too close to the net player, the passing shot can quickly become a gift for the opponent. This sort of error encourages the opponent to keep coming to the net.

As explained in chapter 8, the passing shot can be hit as an aggressive groundstroke (either crosscourt or down the line) or as a short dipper to the opponent's feet. Most of the upcoming passing shot drills provide players with basic technique practice and target practice to ensure that players can pass their opponent effectively. The success of a passing shot is solely dependent on the player's ability to get the shot by the net players. Players not only need to practice passing shots but also practice the shots against a net player so that they get a feel for passing through a specific, confined area to avoid the net player. Unless otherwise specified by the drill, players should use each drill to practice the forehand and backhand sides.

ONE-SHOT CROSSCOURT PASS

Purpose: To develop a one-shot pass off an angled approach shot. The crosscourt pass works best when the approach is hit short and the opponent is not in good court position. This drill helps players learn to move diagonally and aggressively to cut off the shot before it gets deep in the court, giving the opponent time to set up.

Technique practice: The coach or partner feeds balls from just behind the service line. After each feed, the coach or partner takes a couple steps closer to the net to give the player the feeling of a live ball situation. The player receives a down the line feed and moves diagonally toward the ball to cut off the shot and take the ball on the rise. The player moves to the shot with the racket prepared in the backswing and, depending on the strength of the feed, adopts an open stance (if stretched out) or a closed stance (if in position). The player hits the shot crosscourt, flat or with a little topspin, making contact just in front of the lead foot. After each hit, the player recovers back to the baseline. After each set, the coach switches to another feed (flat, topspin, underspin, and so on) so that the player learns to move effectively for all types of passing shots.

Target practice: To use a target, participants place a cone on the court in the service box near the singles line. The closer the cone is to the net, the sharper the angle pass will be.

ONE-SHOT DOWN-THE-LINE PASS

Purpose: To develop a one-shot pass off an angled approach shot. This shot works best when hit off a deeper approach shot that has put the opponent in good position at the net to volley against the crosscourt pass.

Technique practice: The coach or partner starts near the service line and feeds crosscourt angles up and down the singles line. After each feed, the feeder takes a couple steps closer to the net to give the player the feeling of a competitive situation. Depending on the depth of the feed, the player moves diagonally toward the ball to cut off the shot. If it is a particularly deep shot, the player should quickly push off with the outside leg and move sideways, then diagonally to cut off the ball. To redirect the ball down the line, the player uses the rally point of contact just behind the lead foot and hits flat or with a little topspin (to add shape) and height. Adding shape means to hit a ball with height and spin that clears the net with a higher margin for error. The player recovers back to the baseline after each shot. The coach or partner should vary the feeds after each set so that the player learns to move effectively for all types of passing shots.

Target practice: For an added visual target, participants place a cone in the court for the down-the-line shot.

Coaching points: The player will feel the urgency of hitting the ball down the line because of the limited space available down the line and the feeling of the player moving toward the path of the shot. The player needs to stay poised and focus on the execution of the shot rather than the limited area to work with.

ONE-SHOT SHORT DIPPER

Purpose: To practice the first shot of a two-shot pass. This shot works best when the opponent hits the approach short and is still moving to the net.

Technique practice: The coach or partner starts at the service line. The coach or partner feeds balls diagonally near the alley. To mimic a competitive situation, the feeder takes a couple steps closer to the net after each feed. The player moves diagonally toward the ball to cut off the shot and take the ball on the rise. The contact point is just in front of the lead foot. The shot is hit short and with a lot of topspin to cause the ball to drop at the opponent's feet. The player recovers back to the baseline after each shot. The coach or partner should vary the feeds after each set so that the player learns to move effectively for all types of passing shots. This shot can also be hit as a block type shot, a flick of the wrist, or anything else the player can try to get out of a bad position on the court.

Target practice: The target in this drill is the feet of the person feeding the drill.

Coaching points: When getting the ball to drop on the opponent's feet, the player should remember to swing upward while brushing the ball with topspin, meet the ball in the lower- to midlevel strike zone, and use thinner gauge string or polyurethane strings to grab the ball more.

TWO-SHOT PASS

Purpose: To practice the combinations of a two-shot pass. This pass combines a short dipper with a crosscourt or down-the-line passing shot.

Procedure: This drill uses a net and baseline player. The coach or partner, who is the net player, feeds the ball to the baseline player on the other side. The baseline player's goal is to pass the net player by hitting the ball back to that player's feet. After the initial passing shot, the net player volleys or half volleys the shot back to a desired location, and the baseline player tries to pass again, and the point is played out. Both players should use all types of feeds and all types of passing shots to put each other on the defensive or in a position in the court that is less than desirable.

LOB DRILLS

As discussed in chapter 8, the lob can be hit in three ways: topspin lob, backhand slice lob, or bunt lob. The first three drills in this section help players execute these three shots. Then, players can use the Lob Target drill (page 175) to perfect each shot. Once players have mastered the *how* of hitting these types of lobs, they are ready to move on to the *where*. The lob should be practiced off both approach shots and volleys and should be executed to various areas of the court. The goal is to put as much distance between the landing of the ball and the net player as possible.

In terms of options, the lob has similar variety to the passing shot. Players can hit it with one of the following goals: earning an outright winner (usually with a topspin lob), getting a weak or desperate reply from the opponent (with either the topspin lob or backhand slice lob), or getting more time to recover in order to force the opponent to play one more shot (either the backhand slice lob or the bunt lob).

TOPSPIN LOB

Purpose: To develop an offensive lob to hit winners over the head of an opponent at the net. This shot is best hit when the lobbing player is in strong court position on or just inside the baseline with time to set and execute the shot.

Procedure: The player stands on the baseline halfway between the center hash mark and the alley. A coach or partner stands in the middle of the service line on the opposite side of the court and feeds balls alternating between the forehand and backhand. The player disguises the shot with a preparation similar to that of hitting a normal groundstroke passing shot, but the player changes the trajectory of the shot at the last minute by slightly accelerating the takeback and, if needed, shortening the loop. The contact point ranges from attack to defensive, and the ball is hit with great acceleration and topspin. The follow-through should be upward, and the ball should have plenty of height over the opponent's outstretched racket, landing close to the baseline.

Coaching points: If the topspin lob continually lands too short in the court, it may be a result of aiming too low or imparting too much topspin on the ball. If the ball sails past the baseline, the player should be sure to aim crosscourt, imparting enough topspin, and use the feel in the hands to adjust the trajectory of the shot.

BACKHAND SLICE LOB

Purpose: To develop an effective lob that can move the opponent back off the net or win the point outright.

Procedure: The player stands on the baseline halfway between the center hash mark and the alley. A coach or partner, who becomes the net player, stands in the middle of the service line on the opposite side of the court and feeds balls with various speeds and spins, letting the player get a feel for hitting the lob. After 5 or 10 practice lobs, points should be played until one player reaches 11. The net player reacts to each lob, and the point is played until one player makes an error. The baseline player moves sideways or slightly backward and prepares the racket in a manner similar to that for a backhand slice shot. The takeback should be a

little longer, and the racket face should be positioned slightly open so that the player can impart backspin on the ball. The player swings in a high-to-low fashion and tries to cut under the ball to slice the ball so that it goes over the net player but still lands in the court, preferably near the baseline. The contact point occurs in the mid- to lower-level strike zones. The trajectory of the shot should be over the opponent's outstretched arm.

Coaching points: If players' shots continually land too short, they may be imparting too much underspin or misjudging the opponent's reach or ability to hit an overhead. If lobs are too deep, players need to aim crosscourt and make sure to impart enough spin on the shot using the feel in the hands.

BUNT LOB

Purpose: To develop a defensive lob that the player can use to try to extend the rally when a player is on the run or out of position.

Procedure: The player starts on the baseline. A coach or partner stands in the middle of the service line on the opposite side of the court and feeds hard-driving balls to both the forehand and backhand sides. Preparing with an Eastern or Continental grip, the player moves sideways to the ball with the racket out to the side and the racket face open. The stance is open to provide balance because the lob is hit either when out of position or from an outstretched position. With an abbreviated takeback, the player hits the attack point of contact and in the lower-, mid-, or upper-level strike zones. The player focuses on flicking the wrist to gain a high trajectory with little spin while pushing or blocking the shot over the net player's head and in the court.

LOB TARGET

Purpose: To practice placement of the different lobs so that a player can hit them to strategic positions on the court.

Procedure: A coach or partner feeds hard-driving balls from the service line. The player can use the coach or partner as a reference for something to hit over. After feeding the ball, the coach or partner extends a racket upward, providing a gauge for how high the player needs to hit the ball. The player executes the lobs to land in different deep quadrants in the court, mainly crosscourt (slightly earlier contact, just in front of the lead foot) or down the line (slightly later contact, over the lead foot). The player attempts 10 forehand and 10 backhand hits to each spot.

MULTIPLE LOBS

Purpose: To practice the different lobs in a variety of locations in order to improve the feel in the hands and the ability to execute different lobs.

Procedure: The player stands in the middle of the baseline on one side of the court. The coach or partner is on the other side of the court, standing on the midcourt service line. The coach or partner hits a variety of balls (flat, hard, topspin, underspin) softly to the player. The player should hit about 30 to 50 lobs in all, alternating between hitting aggressive topspin lobs, slice lobs, and bunt lobs.

VOLLEY DRILLS

The drills in this section help players practice placing the different volleys to strategic positions on the court. Players should practice both the forehand and backhand sides. The volley is an essential skill for closing off points and adding another dimension to players' games. Development of the volley begins with knowing when to attempt a volley and then how to execute the volley to a certain location. Players should not be discouraged if their execution is deficient. Mastering the volley requires a great deal of trial and error.

STANDARD VOLLEY WITH LEG LOADING

Purpose: To work on the fundamental technique of the volley while emphasizing back leg movement.

Procedure: The coach or partner feeds balls. The player, or volleyer, uses the back leg to generate power to move away from the net. The player starts in a ready position (feet shoulder width apart, knees bent, weight on the toes) on the singles line at the net, in the alley on the side of the volley that the player is drilling. The coach or partner is approximately 3 feet (0.9 m) in front of the player and tosses an easy lofted ball in the air to the player. The player loads the legs and focuses on using the back leg (the leg on the same side of the shot) to push the body forward through the volley, stepping forward with the opposite leg and hitting the ball lightly to the feeder. This motion requires the volleyer to dissipate the energy being created by the legs with a soft touch on the racket and an open racket face. The player then takes one large step backward and resets to the ready position to hit another ball. The player practices 10 forehand and 10 backhand volleys. Moving backward forces the player to use more and more leg action to generate the needed distance on the shot to get it back to the coach or partner.

Coaching points: To control the ball, the player must use a firm wrist and prepare the racket in front and to the side of the body in the direction of the oncoming shot. The player must contact the ball just above waist level with a straight punch to the target and a short follow-through in the same direction. If more depth is needed on the shot, the player should open the racket face slightly back.

Variation: To make the drill more challenging, the player can push the wrist, arm, and racket face through inwardly to create sidespin on the ball. Or, if more underspin is desired for more advanced drilling, the player can push them in a more high-to-low fashion.

Solo variation: This drill can be practiced on a wall. Players should focus on using soft hands to keep the ball in play. Players should practice hitting 10 forehands in a row followed by 10 backhands in a row and then alternate the forehands and backhands.

MOVING VOLLEY

Purpose: To practice the split step and a direct movement to the ball.

Procedure: The player stands without a racket about 1 foot (0.3 m) in front of the middle hash mark on the service line. The coach or partner hand feeds balls from the middle of the service line, starting with balls thrown about 2 feet (0.6 m) to the side and forward of the player and progressing to 4 feet (1.3 m). The player split steps as the ball is released, then quick steps with the outside leg in the direction of the oncoming ball, and steps forward once more to catch the ball. The legs continue to move forward after the catch. The player should focus on taking one or two smaller steps through the contact to balance and then squaring the hips and shoulders to the net in preparation for the next ball. Once the player is consistently moving directly to the shot, the player should add the racket and practice the same movement while volleying.

CRITICAL CUE:

For tougher shots, the step to contact the ball may need to be slightly diagonal to get the player behind the ball in time.

VOLLEY TRACKING

Purpose: To develop the skill of timing the split step and watching the ball off the opponent's racket. This drill improves a player's ability to read an opponent's ball.

Procedure: The player is at the net on the T, halfway between the net and service line. A partner is on the baseline on the other side of the court, positioned midway between the middle hash mark and the alley on the deuce or ad side. The player and partner rally back and forth, lightly at first and then gradually increasing the pace of their shots.

VOLLEY COLLAR

Purpose: To improve coordination of the moving body parts for the volley technique.

Procedure: The player knots together two overwrap grips and ties one side of the grip around the player's neck and the other side around the top of the throat of the racket head; this is a volley collar. The grip should be tight enough so the player's head and the racket head can work in unison but not so tight as to cause danger to the player. The coach or partner stands in the middle of the service line and feeds diagonally to the player across the net, easy balls (slow with loft) at first so the player can get the feeling of the drill. Once the player gets the feel for the volley collar, tougher feeds can be put into play so that the player uses the feet and coordinates the head and the racket with the feet. This forces the player to use the legs more efficiently to get behind and under the ball (emphasizing loading); otherwise, the player will feel a pull on the neck. For safety, the coach or partner should be careful to not to overextend the player. The player and coach or partner can progress to rallying back and forth at the net, continuing to work on the racket head, player head, eyes, and feet all moving in unison. Finally, the volley collar is removed, and the participants perform the drill again, focusing on carrying over the feeling of the coordinated body parts.

Solo variation: To practice on the wall, players should use the procedure as noted and try to keep the ball going for a goal of 10 volleys to the forehand and 10 to the backhand.

HIGH VOLLEY

Purpose: To develop the technique needed to effectively volley a ball above shoulder height, adding power from deeper in the court.

Procedure: The player starts in the middle of the court, halfway between the baseline and service line. A coach or partner feeds balls with loft, targeting a height above the player's shoulder as the ball crosses the service line. The player moves forward to the volley, preparing with a quarter turn of the body and pulling the racket hand slightly behind the head. The player focuses on a high-to-low (aggressive) sweep through the ball to impart pace and a longer, more pushed out follow-through of the racket (closing the face) to impart depth on the ball. The goal is to hit the volley into the back third of the court. The player continues forward with one to two recovery steps for balance and positioning before moving back to the starting location and repeating the drill.

Coaching points: The movement in this drill is essential because the player should generate the pace on this shot by moving through the volley (transferring body weight) and not by swinging the racket.

Solo variation: The solo version of this drill is an excellent way to combine different volleys. When a player hits a high volley toward the wall, the ball will likely rebound to the standard volley location and the player can execute a standard volley.

Variation: This drill can also be executed with three quick, high balls for the player to volley on the way to the net. The recovery steps from the first volley become the approach steps for the second volley, and so on.

CRITICAL CUE: As the hand is drawn back, the racket face opens up so that the butt cap is visible to the other player.

LOB VOLLEY

Purpose: To develop the technique needed to volley high over an opposing player's head.

Procedure: A coach or partner feeds from center court, midway between the net and service line. The player starts in the middle of the court, halfway between the baseline and service line. After the feed, the coach extends the racket above the head to provide a target for the player. On the feed, the player moves up to hit the shot from near the service line. The player executes the shot using standard volley technique, focusing on a more open racket face and a short low-to-high follow-through in the direction of the ball to increase the loft on the ball. The player continues forward with one or two recovery steps for balance and positioning, then moves back to the starting location and repeats the drill. Players should aim to be able to hit 10 shots without the coach reaching the shots.

Solo variation: For an advanced volley drill, players can combine three different volleys on the wall. They should start with a high volley, which will rebound to a standard volley location. Then, players can hit a lob volley, which will rebound to a high volley location, and the drill can start again.

CRITICAL CUE: The ball is hit flat or with slight backspin.

DROP VOLLEY

Purpose: To develop the drop shot off a volley, forcing a baseline opponent to have to come to the net.

Procedure: A coach or partner feeds diagonally from the center of the baseline, hitting balls with medium pace and varying degrees of topspin. The player starts in the middle of the court, 2 feet (0.6 m) behind the service line. On the feed, the player moves up to hit the shot in front of the service line. The player executes the shot using the standard volley technique but focuses on slowing the arm and softening the grip as the racket comes forward and stopping it completely at contact to create the drop volley: a low-bouncing ball that lands in the service box three to five times or bounces once and goes over the singles sideline. The player continues forward with one or two recovery steps for balance and positioning, then moves back to the starting location and repeats the drill.

CRITICAL CUE:

If the player is meeting the ball below net level, a more open racket face with a downward half turn of the wrist will give the shot some height.

LOW VOLLEY

Purpose: To develop the technique needed to effectively volley a ball below waist height.

Procedure: The player starts on the center of the service line. A coach or partner feeds balls diagonally with underspin or topspin to stay low and dip upon clearing the net. The player moves forward to the volley, preparing the racket face forward and to the side of the body, with the racket face open and around knee height. With little to no backswing, the player sweeps the ball with an open racket face, focusing on getting low and holding the knee bend through contact to aid in producing a low-trajectory shot. The player takes one to two recovery steps forward during the short follow-through from low to high, aimed in the direction of the shot.

Solo variation: To practice the low volley on the wall, a player stands a little further back from the standard volley position and lets the ball drop to the low volley position. Players should try to execute 10 forehand low volleys followed by 10 backhand volleys.

CRITICAL CUE:

Keeping the racket face open puts underspin on the ball, which helps prevent loft on the shot and causes the ball to skid quickly through the court and away from the other player.

HALF VOLLEY

Purpose: To develop the technique needed to hit a short ball from the ground.

Procedure: The player starts in the middle of the court, halfway between the baseline and service line. A coach or partner feeds balls as slice shots or flat, angled groundstrokes. The player moves forward to the ball, taking a quarter turn with the body and preparing the racket back and down with a short backswing. The player focuses on keeping steady in the contact stance and pushing the racket forward in a slightly open position with a low-to-high follow-through. The goal is to hit the half volley into the back third of the court. The player continues forward with one or two recovery steps for balance and positioning, then moves back to the starting location and repeats the drill.

Solo variation: When drilling the half volley on the wall, players should stand a little further back than for the low volley, allowing room for the ball to drop, so they can half volley back to the wall. Players should aim to execute 10 forehand and 10 backhand half volleys.

CRITICAL CUE:

The player can help direct the ball to its destination with a firm wrist and quick acceleration upward and outward to the desired target area.

QUICK HANDS AND QUICK FEET VOLLEY

Purpose: To improve tracking skills and reaction time of the hands and feet, while practicing the different volley types in unpredictable combinations.

Procedure: Two players face each other on opposite sides of the court. Both players stand on the service line, either in the middle or crosscourt. Players rally using any volley until someone misses. Games can be played up to 5, 7, or 11 points.

Variation: The advanced version of this drill places the players halfway between the baseline and service line, forcing the focus even more on the footwork and adding the challenge of requiring depth on the volley. Both players hit back and forth, trying to sustain a rally between the service line and halfway back to the baseline. Misses or volleys that land short (in the service box) earn the other player a point. Games can be played to 5, 7, or 11 points.

DEUCE-AD VOLLEY GAME

Purpose: To practice placing volleys to one side of the court or the other, improving the use of all of the volley types.

Procedure: Two players set up on the court. Player 1 plays the net and starts in the middle of the service box between the service line and the net. Player 2 plays the baseline. The goal is for player 1 to hit volleys and overheads to the deuce or ad side (whichever side is being drilled). Player 2 plays on the side being drilled and may hit groundstrokes but is not allowed to hit winners. If the baseline player hits a winner, the point is replayed. Player 1 cannot hit a drop volley on the first ball but may hit one on any ball after that. Games are played to 5, 7, or 11 points.

VOLLEY TARGET

Purpose: To practice placing volleys crosscourt and down the line for accuracy and consistency.

Procedure: Player 1 starts on the deuce side on the baseline. Player 2 starts opposite player 1 at the net, standing in the deuce side service box. Player 1 hits all groundstrokes crosscourt starting with the forehand. Player 2 volleys all balls down the line. Both players work cooperatively, trying to rally crosscourt groundstrokes with down-the-line volleys for 15 seconds, then 30 seconds, and finally 1 minute. After achieving 1 minute, the players switch directions.

LIVE VOLLEY

Purpose: To practice volleys in a live situation.

Procedure: Player 1 is on the baseline, and player 2 is at the net. Both players begin to rally back and forth to each other. All the balls should be hit back through the middle of the court cooperatively until players get to the assigned number of balls hit (2 each). Then the players say *Go,* and the point is played out using the full court. Each time a player misses, the other player receives 1 point; games are played to 11 points.

Coaching points: Proper court coverage is slightly off center in the direction of the shot location. For example, player 2 hits a forehand down the line and takes a position about 2 feet (0.6 m) to the right of the center line. Better volleyers know their strengths and weaknesses and will adjust this according to their skills to find the optimum location.

OVERHEAD DRILLS

If practiced infrequently, the overhead can be one of the toughest shots in tennis. The opponent can impart a choice of spin and trajectory on the ball, so the player is dealing with a shot that the opponent is trying to win with. Other factors include court position and a player's ability to reach the overhead. Finally, environmental conditions (such as wind, sunlight, playing under lights, and so on) have an effect on the ball a player is trying to hit. Once players feel comfortable hitting overheads and can hit them to a variety of locations on the court, they are ready to use them in a game situation.

POWER OVERHEAD

Purpose: To develop a putaway shot to use at the net when the opponent hits a weak, high ball short in the court.

Procedure: The coach or partner feeds lobs from behind the baseline. Feeds may vary so that at first the lob lands on the opposite side of the court and in the service box. Each progressive feed becomes more difficult. The player starts in the service box and then shuffles backward to get behind the ball, then forward just before contact. The contact point is similar to that of a slice or flat serve and is in the upper-level strike zone.

Coaching points: **If the player has trouble with shuffling forward, a helpful reference can be to think of the movement of a baseball centerfielder who is throwing a ball into home plate to get out a player rounding third.**

CRITICAL CUE:

The body angle at contact is slightly forward, and the legs are loaded and used equally, staying balanced throughout the shot for maximum power.

SCISSOR KICK OVERHEAD

Purpose: To develop an overhead technique for balls higher and deeper in the court that do not allow for forward movement and that require an effective jump to make contact.

Procedure: The coach or partner feeds lobs from behind the baseline. The player hitting the overhead starts up at the net with the non-dominant hand on top of the net and turned sideways, ready to move back for the overhead. Upon slapping the nondominant hand on top of the net, the coach or partner feeds a ball deep over the person standing at the net. Pushing off the leg that is closest to the net, the player moves backward. The player times the jump to make contact slightly later than the power overhead (from above to slightly behind the head), scissor kicking the feet after contacting the ball to maintain balance while in the air.

CRITICAL CUE:

The body leans back slightly but stays balanced while elevating upward. The player uses the kick to offset the forward movement of the racket arm.

BACKHAND SMASH

Purpose: To develop overhead technique on the backhand side.

Procedure: The coach or partner feeds lobs from the baseline over the backhand side of the player, who is standing at the net. The player turns and lines up the approaching ball with the elbow of the dominant arm, then extends the bent arm up toward the ball. The attack point of contact is used, and the ball is hit in the upper-level strike zone. The player alternates between placing 10 overheads down the line or at a sharp angle crosscourt.

OVERHEAD TARGET

Purpose: To practice placing overheads crosscourt and down the line for accuracy and consistency.

Procedure: The player divides the court on the other side of the net into four quadrants: the two service boxes and the two deeper halves. The coach or partner feeds the player 8 to 10 lobs in a diagonal fashion. The player chooses the overhead location based on location of the feed and practices hitting balls to each quadrant.

Coaching points: The player should keep the feet in motion, making sure to move around the lob enough to hit inside out to the opponent's backhand side.

LIVE OVERHEAD

Purpose: To improve the shot and shot selection for the overhead.

Procedure: The coach or partner stands at the baseline, and the player is at the net. Players rally back and forth, establishing a rally for two shots each until both players say *Go*. Then the player on the baseline hits a lob, and the point is played out. Games can be played out to 7, 11, or 15 points.

DROP SHOT DRILLS

The drop shot is a highly valuable tool for players to have in their arsenal. The drills in this section can help players improve their drop shot so they can dictate play in a match.

DROP SHOT TARGET

Purpose: To practice hitting quality drop shots.

Procedure: The coach or partner stands by the service line. The coach alternates feeds to the player's forehand and backhand. The player starts off by standing inside the court and hitting drop shots that do the following: drop and stop in the service box on the other side of the court, drop and bounce three to five times in the service box on the side where the ball was fed, or bounce one time in the service box and go over the singles sideline. All three count as successful drop shots.

Coaching points: To hit with backspin, the player should think of hitting the bottom of the incoming ball and going up the backside of the ball with a cupping action of the hand.

DROP SHOT TO DROP SHOT

Purpose: To develop a feel for hitting the drop shot.

Procedure: Two players start on either side of the court in the service boxes. Initially players should start in the middle of the box on the service line. Later they can start in other areas in the boxes. The players hit softly to one another using underspin and backspin. The players try to make the ball bounce at each other's feet. The players rally back and forth establishing a rally for two shots each. After two shots each, both players say *Go*, and then the point is played out. Players can hit a lob, an angled drop shot, or any shot they please. Games can be played out to 7, 11, or 15 points.

CRITICAL CUE:

Players should grip the racket softly with the fingers as if holding a baby bird.

DROP SHOT TECHNIQUE

Purpose: To develop the drop shot, learn the best time to hit a drop shot, and learn how to react to drop shots.

Procedure: Two players are positioned in the middle of the baseline on either side of the court. The two rally back and forth until one player gets a shot to hit a drop shot on. Once the drop shot is hit, the entire court is used, and the point is played out. Games can be played out to 7, 11, or 15 points.

Coaching points: **Participants should vary the rally length. The player can try to disguise when the drop shot is coming by using other shots, such as slice backhands, to rally and then surprising the opponent with a drop shot.**

DESPERATION SHOT DRILLS

These drills develop additional techniques and shot options to keep a player in the point or even win it when totally on the defensive and on a dead run. The following drills practice the forward running shot, the tweener, and the slap shot. Because they are desperation shots, they are not usually practiced for placement, although at advanced levels, they can be.

FORWARD RUNNING SHOT

Purpose: To develop the foot speed, quickness, and technique needed to return a short ball. This shot should be developed on both the forehand and backhand sides.

Procedure: The coach or partner starts by the net, and the retrieving player starts on the baseline. The coach or partner hits a soft drop shot over the net, and the player on the baseline has to retrieve it before it bounces twice. On the coach's or partner's *Go* command, the ball is hit, and the player starts. The player runs as quickly as possible to the ball, pushing the racket in front of the body in the approximate location of the ball, attempting to hit the ball down the line. If successful, the player returns to the baseline and takes one step farther back. When the player reaches the back fence, the player executes 10 on the forehand and 10 on the backhand.

CRITICAL CUE:

The player should start low and pump the arms, as a sprinter would, and keep the racket head pointing in front.

TWEENER SHOT

Purpose: To develop a reply to a lob shot that can be run down but is too deep in the court to get behind. This shot is hit with the forehand side of the racket.

Procedure: The coach or partner feeds short lobs over the player, who is on the opposite side on the service line. The player turns around and runs straight toward the ball with the racket pointing upward and makes adjustment steps that allow the racket head to contact the ball through the open stretched-out legs. The player flicks the wrist downward and toward the body, stopping just slightly through the position of the legs. After contact, the player turns around and recovers back in the court.

SLAP SHOT

Purpose: To develop a reply to an angled lob where the tweener is not an option. This shot should be developed on both the forehand and backhand sides.

Procedure: The coach or partner feeds short lobs over the player, who is on the opposite side on the service line. The player turns around and runs back as fast as possible, making contact in the upper-level strike zone; the ball is at the side of the body behind the head at the attack point of contact. The player runs with the racket out and slaps or flicks the wrists backward and upward, hoping to get enough of the racket head on the ball. After contact, the player turns around and recovers back in the court.

DOUBLE DESPERATION SHOT

Purpose: To practice the different desperation shots in a live ball setting.

Procedure: The player and a partner are at the net on opposite sides of the court hitting reflex volleys. The partner hits (in defense or intentionally) a lob volley over the player's head. The player runs back and hits a tweener or a slap shot. The partner then feeds another ball by hand, which is a drop shot that requires the player to execute an on-the-run forward desperation shot.

Variation: The forward fed ball can be eliminated and the point can be played out from the backward desperation shot. Each time a player misses, the other player receives a point. Games are played to 11 points.

LIVE BALL DRILLS

The previous drills in this chapter are designed for enhancing the technique, accuracy, and consistency of the player's approach shot, lob, volley, overhead, and desperation shots. The following drills put two players in a live situation to blend a variety of shots under pressure.

APPROACH, VOLLEY, AND OVERHEAD

Purpose: To practice shots in combination for effective net play.

Procedure: The player stands in the middle of the court. A coach or partner stands on either the deuce side or the ad side. The coach or partner feeds the ball so that it lands near the service line. The player runs up and hits an approach shot (crosscourt or down the line) to the half that the coach is standing on and continues forward. The coach or partner then hits this shot, and the player volleys the ball back to where the coach or partner is playing. Now the coach or partner throws up a third shot, which is a lob, and the point is played out. The game is played to 11 points. If a ball is missed in the sequence, then it counts as a point to the other player. After 11 points have been played, the players switch sides.

APPROACH AND PASS

Purpose: To hit the approach shots and cover the passing shots in a competitive situation, using all of the options for these shots.

Procedure: Two players start in the middle of the court on opposite sides of the court. Player 1 feeds a series of five short balls to the service line on the opposite side of the court. The feeds can all be to the forehand side, all to the backhand side, or they can alternate sides. Player 2 returns the balls as down-the-line approach shots. Then player 1 replies with a passing shot or a lob. The players then play out the point using the full court. The drill is repeated, and the players switch roles. The players alternate the feeding to play additional points. Games are played to 11 points.

Variation: To increase the challenge, the player hitting the approach shot is allowed to hit to any location. For even more challenge, the player can switch the approach shot to a drop shot. The other player must then try to pass with a return drop shot (if enough time exists to get to the ball) or a forward on-the-run desperation shot.

VOLLEY AND LOB

Purpose: To pit the volley against the lob in a competitive situation, practicing the various options for these shots.

Procedure: Two players rally. Player 1 starts in the middle of the service line. Player 2 starts on the baseline. Either player feeds a ball to start the drill. Player 1 tries to hit good, consistent volleys, and player 2 rallies them back down the middle of the court. Player 1 says *Go* and then hits an offensive volley to the down-the-line corner. Player 2 runs over and hits (based on the strength of the shot) an offensive or defensive lob. The players play out the point on the full court. The winning player earns a point. Players repeat the process and switch roles. Games are played to 11 points.

Variation: A more challenging version is to play crosscourt and then hit the offensive volley down the line after the players exchange a certain number of shots.

NO WINNERS

Purpose: To improve placement, consistency, defense, toughness at the net, and the ability to concentrate for extended periods of time and sustain long rallies at the net or on the baseline. This drill is designed for advanced players who can hit an approach shot, volley, and overhead.

Procedure: Two players rally. Player 1 starts in the middle of the baseline. Player 2 starts midway between the net and the service line in the middle of the court. Either player feeds a ball to the other to begin the drill. Player 1 tries to hit shots that stretch player 2 without hitting winners. The shots may include short dippers, lobs barely within reach of player 2, or shots that player 2 cannot get a good strike on a volley. Points are awarded for any misses or forced errors. When a winner is hit, no points are assigned. The players simply re-feed and start the next point. Games are played to 5 points. A loss by player 2 (net player) indicates a need for improvement in the player's net game.

Variation: To focus on greater accuracy, these drills can be played on a half court using the alleys to the singles half court only. In this scenario the feed can either be a groundstroke or short lob so that the net player replies with either a volley or overhead. Other variations of this drill include using one player transitioning to the net versus two players on the other side. These drills also work well in a timed fashion; players track how long it takes the attacking player to miss 5 or 10 shots.

COACH WILLIAMS SPECIAL

Purpose: To get players ready for attacking tennis quickly and efficiently and to improve mental and physical endurance while working on the transition to the net.

Procedure: Two players start on the baseline on opposite sides of the court. The drill should be timed with a stopwatch. Players perform this drill cooperatively; they work together to sustain the rally as long as possible. Every shot is hit up the middle of the court. Player 1 starts off by hitting a short ball to player 2, who hits the ball as an approach and comes to the net. Once player 2 is at the net, player 1 provides a forehand volley, a backhand volley, and an overhead for which player 2 backpedals. Player 2 then hits the overhead back at three-quarter speed. Player 1 takes the ball from the overhead and now approaches the net, where player 1 receives a forehand volley, a backhand volley, and an overhead. Player 1 responds to these shots at three-quarter speed, hitting up the center of the court. This back-and-forth rallying while approaching and playing the net takes a great deal of focus and endurance; it is tiring. As soon as a player misses, the clock should be stopped and the duration noted. Players should aim to complete the drill uninterrupted and work for lower and lower times.

CRITICAL CUE:

Players must find their rally speed and keep their feet moving throughout the drill. Players cannot perform this drill well if they stand still after hitting shots.

SINGLES STRATEGY AND DRILLS

laying singles tennis is a great test of a player's endurance, movement, court sense, weapons, instincts, and discipline in shot selection. Singles strategy and tactics help the player create a game plan in order to focus on the task at hand. A good singles player has been well coached or has figured out through trial and error what helps to win points. Reading this book can help players determine their favorite shots, how to hit the shots correctly, and the style they have confidence in. If that knowledge is clear, players' practices are more efficient, are more focused, and lead to better results.

Good, sound singles strategy and the intangibles discussed in this chapter can help players become who they want to be on the court. This chapter covers percentage tennis, foundational tactics, strategies, commonly executed shot patterns and opponent responses, and strategies for playing styles. It also guides the player and coach in how to formulate a personal game plan.

PERCENTAGE TENNIS

Before formulating strategies and tactics, it is important to understand the dimensions of the court and how they apply to high percentage tennis. A high percentage shot is one that clears the lowest part of the net and is hit toward the longest part of the court. Essentially a high percentage shot is one that has the best chance of allowing a player to make a shot or win a point. Singles tennis courts are 78 feet (23.7 m) long from baseline to baseline and 82.5 feet (25.14 m) long diagonally (see figure 10.1). When hitting a tennis ball crosscourt the player effectively has 4.5 feet (1.37 m; exactly the width of a doubles alley) of additional court to hit into which makes the crosscourt shot a high percentage shot.

The net on a tennis court is 3 feet (0.9 m) in the center and 3.5 feet (1.06 m) at the sides of the court. When hitting the ball crosscourt the player hits over the lowest part of the net. Crosscourt shots are the highest-percentage shots. Balls hit straight up the middle of the court are the second best percentage plays, and balls hit down the singles lines are the lowest-percentage plays. The net is the first opponent that the player has to beat. If the player misses shots in the net, then the opponent does not get the opportunity to hit the ball. For this reason the best misses are wide or long, but never in the net.

In tennis the player has two serves. Making the first serve is critical. Making a high percentage of first serves keeps pressure on the opponent by requiring a consistent return on a ball over which the player has total control. On the return of serve the player has one or sometimes two looks at the opponent's serve. The player makes the opponent continue play by returning the opponent's serve into the court. In terms of percentage play, the best way to direct returns is crosscourt or up the middle of the court. When leading in the score of a game and receiving a second serve, the player should try to put time pressure on the opponent by hitting the return quickly or taking the return up the line.

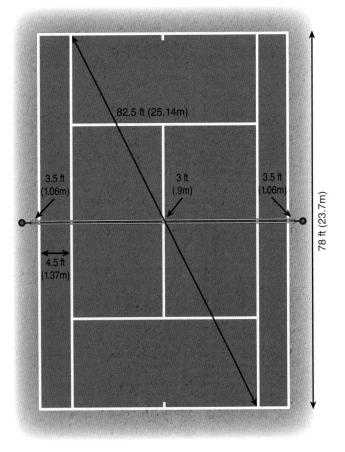

82.5 ft (25.14m)

3.5 ft (1.06m) 3 ft (.9m) 3.5 ft (1.06m)

4.5 ft (1.37m)

78 ft (23.7m)

Figure 10.1 Court measurements.

Approaching the net can put pressure on the opponent in two ways: forcing the opponent to move in a direction that encourages an error, and lessening the opponent's available response time. The rules of percentage play still apply, but if choosing to hit crosscourt in the transition from the baseline to the net, the player had better hit a winner or a highly effective shot. Upon reaching the crosscourt ball, the opponent may choose to hit down the line, giving the player less response time. When a player hits crosscourt to create angle, the opponent has an easier time passing or lobbing over the player. A neutralizing transition shot hit up the middle is not a bad play; it makes it harder for the opponent to create an angled passing shot.

Although it is a lower-percentage shot, the up-the-line transition actually helps the player set up to hit a volley or overhead on the next ball. If the opponent now chooses to pass the player up the line, the player is there; if the opponent goes crosscourt, the player has time because of the longer flight path of the crosscourt pass to move and put the volley away.

SIX FOUNDATIONAL PILLARS FOR STRATEGY AND TACTICS

Players should be able to perform the following six foundational pillars (also called *ball controls*) at the level appropriate to them. Once they have accomplished this step, players are ready to learn tactics and formulate strategies. They can also perform a style of play and improve as competitive players.

Pillar 1: Consistency

Consistency can lead to getting the ball over the net once more than the opponent. Being consistent can lead to feelings of confidence, too. Each time players elevate to a higher level of play, they should try to establish consistency at that level. The following guideposts help players develop that consistency.

- **Basic.** Try to get the ball over the net as often as possible.
- **Intermediate.** Work to be able to hit 50 balls up the middle of the court.
- **Advanced intermediate.** Be able to rally 75 to 100 balls up the middle of the court with varying degrees of spin, including moderate topspin or underspin.
- **Advanced.** Be able to hit, with personal choice of spins, 100 or more balls up the middle or to whichever part of the court is desirable.

Pillar 2: Depth

Players should target three spots along the baseline: deep to the forehand corner, middle of the court, and deep to the backhand corner. Players can use the following guideposts to develop their ability to hit for depth.

- **Basic.** Play the ball deep by being able to hit the ball past the opponent's service line while hitting from behind the baseline.
- **Intermediate.** Be able to do the same as the beginner level but use moderate topspin or underspin shots.
- **Advanced intermediate.** Be able to hit 10 deep balls total to any of the 3 depth spots.
- **Advanced.** Be able to hit 10 deep balls in a row to any of the 3 spots and then alternate hitting 10 balls in a row to all 3 spots.

Pillar 3: Direction

Hitting the ball in the intended direction and being able to place the ball on the court where the player wants it to go, signifies a degree of confidence. The player is now starting to focus on *where*, not *how*, to hit the ball. Players can use the following guideposts to develop their ability to hit in specific directions.

- **Basic.** Be able to direct the ball up the middle of the court.
- **Intermediate.** Be able to alternate hitting 50 balls from one half of the court to the other.
- **Advanced intermediate.** Be able to hit 75 to 100 balls to one half of the court and then the other.
- **Advanced.** This level can consistently rally hitting 100 or more balls to the forehand and backhand corners.

Pillar 4: Height

The ball height over the net is often misunderstood by beginner and lower intermediate players who, because of the camera angle on television from behind the court, incorrectly assume that the professional players are ripping every ball an inch or two (a few cm) over the net. Good players know that clearing the net is very important both for consistency and for creating higher-bouncing balls. The closer a player is to the net, the lower the ball is over the net. The appropriate height for these shots is roughly one to two racket face widths above the net. The farther away a player is from the net, the higher the ball needs to be hit to keep it deep into the opponent's court. For this type of shot, the ball should be anywhere from three to five racket face widths over the net. Players can use the following guideposts to develop their ability to hit for height.

- **Basic.** Depending on level of control, be able to hit on average anywhere from 1 to 10 racket widths over the net. The aim is to be able to get the ball over the net and sustain a rally, so a higher net clearance is needed.
- **Intermediate to advanced intermediate.** Be able to vary heights hitting into the *four square*—each one of the four squares on the opponent's side of the net—at will.
- **Advanced.** Be able to have the full range from 10 or more racket face widths for a topspin lob to 1 or 2 racket face widths over the net on a passing shot. Advanced players are able to control height and are more skilled to handle an opponent's shots.

Pillar 5: Spin

Players hit with these types of spin: topspin, underspin, backspin, sidespin, and flat (even balls hit flat have moderate forward spin on them). Each type of spin has varying levels. Players can use the following guideposts to develop spin in their shots.

- **Basic.** Be able to hit with little or no spin.
- **Intermediate to advanced intermediate.** Learn about and practice topspin, underspin, and backspin. These players should be able to demonstrate ten of each type of spin while being fed from a basket.
- **Advanced.** This level of player can blend spins creating difficulty for their opponents. Advanced players should be able to play the Simon Does game. In this game, they match the spin that their opponent is hitting to them.

Pillar 6: Pace or Speed

When players go out to rally with a friend they use a rally speed with each other, designed to keep the ball to each other and maintain a rally. Once they get good at playing at a rally speed, they can vary the speed of play in various ways. The first is taking speed off the incoming ball (*deflating*), such as by adding height and spin or by softening the grip on the racket. The second is increasing speed (*inflating*), such as by hitting the ball harder or flatter, or by gripping the racket slightly tighter. Players can use the following guide-posts to develop changes in pace or speed in play.

- **Basic.** Develop a rally speed by learning how to rally consecutive shots in a row, starting at the service boxes and backing up to the baseline. About 10 to 25 shots from inside the service boxes, midcourt, and baseline are achievable goals at this level.

- **Intermediate to advanced intermediate.** Be able to start differentiating between slow (30 to 50 percent of maximum possible speed), moderate (50 to 70 percent), and fast (70 percent and up) swing speeds. These levels of players should practice swing speeds by playing the Red, Yellow, and Green Light game. In this game, players call out the color representing the speed they are swinging. Green is fast, yellow is moderate, and red is slow. Players must remember that the slower they hit the ball, the higher they need to aim over the net.

- **Advanced.** Be able to inflate or deflate incoming balls. Players can practice in pairs; one player deflates each shot while the other inflates each shot.

COURT POSITIONING GUIDELINES

When rallying, transitioning, or volleying, the player should always try to position the body by taking more adjusting steps than appear necessary to meet the ball in the ideal strike zone and point of contact for that particular shot. Doing so keeps the player continually trying to get into an improved position when hitting the ball. Knowing where to stand helps the player to anticipate the most likely return of shot from the opponent and cut down on the number of steps needed to meet the ball. The following sections highlight various shots and how court positioning affects them.

Groundstroke Balls Hit to the Middle of the Court If the player and opponent are hitting the ball deep up the middle of the court to one another, then the player should be positioned in the middle of the court and behind the baseline. A groundstroke played through the middle can be played to get a rest in a rally, to reset the point, or to create less of an angle for the opponent's following shot. A player who hits a groundstroke to the middle of the court can also take that opportunity to get in a better court position to set up an attack with the forehand.

Groundstroke Balls Hit Crosscourt When hitting crosscourt from the baseline, the player should remember that the highest-percentage play for the opponent is for the opponent to hit back to where the ball came from. If the player hits a forehand crosscourt with good pace and depth to the opponent, then the player can be positioned about 1 foot (0.3 m) off the center hash mark crosscourt on the forehand side. If the player plays a backhand crosscourt, then the player anticipates the ball to come back to the backhand side and should be positioned just off the center hash mark crosscourt on the forehand side. If looking for a forehand, the player may want to be positioned midway between the center and the alley.

Groundstroke Balls Hit Down the Line   When hitting down the line the player is hoping to hit a winner, hit an aggressive shot, or just change the direction of the shot. If the player does not hit the winner or if the opponent is quick and gets to the shot in time, then the player should immediately start getting into position on the opposite side of the court and be ready for a potential crosscourt reply. Court positioning may also dictate that the player transition to the net following a groundstroke hit down the line, especially when the opponent is late getting to the ball.

Transition Shots   Transition shots are best used when the player expects or gets a good read on a potential opportunity and when a player is used to closing out a point. The player should be positioned inside the baseline for the following situations.

- The opponent is hitting softly.
- The player is trying to lessen the opponent's response time.
- The opponent is in a long rally with the player and is getting tired or nervous, and the player expects the opponent to hit the ball short.
- The player is playing an opponent who likes to hit the ball short on purpose by using drop shots and soft slices.
- The player has just hit a great shot and sees a defensive reply coming back over the net.

   As a rule, unless the player is hitting a winner during the transition crosscourt, the player should keep the ball up the singles line. The correct positioning after the transition is to take two or three steps in the direction the shot was hit and adjust using the split step, waiting for the opponent's response.

First Volley and Second Volley   In singles tennis, the first volley can be hit up the line to keep the ball in front of the player, then the second volley is hit into the open court. The player's volley location can vary, so when the player does not have an effective enough crosscourt shot, hitting down the line or keeping the ball in front of the body gives the player time to get positioned. Regardless of whether the player hits crosscourt or down the line on the first volley, the player should move 1 or 2 feet (0.3 to 0.6 m) from the middle of service box toward the location of the volley. Based on the effectiveness of the first volley, the player may want to move toward the net to anticipate and cut off an angle, or to stay in the current position if anticipating a lob or a down-the-line shot.

Overheads   If the player notices that the opponent throws up lobs well, the player should not close all the way into the net but stay near the service line toward the side, about 1 or 2 feet (0.3 to 0.6 m) from the middle. The player will be in a better position to put the overhead away.

Retrieving an Overhead and Backhand Smash   When a right-handed opponent is hitting an overhead, the player should anticipate that the natural sidespin on the overhead will go to the player's right if the opponent is right-handed and to the left if the opponent is left-handed. If the opponent hits it to the non dominant side, the opponent has hit the harder overhead. If the player successfully hits a lob over the opponent's backhand side, the player should move in a couple of steps to force the opponent to angle the ball sharply crosscourt or retrieve the ball from the direction that it came down the line. Most aggressive overheads will be hit off the court at an angle crosscourt, inside out, or straight down the middle. When an opponent moves back while hitting an overhead, the player should look to retrieve the smash down the line from that overhead. Most retrieval positions are nearer to the baseline for a better lob and farther back behind the baseline for a poor lob.

Return of Serve A right-handed server's natural spin takes the ball to the returner's forehand side, and a left-handed server's spin goes naturally to the returner's backhand side. So, the returner should be positioned in the direction that the serve naturally travels. In other words, the returner should move more to the right when playing a right-handed player and more to the left when playing a left-handed player.

For more powerful, flatter serves coming through the court, the returner should move back. This move should not occur too soon or the returner will be open for an ace out wide. Just as the server tosses the ball up in the air, the returner should back up. The same move is necessary against a really strong kick serve. If the server is acing the returner to one side, the player should get ready to return in the location where most of the aces have occurred in order to take that spot away from the server. Thus, the returner can force the server to go to a different location to break up the server's rhythm.

Serve When left-handed players play against right-handed players, they position themselves wide on the ad side to create a more severe angle to the opponent's backhand. Right-handed players can do the same thing on the deuce side: By standing a bit wider and serving out wide, they can hit a challenging serve to return for left-handed opponents. Varying the position on the serve can keep opponents guessing where players will serve next.

FOUR PHASES OF PLAY

Anytime a rally ensues, the player is jockeying for position. Presumably, the player wants to play more offensive tennis and put the opponent on defense. However, this is often determined by the strength of the opponent's shots, the player's and opponent's movement in the court, and the effectiveness of their shots. The notion that the player can play offensive shots all the time is wishful thinking; in reality, the player needs to be smart regarding shot selection and must be able to blend offensive shots with neutral shots, counterattacking shots, and defensive shots to properly construct a point.

A simple way to learn the four phases of play is to attach colors to the coordinating phase of play. Knowing the types of shots to hit in each phase of play and the responses to those shots can greatly enhance a player's intelligence and anticipation skills on the court. A green phase of play represents the attacking phase, or a *Go* situation, during which the player can play offensively. The red phase of play is defensive, during which the player can buy time to attempt to reestablish the point, such as by using a defensive lob. A yellow phase of play is the rally phase, during which the player can hit a shot to set up another shot or the player can take a red ball and, with good preparation, make it a yellow one. Counterattacking phases of play are orange because the player effectively turns around a defensive situation and makes it an offensive one, such as with a reflex volley that gets the opponent off balance.

Attack Phase of Play

In this phase, the player is on offense. The player sees that the opponent is in trouble from the last shot that forced the opponent to be out of position or on defense. This situation gives the player confidence to either place or attack the ball for a winner. An opponent's shot that gives the player a green phase is usually a ball that lands inside or near the service line or is hit more slowly, which gives the player a better chance to be offensive. The choices on a green phase shot are a winner or a shot hit with power, an approach shot, or a shot with which the player can improve court position and keep the opponent on the defensive. The attack phase of play is usually played with flat drives and aggressively played topspin shots that have a lower trajectory over the net. The shots are hit for depth or angles.

Even though an opponent's shot can signify an attack phase for the player, ultimately the player's racket preparation and movement to the ball determines the execution and success of the shot. An attacking shot for which the player is not properly prepared or to which a player moves poorly, turns into a yellow ball. This situation is equal to a missed opportunity in a rally. The player should always focus on when an opponent makes a mistake in a rally. A mistake at any level is a poorly hit ball or a ball that lands short, where the player could take advantage of the opponent. A player who focuses on this aspect and is able to effectively execute the desired shot shows signs of being intelligent and opportunistic with an attacking mentality.

Rally Phase of Play

In this phase, the player is comfortably and consistently hitting spots on the tennis court. For example, the player can win matches by maintaining a consistent ball speed and running the opponent all over the court. An opponent's shot that allows the player to rally is hit with medium speed and usually lands between the baseline and the service line. A rally shot is played offensively when the player is in good position for the shot and can use a weapon and defensively when the player's preparation was late or the player got a late read on the ball. A rally shot, usually a neutral type shot, can also be played more offensively if the player has good movement or has an attacking style of play. For example, an offensive player can use rally shots as an opportunity to be more offensive by running the opponent with this type of shot.

Another time to play a rally ball is when the player prefers to be more patient or does not feel as though the court position is strong enough to be more offensive. The best way to improve a rally ball situation is to hit with power or depth and location. In addition, the player can take standard rally balls on the rise, giving the opponent less time. The player can also use a high, heavy ball or a ball hit with more angle to be more offensive. A player can use a rally shot to set up a point by hitting a shot that has the chance of leading to a more favorable and offensive shot on the next ball. In other words, the rally shot can be the shot before the offensive shot; it makes the offensive shot possible. Players who give their rally shots a purpose in this way have an effective strategy for building points.

When a player misses an opportunity to be more aggressive with a yellow ball, the player turns the reply into a red (defensive) shot. A common mistake tennis players make is feeling they have to or want to go for too much on their shots even when they are in a bad position in the court. Striking a delicate balance between going for too much or too little takes a great deal of patience. One could call it *controlled aggressiveness*; it is a good mentality to adopt when playing points.

Defensive Phase of Play

A red ball is an opponent's shot that forces the player to play a defensive shot. This ball usually lands near the baseline. It could be a ball hit with great spin that bounces out of the player's strike zone, or it could be a shot hit when the player's movement was poor. With defensive shots, the player tries to stay in the point to establish or reestablish more favorable court positioning or an advantage. To keep the opponent from going on offense, the player should look to clear the net with some extra height and spin.

Hitting a defensive shot doesn't mean the player can't hit a shot that leads to getting back on offense; as a matter of fact, that is the player's goal. The player's goal should be to hit offensive high, heavy replies crosscourt, or up the middle if a defensive shot is preferred. If the player is on the run or out of position, then using a shot with greater loft or trajectory, giving the player ample time to recover, is sufficient. Often recovering back in the court after a deep shot from an opponent can help the player gain an advantage for subsequent shots.

Court positioning in a defensive position is usually behind the baseline or off the court. The player should pay attention to where the recovery is made after hitting a defensive ball. The player should focus on recovering closer to the baseline in order to be better prepared in the event of a short ball, a weak reply, or the possibility for an attacking shot. If the opponent is continually putting the player on the defensive, or if the player's game style is more patient, then hitting balls with greater depth or with spin and power can sustain the player in the point until the player gains an advantage. Defensive shots in which the player is in a bad position or does not properly execute a more offensive shot can keep the player on the defensive and give the opponent an advantage.

Counterattacking Phase of Play

This phase of play is when the player attacks from a defensive position. For example, a player is being run by an opponent and is on defense. The player goes for broke, hitting a shot with added pace, spin, and placement designed to go on offense. An example of an counterattack would be when a player's opponent hits a drop shot. Upon reaching the ball, the player is on the defensive and tries to get the ball over the net. The opponent approaches the net and sees that the player is in trouble. The opponent expects an easy put-away volley, but instead the player lobs the ball up over the opponent's head for a winner.

Another great counterattacking position is deep behind the baseline. Usually a player tries to give the ball some height and depth, attempting to keep the ball deep in the opponent's court. Sometimes if a player sees an opponent approaching the net, the player can aim lower over the net and dip the ball at the opponent's feet with additional spin, forcing the opponent to volley or half volley the ball up and over the net; here, the player can move in and go on offense.

The effectiveness of the counterattacking phase of play is based on the player's reflexes, reactions, and ability to counter an opponent's strengths. The counterattacking phase is also based on hitting a riskier, more aggressive shot off an opponent's aggressive shot, so the player's counterattacking skill needs to be advanced. The real goal is to surprise the opponent with aggressive play and possibly force an error. The counterattacking phase of play hits any type of shot that shortens the opponent's available reaction time and uses all different heights, spins, and locations. The art of the counterattack is about what shots the player develops to counter and how they fit into the player's style, such as a serve-and-volley style player who learns how to counterattack aggressively and is constantly looking for different ways to get to the net.

COMMON PATTERNS OF PLAY AND OPPONENT RESPONSES

Tennis is a game of strategy. Players must be aware of where they are on the court, where the opponent is positioned, and where the ball is. One move in tennis can set up another move; one shot can set up another great shot.

Service Patterns

When playing points, the service patterns are used to set up the player's best strategy. When players know that serving to a particular location will likely produce a particular reply, they can then begin to anticipate and be more offensive as players. The out-wide serve, the body serve, and the T serve are all effective, especially when the server mixes up the serve or uses opportune moments to hit a particular serve, such as hitting out-wide serves in the beginning of a game and then going to the T on a big point.

Out-Wide Serves

Ideally when serving wide the player wants the serve to land as close as possible up the singles line near the net and move off the court to pull the opponent wide and outside the court.

Opponent's response: An opponent who catches a great out-wide serve late is forced to hit down the line. If the opponent is early and can get the racket head on the outside of the ball, the opponent is in a position to go big crosscourt or up the middle of the court.

Jam or Body Serves

A serve hit at the opponent's body may create problems for the opponent. The body serve can handcuff an opponent and may keep the returner from achieving a full swing. A well-executed jam serve can make the ball unreturnable because it is placed intentionally into the left hip of a right-handed player and the right hip of a left-handed player.

Opponent's response: If the opponent is quick to move around the ball, the return can be a forehand. It is also possible that the returner likes body serves and can direct them to any location. Most of the time the player feels handcuffed by the serve, in which case the server should anticipate a potential mishit or short ball.

T Serves

Serves hit up the T line (where the centerline connects to the service line) give your opponent little time to react and generally results in a ball coming back through the middle of the court.

Opponent's response: If the player has hit a serve up the T that has stretched the opponent, then the ball will come back up the middle of the court, setting up the player to attack on the next shot. If the opponent is early taking the ball, then the ball is hit up the line.

Return Patterns

Return patterns are used to give the player the best possible position to start the point, neutralize an opponent's serve, and minimize the server's next shot. Returning crosscourt or down the middle are the most used return patterns (mainly offensive or neutralizing), and the down-the-line return is mainly used in either an offensive or defensive position. Most players prefer a particular return pattern, but it is important that players use variety on return patterns.

Deep Return Crosscourt, Down the Middle, or Down the Line

Players use deep returns crosscourt because the net is lower in the middle, there is more court to use, and it is the best return for starting a rally. The main consideration on the deep crosscourt return is whether the player is able to hit it with power and depth.

Opponent's response to the crosscourt return: If the player returns deep crosscourt, the opponent will generally hit the next ball back crosscourt. If the player returns a sharp angle crosscourt, depending on the opponent's strengths, the opponent will hit an angle back crosscourt or hit down the line to make the player run. A poorly hit crosscourt return can lead to an easier transition ball for the opponent.

Opponent's response to the down-the-middle return: After a down-the-middle return, the next shot generally comes back down the middle of the court. If the return is short, the opponent will be in a strong court position to win the point.

Opponent's response to the down-the-line return: The most common response off a down-the-line return is hitting the ball crosscourt, so it is vital that the return has power and depth and keeps the opponent from hitting aggressively crosscourt and putting the player on the run. If the return is strong, the player can look to sneak in on a floating shot. If a right-handed server is serving to the deuce side, a well-hit return down the line forces the server to rotate the body completely to reach the ball that is moving behind the body. The response may be a floating shot that is directed back toward the center of the court. The returner can take advantage of this floating shot by taking it out of the air and directing it into the open court. On the ad side a return hit down the line to a right-handed server will be going to that server's forehand. Since a later point of contact is possible on the forehand side, the server often can direct this shot more sharply crosscourt. Again, if the returner hits a great return down the line, then the returner moves forward for what will be a defensive reply.

Short Return Down the Line, Middle, or Crosscourt

The player is now taking advantage of the opponent's second serve, or maybe the player is up in the score, or perhaps the player is just feeling creative on a particular play. Either way, if used wisely, the short return can be very effective. This return is effective also if the server doesn't move forward well.

Opponent's response: If the opponent has anticipated a short return to any location, the opponent will be there quickly and hit the ball wherever is desired. However, if the opponent does not get off to a good start, the player can look for the next shot to be a low-angled crosscourt shot hit over the lowest part of the net. On a ball down the middle the player will have to guess whether the ball will sit up above the net. If the ball is low, the opponent is going to hit the ball shorter into the court and to the player's perceived weaker side. Anytime a player hits a really short ball by accident, such as a net roller, or intentionally, such as a drop shot, the player should move in a couple of steps because the opponent will be forced to lift the ball up over the net, causing the ball to land short in the court.

Groundstroke and Net Play Patterns

When a player faces a competitor of similar ability, the clock is running to see who can figure out the correct combination of patterns to win the match. Figuring out what is working with an opponent increases the player's focus and confidence when competing. Each of the following patterns may also be increased incrementally. For example, instead of a 12 pattern, the player can make it a 13, hitting 3 balls to the backhand first before hitting to the forehand.

One-to-One Pattern

A one-to-one pattern is alternating one shot to one half of the court and the next shot to the other half of the court (see figure 10.2 on page 198). This pattern can be used to open the court to hit a winner or to transition and play at the net (attacking phase), to repeatedly run the opponent on the baseline (rally phase), or to counter an opponent's aggression by shortening reaction time or changing the pattern of attack (counterattacking phase). It may also be used with increased height and spin to buy more time when the player is put on the run (defensive phase). The following are some pattern examples:

- Alternating crosscourt and down-the-line groundstrokes (all phases)
- An inside-out forehand followed by an inside-in groundstroke (attacking or counterattacking)

- An inside-out forehand followed by a backhand down-the-line (attacking or counterattacking)
- Transitioning to the net with a crosscourt groundstroke followed by an approach shot to the other side of the court or down the line (attacking)
- Executing a deep volley that produces an overhead (attacking)
- Serving out wide and then hitting a groundstroke or approach shot to the open court for either a winner (attack phase) or with the goal of getting the opponent out of position and keeping the opponent running (rally phase)

Opponent's response: If the player is running the opponent left and right, the opponent will try to step it up and go for something big to stop the prolonged agony of being run into the ground. The player should be on the alert for a counterattack: sudden increase of speed or direction as the opponent tries to put the player on defense.

Two-to-One Pattern

The Two-to-One pattern is two shots hit to one side of the court followed by one shot hit to the other side (see figure 10.3). This pattern is generally used when the player is attacking with a goal of wrong-footing an opponent to create an opening, or rallying to use shots to expose a weakness. A great way to use this pattern is two shots hit to the opponent's weaker side followed by a surprise shot hit to the opponent's strong side. For example, against a right-handed player with a powerful forehand, this pattern would go

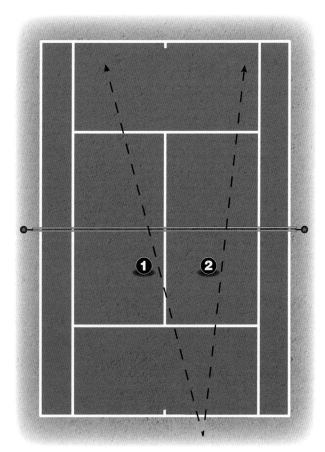

Figure 10.2 One-to-one pattern.

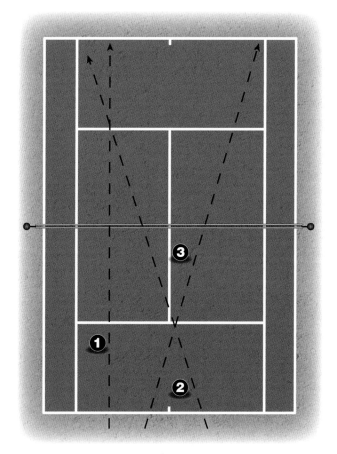

Figure 10.3 Two-to-one pattern.

crosscourt to the backhand twice, followed by a shot to the forehand. If challenging an opponent's strength, the player may choose to hit two balls to the opponent's strength and then attack the opponent's weakness. Here are some additional examples of the two-to-one pattern:

- The player hits two groundstrokes crosscourt (to a groundstroke weakness in the opponent) and then one out to the opponent's strength in the hopes of opening up the court and further exposing the weakness.

- When transitioning, the player uses two groundstroke shots to pull the opponent in a certain direction and then uses the transition shot to potentially put the opponent on the run.

- When in net play, the player hits two volleys to pull the opponent back or off the court and uses another shot as a put-away.

- The player serves out wide and then hits a groundstroke to the same area (potentially going behind the opponent, who will be running to get back in the court) and then follows with a shot to the opposite corner of the open court.

Opponent's response: A smart opponent will try to make it more difficult for the player to get two shots to the opponent's weakness by staying as long as possible on the weaker corner in hopes of running around the weakness. Hitting to the side of the court that is opposite to the opponent's strength can then open the weakness up for attack.

One-to-Two Pattern

The one-to-two pattern is one shot to one half of the court and two shots to the other half (see figure 10.4). As with the two-to-one pattern, this pattern is used for attacking and rallying. The player starts by opening up the court with the first shot, followed by a shot to the opposite side, forcing the opponent to run. The third shot is hit to the same location and behind the opponent as the player is moving back to the center of the court in anticipation of a one-to-one pattern. A player can implement this pattern in several ways:

- The player can hit one groundstroke crosscourt (to open up the court or expose a weakness), followed by two groundstrokes down the line.

- When transitioning, the player can use the first groundstroke to go down the line (to open up the court), followed by a crosscourt volley into the open court and either a second volley or an overhead to the same location; for example, back behind the player as the opponent moves to cover the other side of the court.

- The player can serve out wide and then hit two groundstrokes to the opposite corner.

Opponent's response: The opponent should focus more on the first shot (return) and try to take away the server's court position and ability to attack effectively.

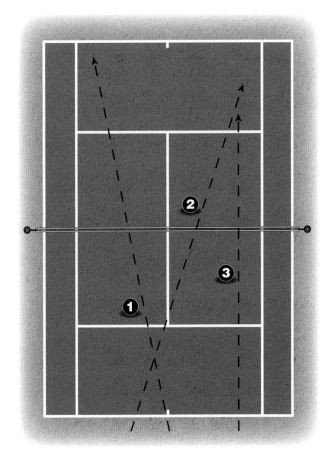

Figure 10.4 One-to-two pattern.

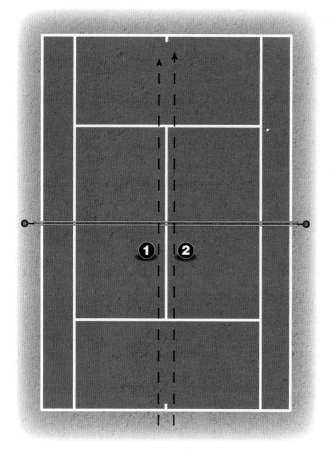

Figure 10.5 Neutralizing pattern.

Neutralizing Pattern

The neutralizing pattern is generally two or more balls through the middle of the court or mildly crosscourt (see figure 10.5), countering an opponent's pace or pattern by hitting deep up the middle to keep the player in the point and aid in recovery. When in the defensive and counterattacking phases of play, this pattern gives a player the most time to gain balance and focus to mount an attack or counterattack. This pattern can also be used in the rally phase to keep the opponent from being more offensive. The following are possible implementations of the neutralizing pattern:

- The player can hit groundstrokes through the middle that bounce higher, stay lower, or are just powerful enough to make it harder for the opponent to hit a more aggressive shot.

- A neutralizing volley can be hit from a defensive position (stretched out) to deep in the court and in a great location that allows the player to recover and hit an easier next volley or overhead.

- Neutralizing transition shots can be hit as a chip return (counterattacking phase) or as a slice transition shot (rally or attacking phase) to approach the net.

Opponent's response: If a player moves around a ball well, this player will try to get on offense (attack phase) by hitting a deep ball to one of the corners. The opponent may also play a rally shot to attack on the next ball.

STRATEGIES

Strategies are plans that give a player a sense of purpose when on the tennis court and that build on the common patterns of play. Simply put, the player executes shots in combinations that the player feels confident with and that help the player dictate play and win points.

The player's level of skill and specific shots (weapons) determine which of the following strategies to focus on and tailor to the player's individual style. For example, players who want to employ the strategy of pulling an opponent off the court should have a good inside-out forehand, have wide serves, and be able to use angles. Players can always add shots to enhance their game and add variety, but the strategy they should use most is the one that matches the shots they can hit consistently and with confidence.

All advanced strategy is based on fundamental strategy; advanced players are advanced because they didn't skip over the fundamentals. Understanding the true meaning of the shots and how they fit into the individual overall game plan gives the player a foundation of knowledge to build on. The following strategies build from fundamental to advanced.

Basic Strategy #1: Hitting to the Open Court

In this strategy, the player hits the ball to where the opponent is not standing. This strategy begins a player's development of soft focus, which is seeing where the opponent is while focusing on the player's own court positioning and the incoming ball. The player will start using ball control in an attempt to get the ball to the open court.

Common patterns of play: One-to-one pattern, hitting the ball deep, short, high, low (defensive, rally or attack phase).

Basic Strategy #2: Covering a Weakness

When the goal is to hit a weapon in a rally, the player can use the tactic of running around the weakness. Doing so takes great speed and athleticism. Consistently running around a weakness does not improve the weakness, so this tactic relegates a player to this style of play; all subsequent shots have to be developed to help that strategy.

The most popular weakness initially is the backhand, so the inside-out forehand is the answer. To effectively run around a weakness, the player must look for a short, midcourt ball with slower pace and more height. (The Three-Quarter Court drill in the upcoming strategy can help players practice covering for a weakness.) Alternatively, to set up the opponent to hit to a strength, the player can recover to the weaker side, leaving more room to hit the stronger stroke. Recovering to the weaker side also shrinks the court for the opponent, making it harder to hit it to the weakness. This is the goal of proper court positioning.

Common patterns of play: One-to-one, one-to two, and two-to-one patterns keeping the ball crosscourt as often as possible.

Basic Strategy #3: Weapon to Weakness

For most players, the serve and the forehand are the main weapons in their games. However, it doesn't mean a backhand, speed, or net play can't also be developed and used as weapons. Whatever the player's strengths may be, the goal when playing winning tennis is getting in position to hit a weapon to the opponent's weakness. The best way to do this is to use the three-quarter court strategy. This strategy says the player will try to be positioned midway between the middle hash mark and the alley on the baseline or near the baseline on the side of the player's weaker shot. The player will recover to this location on rallies, after a serve, and after a return. Because the opponent is hitting his or her strength, the opponent's net play could improve as a result of hitting a more effective approach shot, too.

Common patterns of play: One-to-one, two-to-two, two-to-one, and neutralizing (by keeping the ball up the middle of the court).

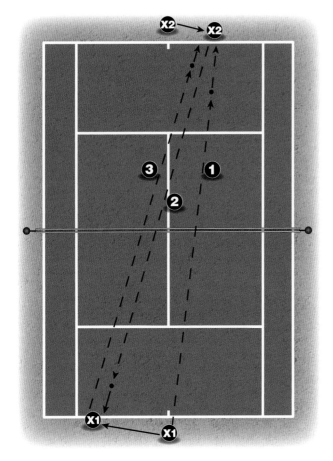

Figure 10.6 Hitting forehands from three quarters of the court.

THREE-QUARTER COURT DRILL

Purpose: To teach how to cover a weakness and use a weapon.

Procedure: Both players start in the middle of the baseline on opposite sides of the court (see figure 10.6). Player 1 feeds a ball to land midway between the middle of the baseline and the alley near the baseline. Player 2 runs around the backhand and hits a forehand inside out to midway between the middle of the baseline and alley near the baseline. Player 1 responds by running around the backhand and also hitting an inside-out forehand. After two inside-out forehands have been hit, the players play the point out whole court. The first person to 7 points wins the round; players play to the best of 5 rounds.

Coaching points: This strategy is usually used when the forehand is the weapon and the player wants to be in a position to hit more forehands in a match. For drilling to strengthen one's backhand, the player can also practice running around the forehand, but this is not recommended for match play.

Intermediate Strategy #1: Pulling an Opponent off the Court

This strategy is used to test an opponent's ability to move and also is a great way to open up the court. There are a variety of ways to pull your opponent off the court, including a deeper crosscourt ball or a shorter-angled crosscourt shot. A serve and return can also be played to pull the player off the court as well as a volley. How powerful and well placed this shot is hit, dictates the player's next shot. A weaker shot that misses its mark can give the opponent an easier next shot. A powerful and well-hit crosscourt shot can force an error or a short ball.

The goal of pulling a player off the court is to hit the next shot into the open court or behind the opponent to wrong-foot the opponent. Two very common plays are to hit a forehand or backhand crosscourt and then hit the next ball down the line. The player can use this strategy with the rush-and-crush strategy (Intermediate Strategy #2) to put additional pressure on the opponent.

Common patterns of play: One-to-one, one-to-two, and two-to-one patterns.

ALLEY DRILL

Purpose: To emphasize hitting the outside of the ball and opening the court to pull the opponent off the court.

Procedure: Each player stands on the deuce side of the court and behind the doubles alley on each side of the court. Player 1 feeds the ball into play and aims for player 2's doubles alley (see figure 10.7). Player 2 responds by also hitting to player 1's alley. After two alley shots are executed, the point is played in the singles lines only. Each player should hit on the outside of the ball with the intent of opening the court. The feed does not count as a point but every forehand crosscourt hit into the alley does count as a point. The game is played to 7 points and then switched to the backhand side. Players should also alternate between being player 1 and player 2.

Coaching points: Spin and height are essential for winning this game. The player should relax and continue to accelerate on the ball.

Variation: Players can play this game from around the service line to develop angles, midway between the service line and baseline to develop a heavy rally ball, and deep behind the baseline to practice hitting from a defensive phase.

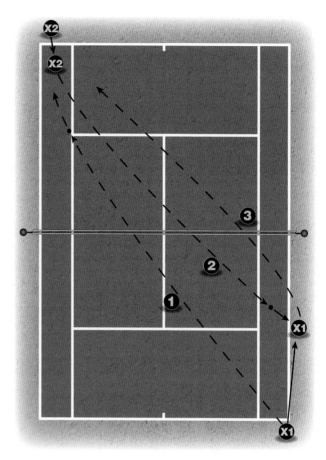

Figure 10.7 Hitting into the alleys.

Intermediate Strategy #2: Rush and Crush

With rush and crush, the player is looking for ways to get to the net. Several plays can be used to execute this strategy, starting with the serve-and-volley or return-and-volley. Or, the player can get an opponent on defense with a weapon and move in to hit a swinging volley or block volley. Another option is to throw up a high, heavy ball to the opponent's weakness and sneak in behind it. Or, the player can hit a drop shot, bring the opponent forward, and then lob over the opponent, approaching the net as the opponent runs back to recover the shot.

Common patterns of play: Serving and volleying, chipping the return or hitting and coming in, or transitioning shots of any kind are used to rush and crush. With the strategy of rushing and crushing, the player is taking every opportunity to get to the net, including one-to-one, two-to-two, and two-to-one neutralizing patterns of play. Players can also use short to deep shots to transition to the net.

WALK-IN DRILL

Purpose: To develop players' ability to volley from all parts of the court and on their way to net. This is a great decision-making drill for the *walking volleyer*, who must decide to block or swing at the incoming ball.

Procedure: Two players play out points crosscourt only. Player 1 serves crosscourt, and player 2 returns crosscourt. After the serve, player 1 walks two steps forward and then takes a transition volley out of the air followed by two more steps forward (see figure 10.8). If the reply from player 2 is within the recommended volley range, then player 1 volleys. If the reply from player 2 lands shorter than the two steps, player 1 can work on the half volley or block approach and keep advancing. The goal for player 1 is to practice volleying all the way from the baseline to the net. Player 2 continues to play crosscourt, reacting to player 1's volleys. If either player misses a shot crosscourt, they lose the point. Points are played to 11; one player is the volleyer for the entire game or alternates feeds every 5 points.

Variation: The player should not walk to the net but accelerate to the net, taking every ball out of the air. A scorekeeping variation is for player 1 to lose a point when missing a volley.

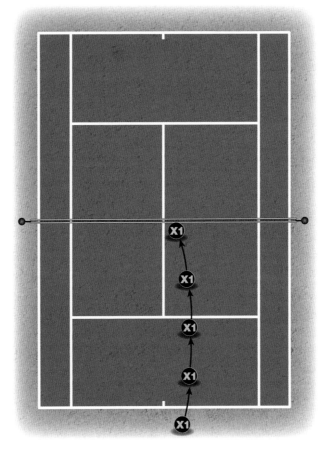

Figure 10.8 Player 1's movement to the net.

Intermediate Strategy #3: Running the Opponent Into the Court

Movement strategy is based on the fact that most tennis players either move better laterally, toward the ball, or around the ball. The most unusual movement for everyone is backward. While playing, the player should use shots that explore the opponent's movement strengths and weaknesses. The player should use the drop shot to check reaction time and speed to the ball forward. A high, heavy shot is a good test to see whether the player can effectively move back in the court. The player can use the one-to-one pattern to test lateral movement. The one-to-one pattern can also be used short and deep to test the ability to transition between forward and backward movement. Finally, the player can test the opponent's movement around the ball by hitting it right at them. Once the player knows the opponent's weaknesses, the player can execute patterns of play that have the opponent running in uncomfortable movement patterns.

Common patterns of play: One-to-one, one-to-two, two-to-one, and neutralizing patterns.

RUNNING THE OPPONENT

Purpose: To practice extended rallies and the patterns that create them.

Procedure: Two players set a rally goal of 4 shots each. The drill starts with one player serving followed by the rally phase. Once the rally goal has been reached, player 1 hits one of the test shots, such as a drop shot or slice, and the point is played out. For more of a challenge during the rally phase, player 1 hits all crosscourt shots while player 2 hits all replies down the line (see figure 10.9). Players play games to 7 points and then switch roles.

Coaching points: This is a cooperative style drill in which both players have a common purpose of reaching a goal and then battling one another. Maintaining the rally speed together is crucial or the common goal cannot be reached.

Variation: Players practice doing two-to-one and one-to-two patterns.

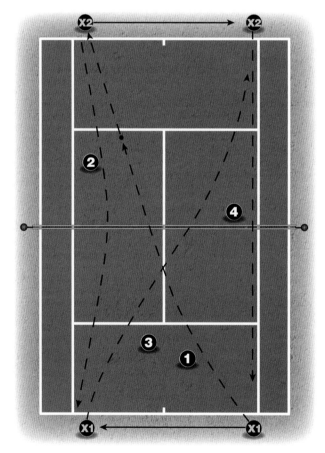

Figure 10.9 Rally phase pattern.

Intermediate Strategy #4: First Strike

First strike is using a weapon to put the opponent on defense early in the point so that the player can dictate from the start (as opposed to working one's way into the point). This strategy emphasizes a quicker point that doesn't allow for the opponent to get into a rhythm. First strike can be accomplished from the start by placing the serve in a location that puts the player in the best possible position to hit a weapon. Or, the player can return to a location that allows for using a weapon. Most players back up to allow themselves additional time to attack the return or to cover up their returning weakness. When into the point, hitting a shot behind the opponent can get the opponent off balance and set the player up for the winning shot.

Common patterns of play: Two-to-one and one-to-two.

FIRST STRIKE

Purpose: To practice playing quicker points to prevent an opponent from establishing a rhythm.

Procedure: The drill starts with one player serving to the other followed by a rally. The goal of the server is to end the point within four touches of the ball for either the server or the returner. The goal of the returner is to force an error from the server or survive the server's first four shots. The server earns a point for winning the point within four shots. The returner earns a point if the server errs or if the rally goes on for longer than the server's first four touches. The game should be played to 11 points. Players can alternate serving after every 5 serves.

Variation: Players can increase point totals for more aggressive first strikes, such as a serve and overhead winner or an ace on the serve.

Advanced Strategy #1: Hitting Shots to Set Up Strengths

Advanced strategies require players to do more. They require that the player start anticipating the responses expected off the shot that the player sent. If the player can anticipate the opponent's response, the player can use that information to place shots in the best possible position and reply with weapons. Here are some common ways to set up strengths:

- The player can hit a weaker shot down the line to have an opponent answer cross-court to a strength.
- The player can serve out wide on the ad side and look for a ball down the middle of the court.
- The player can hit a heavy ball to gain more time to run around a weakness and use a weapon.
- The player can hit a dipping ball or short ball on the opponent's feet to get a pop-up, which the player can move in and put away.
- If a player has great speed and passing shots, the player can hit a short ball and anticipate the next ball to pass the opponent, who has moved forward.
- The player can hit great lobs to make the opponent nervous about coming to the net.
- The player can hit a ball directly at an opponent at the net and look for the short ball to pass.

Common patterns of play: One-to-one, one-to-two, two-to-one, and neutralizing patterns.

HITTING SHOTS TO SET UP STRENGTHS

Purpose: To learn how to build a point and hit to a location that gives the best chance to use a weapon.

Procedure: Player 1 and player 2 rally crosscourt, working deep shots to the back corner. After an agreed upon number of crosscourt shots (usually two), the designated player says *Go*, signifying they are hitting down the line (see figure 10.10). After the player says *Go*, the point is played on a full court. Players play a game to 7 or 11 points, counting any misses as a point. Players should alternate feeds every 5 points. The same players repeat the process again for one full game, and then they reverse roles for the next game.

Coaching points: Most tennis players are programmed to hit crosscourt. A high, heavy ball hit down the line on the *Go* signal will give the player more time to recover. This drill also teaches patience and endurance. The receiving player has to read the opponent's intentions very carefully and try to anticipate the down-the-line shot.

Variation: Players play the initial rally hitting down the line and then hit crosscourt to start the point.

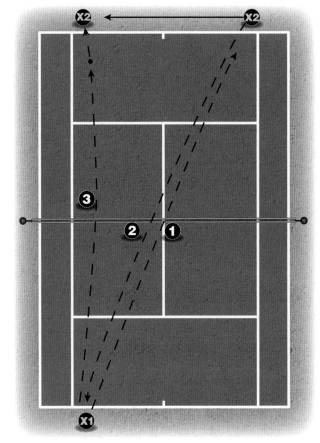

Figure 10.10 Two crosscourt shots and the *Go* ball.

Advanced Strategy #2: Deflating and Inflating or Inflating and Deflating

This strategy is a more advanced version of Intermediate Strategy #3 but uses different techniques to move the opponent up and back in the court. Deflating balls can be done by aiming shorter in the court, adding spin, taking pace off the ball, or decreasing height of the ball. Increasing pace or depth, increasing height, or reducing spin can inflate balls.

The deflating and inflating pattern tests the opponent's ability to move forward, the ability to handle shorter shots including shorter angles, and the ability to move backward for a high and heavy ball. It is also used to potentially catch the opponent out of position. The following shot combinations are useful for deflating and then inflating:

- Drop shot and lob
- Drop shot and pass deep
- Short, soft slice and flat, deep ball
- Short, soft slice and heavy ball
- Crosscourt angle and drive up the line

The inflate and deflate pattern tests the opponent's ability to move backward first or handle increased height, spin, depth and pace. Common ways to inflate and deflate include the following:

- The player can hit heavy and deep, followed by a short angle.
- The player can drive the ball through the court, followed by a short ball with touch, such as the drop shot.

   Common patterns of play for both patterns: One-to-one, one-to-two, two-to-one, and neutralizing patterns.

DEFLATE AND INFLATE OR INFLATE AND DEFLATE

Purpose: To work on blending differing tactics of direction, speed, spins, height, and depth.

Procedure: Players divide the court into four squares on both sides of the court. The players establish the rules regarding each box on the court. For example, *all balls hit to the service boxes must be deflated with backspin or underspin. All balls hit past the service line must be hit flat or with topspin.* (See figure 10.11.) Both players are positioned on the middle hash mark opposite one another on the baseline. Players should feed the ball to the four possible locations on the court based on the type of shot they are working on. The possibilities are short to short, short to deep down the line, short to deep crosscourt, plus the all the deep to short combinations. After two shots have been successfully executed, players should play out the point on the full court. A point is awarded after a player misses a shot after 2 shots have been executed successfully. Games should be played to 11 points. Players alternate feeds after every 5 points.

Variation: Players can change the rules by saying that they have to inflate (hit with topspin) to the service boxes and deflate (hit with underspin) past the service line. This game can also be played randomly—players don't have designated areas to hit.

CRITICAL CUE:

The player should watch the opponent's racket face closely to see what types of shots the opponent is trying to use against the player.

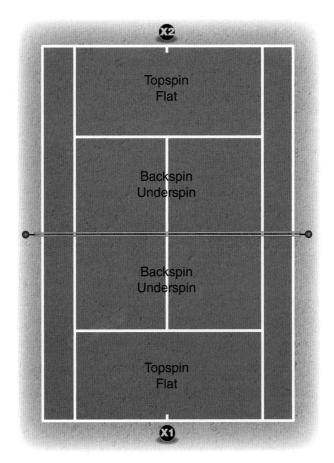

Figure 10.11 Rules for court boxes.

Advanced Strategy #3: Deflating and Deflating or Inflating and Inflating

A player using the deflating and deflating strategy constantly takes pace off the opponent's shot, forcing the opponent to finish the shot by always adding pace. One option is to use underspin and backspin, which force the opponent to move up to the ball. Or, the player can soften the grip on the racket and use topspin to take pace off the incoming ball.

A player who is using the inflating and inflating strategy, or going for broke, should be sure to play the percentages by aiming crosscourt and well inside the lines, hitting hard and flat to the corners or hitting heavy and deep to the corners.

Common patterns of play: One-to-one, one-to-two, two-to-one, and neutralizing patterns.

OFFENSIVE INFLATION VERSUS DEFENSIVE DEFLATION

Purpose: To practice inflation and deflation tactics and techniques against an opponent.

Procedure: Players can play this game in two different ways, either with a feed or a serve. Players can determine who will be on offense and defense, but the offensive player will always serve. The player on offense is going for broke and will inflate all shots, trying to hit bigger and more aggressively. The player on defense uses the deflation strategy and takes pace off and reduces the height of the offensive player's ball. Players play games to 7 points and then switch roles.

Coaching points: **The offensive player should practice high-percentage aggressive plays such as runaround forehands hit crosscourt. The defensive player should work on each point to get as many balls back to the opponent to wear down the opponent and force an error.**

Variation: Players play again, but the returner is on offense, and the server is on defense hitting second serves only.

CRITICAL CUE:

Players inflate balls by increasing height, depth, spin, pace, or by sharpening the direction change. They deflate balls by reducing height, depth, spin, pace, or lessening the direction change.

STRATEGIES AND TACTICS FOR STYLES OF PLAY

As previously explained in the book, the style players choose depends on their favorite shots, weapons, strengths and weaknesses, on-court personality, and passion when playing a style. A vision of how the player ultimately sees the game helps the player choose a style and keeps the player's focus on improving the specific skills used to play that style. The player's dedication and hard work dictate the eventual success of the style of play.

Although players' strengths and on-court personalities help determine playing style, the ultimate test is being able to use and execute the best strategies for their style of play. The upcoming examinations of each style and the game style form in figure 10.12 on page 210 can help players determine their two best playing styles.

FIGURE 10.12 DEFINING YOUR GAME STYLE

Check the descriptions that best describe your game.

- ○ Your play is patient, and you like to work a point. (A)
- ○ When reading passing shots, you pick the right side often. (D)
- ○ You like to dictate play from the baseline and go for your shots. (B)
- ○ Having a balanced attack of aggressive groundstroke play and net play is your goal. (C)
- ○ You understand that this game style has a high risk factor and takes time to develop. (D)
- ○ You are as comfortable at the net as you are on the baseline. (C)
- ○ The longer the rally, the better. (A)
- ○ You have an effective slice to mix up your opponent and change the rhythm of the rally. (C)
- ○ You enjoy the role of the intimidator or aggressor. (D)
- ○ Mentally you are the aggressor. (B)
- ○ Changing speeds is something that you enjoy doing to throw off your opponent. (C)
- ○ Your mind is your weapon. (A)
- ○ Power and accuracy are how you like to win points. (B)
- ○ You have a weakness that doesn't allow for great improvement (e.g., a great forehand and a weak backhand). (A)
- ○ People describe your game as being very athletic. (D)
- ○ You choose to attack with multiple options. (C)
- ○ You will hit an approach shot and transition to the net when given a good opportunity. (A)
- ○ You enjoy following your serve into the net and putting bodily pressure on the opponent. (D)
- ○ Physically you are in better shape than your opponent is. (A)
- ○ You have more than one weapon in your arsenal. (B)
- ○ You enjoy outrallying your opponent. (A)
- ○ Mentally you are willing to adapt and play whatever style is necessary to win on that day. (C)
- ○ People describe you as having great movement on the court, and you use speed to maintain offense. (B)
- ○ You prefer running forward and backward instead of side to side. (D)
- ○ When you are on, you're on, but when you are off, you spray your shots. (B)
- ○ People comment on your eloquence when you play. (C)
- ○ You enjoy finishing points at the net and look for every opportunity to transition to the net. (D)
- ○ Mentally you know that you can outlast your opponent. (A)
- ○ You don't mind the errors that come with going for more on your shots. (B)
- ○ You use a variety of shots to transition to the net. (C)
- ○ You are committed to this style of play, choosing to live by the sword or die by the sword. (B)
- ○ You have quick reflexes. (D)
- ○ You have one stroke that is superior to all the others (a weapon). (A)
- ○ You like to be in control of your destiny. (B)

○ You enjoy staying back on the baseline and using groundstrokes to control points. (A)

○ You love winning with variety. (C)

○ You come into the match to put your opponent on defense. (B)

○ Being passed at the net is something you get over quickly. (D)

○ Keeping your opponent guessing is something that you enjoy doing while on the court. (C)

○ Your favorite transitions to the net are outright winners (e.g., block transition volleys, swinging volleys). (B)

○ Mentally you like taking risks. (D)

___ **Total number of As**   ___ **Total number of Bs**

___ **Total number of Cs**   ___ **Total number of Ds**

The letter with the largest number of responses indicates the style that is likely the most comfortable. A = rallying or defensive baseline player, B = aggressive baseline player, C = all-court style player, and D = serve-and-volley style player.

Rallying or Defensive Baseline Player

A rallying or defensive baseline player has a foundation to one day be an aggressive player, but doesn't quite have the tools of the aggressive baseline player yet. Maybe this player's weapons aren't big enough, or the player has a weakness that an opponent can exploit. Maybe the player's personality is more neutral (passive), or the player lacks the confidence to take the game to another level. The movement of the player can also keep the rallying baseline player from being more aggressive. Either way, the rallying baseline player should try to improve speed around the court to become more of a counterpuncher, or increase the power to become an aggressive baseline player.

The mindset and personality of the rallying baseline player is one of patience and endurance. The rallying baseline player likes to win points two ways: by outlasting someone or by working the point to an extent where the opponent gets out of position or off balance enough for the player to finish with a killer shot. This doesn't mean the rallying baseline player can't volley or doesn't like to volley, but this player prefers to win points by baseline strategy and has a good use of basic strategies such as hitting behind an opponent, hitting into the open court, and knowing when to hit back through the middle of the court.

The rallying baseline player possesses the following strengths:

- **Groundstroke weapon.** The rallying baseline player has a weapon to be able to keep the opponent on the defensive. A weapon has different facets, such as being able to hit a weapon from anywhere on the court or good defensive skills (speed).

- **Consistency.** The rallying baseline player consistently makes good decisions and is steady in technique, avoiding errors. An extreme version of being consistent is what one would call a *grinder* or a *pusher*. This type of player thrives on getting a lot of balls back (think, human backboard). This type of player also wants to give the opponent the feeling that the player will not miss and will outlast the opponent.

- **Ability to use depth on shots effectively.** The rallying baseline player keeps the opponent from gaining an advantage by keeping shots deep. Doing so gives the baseline player the opportunity to receive more short balls, gives extra time to run around weaker shots, and keeps the opponent from attacking.

- **Good anticipation and tracking skills.** The rallying baseline player reads opponents' tendencies and employs smart movement for maximum court positioning.

- **Ability to play good defense.** Lacking a big weapon, the rallying baseline player must know when to attack and when to be scrappy and get a ball back for another chance at an attackable ball. Good defense is also used to mix up shots effectively, including the slice or high, heavy ball to make opponents feel uncomfortable during the point.

- **Mental and physical toughness for enduring long rallies.** A successful rallying baseline player has the conditioning to go the distance and the mental focus to not fatigue during the long rallies (and matches) associated with this style of play. This mental and physical toughness can further wear down an opponent who is less solid in these areas.

From the strategies presented earlier in this chapter, the ones best suited to a rallying baseline player are hitting to the open court, covering a weakness, and using a weapon to the opponent's weakness. Besides these overall strategies, there are two other strategies specific to successful rallying baseline players:

- **Playing high and heavy balls deep to keep opponents pinned back in the court.** Some rallying baseline players adopt a style of hitting only flat balls. It can be very effective, but invariably, opportunities always come where the player must play a more defensive style of offense. This strategy is used to play a shot with a higher trajectory, allowing the player more time to recover back into the court and set up more offensive shots.

- **Minimizing direction changes in shots.** This strategy empowers players to play the percentages when in a rally situation. The thought process should be to keep shots going predominately crosscourt or more to the middle when the opponent has hit an offensive shot and only change the direction of the shot when in a more favorable position.

Aggressive Baseline player

The aggressive baseline player has most of the components of the rallying baseline player, but this style is based more on hitting with power, hitting more aggressive shots, and causing errors. The mindset and personality of the aggressive baseline player is very different from that of the rallying baseline player. The player who likes this style prefers to be in control of the point and needs weapons to be successful. This style has the mentality of a serve-and-volley player but from the baseline, preferring to hit a winner rather than come to the net to end the point.

This style centers on using power strokes, dictating play, taking time away from an opponent, and going for more on shots. The ability to run around balls that are hit to the backhand and create angles inside out are hallmarks of the aggressive baseline player. This style goes for shorter points than the rallying baseline player.

The aggressive baseline player possesses the following strengths:

- **Lethal serve and forehand combination.** The player using this style usually tries to anchor the game with one shot. It is usually a forehand, and the player uses three quarters of the court positioning to hit the forehand. A big serve combined with a big forehand can prove to be lethal.

- ***Go-for-it* mindset.** This is a great style for a player who has the mindset to hit hard and hit winners. This style works on first-strike capabilities including a good serve, a big forehand, a good swinging volley, and putaways.

- **Ability to control the baseline.** Players using this style constantly look for opportunities presented by the opponent.

- **Aggressiveness.** Successful aggressive baseline players have great movement to keep the opponent on the defensive.

Just like the rallying baseline player, the aggressive baseline player uses depth, accuracy, court positioning, and movement to be able to hit favorite shots, which are probably weapons. However, because this player is more aggressive, the strategy and tactics are more closely related to the all-court player. The strategies best suited to an aggressive baseline player are weapon to weakness, running the opponent into the court, first strike, and deflating and inflating.

Besides these overall strategies, two other strategies are specific to successful aggressive baseline players. Stepping up in the court, the player takes balls on the rise and hits winners from deeper in the court. While sticking with the strategy of hitting mainly the forehand, the player is also able to hit an aggressive backhand down the line.

All-Court Player

Adept at both offense and defense, the all-court player is considered a jack of all trades and enjoys all the different components of a point. Equally comfortable coming to the net as staying back on the baseline, an all-court player's mind and personality is whatever it needs to be in the given situation. An all-court player can be patient and wear an opponent down, or can attack. This player feels comfortable playing any type of opponent. Part of the psyche of an all-court player is built around the knowledge that the player can handle playing and beating any style of play. The balanced game allows this player to combat any type of play, whether it is the faster pace of an attacker or the more patient style of the baseline player.

Commonly referred to as ballet on the tennis court, all-court players typically make playing tennis look easy. What is deceiving is the amount of hard work that an all-round player has put in to be able to perform all the playing styles well.

The all-court player possesses the following strengths:

- **Wide variety of shots to use in a rally.** This is very intimidating to opponents, plus it creates more opportunities to stay in a point and go on the offensive.

- **Versatility and flexibility.** This player explores different ways to exploit an opponent. Because of this player's versatility, the all-court player possesses a built-in plan A and plan B. The player's wide variety of shots allows the ability to try different strategies when things aren't going well against an opponent.

- **Great movement in both areas of the court.** This player has a quick first step to the ball and is just as adept at moving forward and backward as side to side.

- **Ability to use the court to personal advantage.** To play an all-court style of play, the player must understand an opponent's tendencies and anticipate the next move. This knowledge takes time to master and a great deal of trial and error, but ultimately the player is rewarded.

The all-court player uses shot variety as the strategic foundation. This player has the ability to come to the net and put away a volley, or can stay on the baseline and outrally an opponent. This player can also mix up shots, which becomes very unnerving to an opponent and is very effective in keeping an opponent on the defensive and creating opportunities.

The all-court player also uses the speed of the court to an advantage. The faster the surfaces or lower the bounce of the ball, the shorter the player's backswings need to be. Because all-courters have a wide range of abilities, they have an easier time adapting to different surfaces. They can adapt with their swings and footwork to the slower clay surface as well as a faster indoor, carpet, or grass court. Their strength is that their strategy is not tied into a particular surface, such as a baseline player playing on a faster surface, or a fast-paced player playing on a slower surface.

The strategies best suited to the all-court player are pulling an opponent off the court, rush and crush, first strike, hitting shots to set up strengths, deflating and inflating, deflating and deflating, and inflating and inflating. Besides these overall strategies, all-court players often use a few other strategies successfully:

- **Taking time away from the opponent.** All-court players try to take time away by hitting the ball early (as it is rising off the court), moving toward the ball to cut off angles, and being in a good location for the return of the opponent's shot. All-court players strategically place themselves so that they can hit more favored shots, keeping the opponent on the defensive, thus taking reaction time away from the opponent.

- **Breaking up rhythm.** This strategy comes with the variety and shot selection the all-court player possesses. If the all-court player is creative enough and uses different strategies and patterns of play, then this player will effectively break up any rhythm a baseline player or serve-and-volley style player is trying to develop.

- **Using the slice.** The all-court player uses the slice effectively to mix up shots and neutralize the opponent's strengths.

Serve-and-Volley Style Player

The serve-and-volley style is the most attacking style of play. This player emphasizes fast-paced action by following the serve to the net or looking for the first instance to approach the net. This player is not only going to put pressure on the opponent with good serves, returns, approach shots, volleys, and overheads, but is going to give the opponent less time to respond. This player's goal is to apply body pressure on the opponent so that the opponent feels rushed and makes mistakes. In terms of the points they enjoy playing, the serve-and-volley style player is a sprinter as opposed to a marathoner.

Because this style takes so much focus to develop, players who choose this style may initially develop insecurities with their ability to be effective from the baseline. The net rusher's goal is to get to the net. This player will take time to develop the art of rallying. The net rusher's goal is to learn how to rally effectively from the baseline using depth, angles, or changes in pace and spin to complement the game and be strong enough on groundstrokes to effectively get to the net. Serve-and-volley style players should not spend extended periods of time on the baseline if it is not their strength.

Serve-and-volley style players possess the following strengths:

- **Good serve.** As previously discussed, a good serve has power and good placement. The quality of the serve affects how tough the volley will be when the player approaches the net; in other words, it affects the player's ability to get aggressive shots to the opponent's weaker side.

- **Variety of volleys.** Good volleys are mandatory for employing this style of play. Not only must they be reliable, they should be hit to the correct location. Good volleys allow players to put a ball away, or set themselves up for a better opportunity to put away the next volley.

- **Strong overhead.** A good overhead is an opportunity to end the point, and it can intimidate an opponent. An overhead can be precisely placed to improve court positioning in a manner similar to a volley, or it can be hit hard with power.

- **Quick footwork.** Playing the net takes good footwork. Being balanced, in good position, and closing off volleys are all skills that require athleticism, strength, and good instincts. It is imperative the serve and volley player has a great first move to the net after the serve, a great split step, and a first step to the volley.

- **Ability to make shots.** Serve-and-volley style players, or *attackers*, favor themselves as shot makers. They bring the action to the opponent and therefore feel confident in their ability to make tough shots in every situation.

The strategies best suited to a serve and volley player are rush and crush, first strike, covering a weakness, hitting to the open court, and inflating and inflating. Besides these overall strategies, successful serve-and-volley style players often use several other strategies:

- **Using a variety of serves to attack the opponent.** This player uses the serve effectively by placing it in locations that have the returner hit the ball out of reach, out of the strike zone, or directly at the server to get a weak reply for the first volley.

- **Placing volleys strategically.** Usually this player approaches the net looking to put the ball away, but often that opportunity doesn't present itself until the second, third, or fourth shot, so the player must use a strategy to successfully stay in the point to hit a volley winner. Volleys down the line on stretched-out balls, balls slightly out of reach, shots for which the opponent is slightly out of position, and crosscourt on putaways are examples of great volley strategy.

- **Coming in on the next ball.** Serve-and-volley style players should follow their serves to the net but sometimes a returner is hitting great returns (hitting the balls to the server's feet or ripping them to the corners) and the server is not winning as many points as necessary. Coming in on the next shot is an effective way to break up the returner's rhythm. If played correctly by mixing up the times coming to the net, this strategy can create an opportunity to receive a short ball that is easier to hit as an approach shot.

ESTABLISHING A GAME PLAN

A game plan is vitally important to the player's overall success in match play because it provides an initial direction from the start of a match. At the beginnings of matches, usually players focus on being competitive and getting off to a good start. A game plan can add more purpose. Players must be careful when establishing a game plan because its success is contingent on the execution of shots, and sometimes what the player thinks will work may not work as well as was hoped.

When it comes to creating a distinct game plan for each opponent, each player is different. Some may prefer specifics that include a strategy for each phase of the game. For example, a player might choose to use mostly kick serves, hit high and heavy balls to the backhand side on returns, go back behind the player on transition shots, or explore the opponent's speed moving forward. Other players prefer to just focus on what they do best, and may use their own game style as the basis for the game plan. When a player uses the preferred game style, it is important to know the opponent's tendencies. Regardless of how specific the game plan is, the ultimate goal is to remain flexible, stay with what the player does best, and be prepared to explore different ways of executing the game plan.

Game Planning Process

The game planning process is exactly that—a process—and it should be used to help the player formulate the best possible scenario to help the player's competitive level. The following steps can help players and coaches design a basic game plan:

1. **Prioritizing game styles.** The player can list the game styles in order from favorite to least favorite based on what has been established through the questionnaire in figure 10.12 on page 210, but mainly focus on the distinct style the player feels comfortable with and a style that helps to win points. Players must have their best game plan in mind, followed by their second, third, and fourth best plan of action.

2. **Assessing strengths and weakness for first and second favorite styles.** Players assess their strengths and weaknesses in their number one and two playing styles. For example, if a player's top style is serve-and-volley style, the player's strengths might be the serve and the first volley, and a weakness could be rallying from the baseline. If the player's number two style is the aggressive baseline style, a strength might be the attacking forehand inside out, and a weakness might be the backhand up the line.

3. **Prioritizing patterns of play within the style.** These patterns of play are options within a style. Players should prioritize options for both serving and receiving games. For example, if a player's game style is a serve-and-volley and attacking baseline play hybrid, this player might use the following options for the service game:

   Option 1: Slice serve out wide on the deuce side, approach the net, and volley into the open court. Kick serve on the ad side, approach the net, and volley into the open court.

   Option 2: Serve up the T, look to move around the next ball, and attack with a forehand.

   Option 3: Jam serve into the opponent's body and volley into the open court.

   The player might use the following options for return games:

   Option 1: Neutralize the return up the middle of the court, try to apply pressure with the forehand to the opponent's backhand, and come to the net.

   Option 2: Take the opponent's second serve and hit it up the line coming to the net behind it.

4. **Practicing the options.** Players should practice each option two or three times a week by playing games with a friend to 7 points. If the option the player is working on is to return up the line and the player mistakenly hits crosscourt, then the point must be replayed. The player should practice each option slowly and deliberately.

5. **Playing practice sets and recording results.** The player should play three to five practice sets a week and keep a journal on performance with different options within the playing style. The player can use practice sets to record emotions, focus, intensity, and any positive or negative strategic adjustments made during the practice sets. Players should rate these categories from 1 to 10. These ratings can be referred to later, and players can analyze their practice sets and how they connect to improved match play.

6. **Playing under pressure.** The player should enter a tournament or league competition and be diligent playing the options under pressure. Competition will be the test of the player's perseverance and discipline.

7. **Evaluating matches.** After each match, the player must consider whether any action or lack of action might have helped the player play better. The player should do this for a month after each practice set, practice match, or real match. Doing

this helps all players learn about themselves and their game. They effectively create a blueprint for reproducible top performances.

Although having a good, sound strategy against an opponent is important, the game plan should be simple. A few simple points can go a long way toward helping a player in times of need, but more important, it can keep the player from being too bogged down with details. Some tennis players like to obtain a lot of information on their next opponents and some like to know less. Regardless of preference, the player should keep the information simple and remember to focus more on things that can be controlled, such as the player's own skills, attitude, and confidence. The following section includes additional tips that can help make the game plan more effective.

Game Plan in Action

The following tips for assessing game plans in action are based on a player maintaining flexibility for what is working on a particular day, staying with what is working, and evaluating and making any needed adjustments. Oftentimes during a match, a player's technique can break down, so self-correcting techniques such as triggers can help the player refocus. However, at the end of the day, players need to learn how to compete regardless of how well they are playing or how good they feel. Following are some tips for implementing a game plan:

- **Being flexible.** One of the best forms of a good game plan is acquired while playing an opponent. Perhaps something the player thought would be effective is not working because the player is not hitting a particular shot well on that day, or maybe it is a bad game style matchup. Regardless of the situation, a game plan is subject to change, and a player must be flexible when change occurs. As a matter of fact, rarely do competitors play a match in which every attempt works perfectly. When playing a match the player should try seeing oneself as an accountant who constantly tries things, notes the reply, and then stores the information for a later use.

- **Assessing the game plan.** Evaluating how well the player can counter an opponent's shots is the beginning of the process of assessing how well the game plan is doing in any given situation. The player should keep in mind the following strategies for countering an opponent's shots to get an idea of how the competitors' game plans match up.

    - Going toe to toe—Part of a good defensive strategy is to be able to go toe to toe with an opponent. The player must assess this immediately and quickly decide whether to keep doing it or whether to change the game with a variety of shots. Going toe to toe with an opponent either makes the opponent change the game or causes the opponent to make more errors. In this situation, the player is effectively doing what the opponent likes to do and reacting to the opponent's shots. This strategy can be very intimidating and forces the player to revaluate his or her own methods of winning points.

    - Defense to offense—The ability to take an opponent's better shots and create an offense off them is very effective. This can and should be done because it gives players the best chance to win points. When players shift from defense to offense, they take the ball earlier or they reply to a shot with a better shot. Each point vacillates between offense and defense and vice versa, so consciously thinking of it improves footwork and shot selection.

- **Making tactical changes when needed.** If the player is winning with a game plan, the player should not change it. If the player is losing with a particular plan, then it may be that the chosen game plan is playing into the opponent's strengths. For example, a player has chosen to play like an aggressive baseline player but now switches to counterattacking. The player's shot pace is feeding into what the opponent likes. It is then imperative that the player make tactical changes in the game style. For example, a player can try to apply more time pressure by taking the ball earlier as opposed to using stroke pressure by hitting the ball harder. If that does not work, the player should try switching to a predetermined alternative plan or strategy within his or her chosen game style.

- **Being aware of breakdowns in technique.** It is important to note that a game plan can fail as a result of a breakdown in technique. Having good technique allows the player to counter an opponent's shots more effectively. When the player has poor technique, a weakness can hinder the player from hitting an effective enough shot to recover offensively.

- **Not getting caught up on feel.** Some players show excessive emotion and frustration at missing shots, including banging their rackets, checking the tension, wondering why it doesn't feel right, and shouting that they don't feel it. When everything a player does on a particular day works and every shot feels good, the player is in the zone and can do no wrong. However, achieving this zone can be elusive, so a better approach is to compete and work hard during every point. Players who allow frustration about their lack of feel on a particular day to overwhelm them have no chance of achieving the zone.

DOUBLES STRATEGY AND DRILLS

Doubles is a great game because of the exciting pace of the match, the fast hands and instincts, the strategy, and the bonding created with a partner. A doubles team's strength lies in the players' physical, mental, and emotional collaboration. Great doubles teams that exemplified these qualities, not to mention who have won many Grand Slam titles, include Bob and Mike Bryan, Mark Woodforde and Todd Woodbridge, John McEnroe and Peter Fleming, Martina Navratilova and Pam Shriver, Gigi Fernández and Natasha Zvereva, and Venus and Serena Williams.

People play doubles for a variety of reasons, including the following:

- **Enjoyment.** Playing doubles is fun and gets the creative juices flowing. The rapid-fire exchanges and working with a teammate to get the best out of each other make doubles very exciting. It can be fun to have a partner to communicate, compete, and develop a relationship with in a spirit of teamwork.

- **Singles game improvements.** Playing doubles is great for a player's singles game. Many singles players focus solely on the singles game and do not want to bother with the work needed to find a good doubles partner. However, playing doubles is advantageous and even necessary for many reasons. The serve-and-volley component, which is restricted to half the court, becomes better. Playing doubles also develops the player's net game and teaches the player a faster-paced game. Playing with or against a higher-ranked singles competitor in a doubles match provides the opportunity to learn from the better player. Playing with or beating a higher-ranked singles competitor, even as part of a doubles match, gives players more confidence when they meet these players again in singles competition.

- **Niche fit.** Not all players are destined to be great singles players; for some, doubles is the answer. A player can develop doubles play by practicing it often and playing tournaments. Many singles players cheat themselves out of better opportunities that doubles may have to offer. This doesn't mean players shouldn't aim for success in singles. However, for myriad reasons, such as a preference for playing on a team or a great net game that is muted on the singles tour, for some players, doubles may be a better fit. The professional game includes plenty of doubles only players and teams, including Bob Bryan and Mike Bryan, Daniel Nestor and Max Mirnyi, and Cara Black and Liezel Huber.

- **Ageless game.** Doubles is a game a player can play at any age. Every club includes some doubles players who can't walk well, but they continue to play their doubles game. Anyone from age 8 to 80 can play doubles; that is why it is called the game for life.

CHARACTERISTICS OF GOOD DOUBLES PLAYERS

Successful doubles players share many of the same characteristics of singles players, such as an effective serve and return. An additional quality of good doubles players is the strength of their movement to the net and their net play skills. Playing more doubles can greatly enhance singles play in this area.

Good doubles players can come from any style of play. The serve-and-volley and all-court play styles use net play extensively, so their volley instincts are more naturally and keenly developed. These styles specialize in variety and aggressive play similar to those found in doubles. The aggressive baseline player can also be a good doubles player when using power on groundstrokes and volleys. The defensive baseliner would use steady play, defense, and shot placement to be a good doubles player. No matter what player styles make up a doubles team, though, the best teams also excel at teamwork, communication, and energy.

Teamwork

Good teamwork is essential to playing good doubles. Teams that work together have greater success by supporting each other and working toward a common goal. When they play, players are as one; no one person is greater than the other in wins and losses or in glory. The skill of good teamwork can be learned and is a great attribute to have for other venues in life. One way to show support and build a doubles partnership is for the players to watch each other's singles matches to get a feel for each other's plays and preferences on the court. Attending also shows an interest in the person's success, which can lead to success together as a doubles team.

Partners should also support each other in tough doubles matches. On a particular day one partner may be so badly off that the other partner carries a heavy load, then all of a sudden the first partner hits one great shot, and the match is over. This is a scenario unique to the doubles environment, and makes it an interesting way to play. Players should never leave their partners spiritually, emotionally, or mentally because they never know what it will take to win the match.

Communication

Verbal and nonverbal communication is a large part of the success of a good doubles team. It is important that the player be able to tell a partner anything that is relevant to the player's success, such as where the player might be serving or about a possible plan to employ a different strategy. Sometimes, even making a comment that is not relevant to the match but loosens up the partner can be helpful. Communication during a point on the court is also a key to greater success. Informing the partner when the player is switching sides or talking about which ball to get is also an effective form of communication. For nonverbal communication, teams use hand signals to indicate to one another where to serve and whether they are attempting as a team to poach, fake, or stay in one location.

Good Energy

Since doubles is a team effort, it is important that both partners bring good energy to the contest. Thoughts and discussions of injury, or partners who can't play because they got into another tournament, or they are out of singles and their heart is out of it, can really cause friction between partners. The best way to approach an event is for both players on the team to begin with the notion that they will finish the event. Doubles matches are won and lost on energy, and energy helps teams remain competitive.

PICKING THE RIGHT PARTNER

One of the first steps to picking the right partner is for the player to understand his or her own preferred game styles, strengths, and weaknesses and to practice and play doubles. Once a player has become established as someone who wants to play doubles more competitively, the player needs to select a partner who compliments the game style and helps to build the doubles team based on both players' strengths and weaknesses.

Just as in singles tennis, as soon as a player is sure of the preferred doubles style, the player should assess which styles work best with individual strengths and weaknesses.

The player can choose someone with the same style or a contrasting style that may complement it. Deciding what style of play suits the player's game style is a personal choice, so it is important to play partners of different styles to assess it.

The next component of the partnership is how the players get along with and respect each other both on and off the court This component is important to experiment with. A player may be surprised to find that the partner who initially seemed to be a mismatch is actually the best partner.

After a player chooses a partner who seems to fit all the criteria, then the two players play together for a while to properly assess whether their team can be successful. Players should avoid expecting initial great results; doing so is short sighted and players should avoid it. Success is not impossible when two doubles players who know how to play good doubles pair up for the first time, but it should not be expected. Most teams take awhile (six months to years) to gel and get used to each other.

After picking a partner and practicing a bit, the player will start to get a sense of how the partner plays and can then discuss who will play the deuce side and the ad side, who should serve first, and who should take balls in the middle. Answering these questions can help the players focus more on the task at hand, which is beating their opponents. Alternatively, an experienced doubles player with an already developed preference for playing a particular side can use that knowledge to more quickly narrow the search for a compatible partner.

Choosing Sides

When deciding who should play the deuce court or the ad-court, players should always start the discussion with who is the better returner on that particular side. Players must be gentle handling this matter; sometimes it is clear, and sometimes it is not, so they should discuss it logically and take into consideration recent tournaments, great weapons, or who is more likely to perform better in clutch situations.

The next thing to consider and discuss is what shots players like to hit on subsequent shots such as transition shots to the net, volleys, and overheads. For example, some players volley better on one side or the other. This discussion is very important if both players are evenly matched when it comes to returns.

The better player usually has the higher singles or doubles ranking, and traditionally this player plays on the ad side because the rationale is that the better player can come through in more clutch situations. Clutch situations arise when trying to break the opponent's serve or when hitting a return to tie up a game, so it is important that the best player or best returner plays on the ad side. With the stronger player on the ad side the team can also build on any leads initiated by the deuce player.

The deuce court player is responsible for winning the majority of setup points, points that bring the team 1 point away from winning a game (30-all, 40-all, 30-love). This player has a few additional roles to develop, including starting the team off well (essential to doubles success), being creative (especially in the beginning of matches), being aggressive (especially if the ad-court player is consistent and reliable), and setting the tempo for the team since the deuce court player gets the first opportunity to return the opponents' serve.

Based on years of observation of how deuce and ad-court players perform, the deuce player generally seems to be wilder, takes more chances, and creates a major influence on the tempo and results of the team. Because ad-court players are the last to return a serve and the last line of defense, they are usually credited with coming up with the big shot or the steady defense that helps a team's chances of winning. When Martina Navratilova and Pam Shriver played, many people assumed Navratilova was a more integral part of the team because of her singles success. However, Shriver created the mood and tempo for their team, allowing Navratilova to flourish in doubles too. In doubles, each player has an important role, regardless of whether it is from the deuce side or the ad side.

When choosing a side, the ultimate goal is matching the players' stronger weapons on the groundstrokes, returns, and volleys so that they hit more shots with them. Players should consider which shots are their best on a ball hit down the middle of the court and out wide, in addition to returning preferences. When it comes to the groundstrokes, maybe a player has a great inside-out forehand, so playing the ad side would be a great choice. It is possible that the backhand volley is the player's weapon, in which case the deuce side would be wise because when poaching, the player can put the ball away with the backhand volley. Finally, perhaps the player hits a one-handed backhand inside out; the deuce side is a great choice for this player. Other important factors to consider are the temperament, experience, and success of the player playing on that side, and mainly what works for the team's overall success.

Deciding Who Serves First

Who serves first on the team is a big decision. Matches are won and lost in doubles because of the type of start teams get, so holding serve on the first service game is important. Three considerations should factor in to the decision of who serves first on a doubles team:

- Which player has the stronger serve based on possessing great power, having good placement, or being able to hold serve?
- Which player likes to start serving and has a certain confidence regarding the serve?
- Which player is good at the net and can help the team hold the serve?

Deciding Who Takes Shots in the Middle

Invariably, situations always exist in which a ball played by an opponent lands in the middle of the court at the net or at the baseline. Both players should react to the middle shot and get in position. Usually, the player with the stronger down-the-middle shot takes these shots, but the shot can also be played by the person who has the forehand in the middle because that player can be a bit late and still make the shot. Choosing who takes this ball is not an exact science but it is worth a discussion because the ball hit in the middle can cause players to freeze.

PERCENTAGE DOUBLES

Percentage play in doubles is the foundation to a good team, and it is the key to sound doubles strategy. First, players should understand the dimensions of the doubles court. The net height is the same as for singles: 3 feet (0.9 m) in the middle of the net and 3.5 feet (1.06 m) at the sides. The court length is also 78 feet (23.7 m) but the doubles court is wider (36 ft, or 11.85 m) to accommodate two players on the court.

Strategy in doubles starts with the serve and return. Because two players are on the court the placement of the serve, return, net play, and location of shots either set the partner up to put the ball away or set both players up to be put away. Similar to volleyball, one player sets up the partner to spike, or put the ball away.

The following are several basic strategies for playing percentage doubles. How well these basic strategies are executed gives the team the ability to become more offensive and control the net; that is the main goal in doubles. The team that controls the net usually wins doubles matches, and percentage plays give teams the best opportunities to win.

Percentage Serving

Serving in doubles is paramount to the success of a doubles team. Ideally, the team should use a variety of service types (slice, kick, flat) and placements to keep the opposing team guessing. Whatever mix of serves the players decide to use, a first-serve percentage of 80 or higher gives the team the best opportunity to control play and the net. A high first-serve percentage can keep the returning team from gaining confidence and becoming more aggressive on the returns.

Doubles players should serve from halfway between the center mark on the baseline and the singles line. If the opposing team has a tough crosscourt return, then the server should stand out wider to cover the doubles alley more easily. Service placement will be predominately to the body (also called *jam serves*) or the backhand.

When moving forward to volley, players have a variety of choices. For example, players serve and volley and are now approaching the net to the deuce side and receive a low first volley. If possible, the player will aim down the middle or deep crosscourt. If a player receives a high volley or sees an opponent at the net moving to attack the upcoming volley, then redirecting the return down the line is a wise play. As a rule, players approaching the net on the deuce side of the court should rely on the forehand volley (for right-handed players) for a ball coming crosscourt, and players approaching the net on the ad side of the court should rely on the backhand volley. The reason for this is simple: It is easier to redirect the volley down the line this way or crosscourt.

Percentage Returns

The main goal for the return is to make the return first and then try to build confidence on subsequent returns. The best returns are hit low to an oncoming server or pull a player off the court or back in the court. The highest-percentage return is hit crosscourt. A return crosscourt and deep in the court, gives the best opportunity to get the doubles partner up to the net.

Although it is tempting, hitting down the line is a low-percentage return, especially in doubles. Just as in singles players are hitting over the highest part of the net and into the shortest part of the court (78 ft, or 23.7 m) but doubles adds in a net player standing at the net. An exception to this rule occurs when the returner is pulled way off the court, such as by a serve, or if the player chooses to surprise the opponent at the net, especially if the player is not comfortable at the net or is not expecting the return to be drilled right at the body. The down-the-line return can also be used offensively to target the uncovered line when the net player is shaded to the other side in attempts to poach.

Percentage Net Play and Transition Shots

When it comes to volleying, there are two general rules. First, when a player volleys crosscourt, the player maintains high-percentage play in doubles. Since the net height is lower across the middle, this volley is theoretically easier to execute. Second, the players can alternately volley down the line when in an offensive position. The net height is higher down the line, so the execution of this shot is usually used on higher volleys (higher than the net level). Volleying down the line is an effective high-percentage play, when the ball hit from the opponent goes outside of the shoulder level of the players at the net. It is easier to change the direction of the ball hit to a player's outside shoulder. It gives the player a strong offensive position at the net, and it can make the opponents vulnerable if they are at the net.

Server's Partner at the Net

The first job of the server's partner at the net is to help the serving partner hold serve. The server's job is to set up the partner so that the partner can put the ball away. For example, if a server plans to make a well-placed first serve up the T, the net partner should be covering more of the middle of the court. As the opponents' return comes back down the middle, the partner aims the first volley down the middle of the court or directly at the net player on the other side. Because the partner will have moved naturally in the direction of cutting off the return, the momentum toward the opposing net player makes this volley a high-percentage shot. If a lob is used on the return, the overhead can be put away through the middle or toward the alley if the returner is moving away or covering the middle.

When the server plans to jam the returner, the net player's goal is to judge the movement of the returner. If the serve is strong or the returner appears to be fooled, the net player can be more aggressive. If the serve is not strong, the net player should be ready to reflex a volley because the opponent's most likely target will be the net player or down the line. When the return is hit at the net player, the net player should volley it through the middle or hit more aggressively toward the other net player. When the return is down the line, the best reply is through the middle, a quick reflex back to the returner, or on an easier return, a drop volley. If the return is a lob, the net player should put away the overhead toward the middle.

On a serve out wide, the net player must prepare to cover down the line. The most likely return is a more angled return, a ball hit down the line or a lob, and the angle keeps the net partner covering the line. The player can reflex volley a ball hit down the line and look to hit the ball toward the middle, or can go aggressively at the returner and hit a drop volley. If the returner lobs, the player should hit the overhead toward the middle, and only go for an angle when in a good position on the court. Hitting a poorly executed crosscourt volley shot spreads the defense for the next ball and requires a lot of recovery to get back in good position. One consideration is to be careful serving out wide and then volleying back to the returner. Unless that ball is hit well, the player will be giving the returner the potential to hit down the line. Great doubles players can still hold the line, poach, and be aggressive, all while covering a larger area.

Out-wide serves limit the net player's ability to set up the serving partner through the middle. The net player should look to help on more easily struck balls through the middle, but prepare for a ball to be returned down the line or lobbed. The player can put away easier middle shots or go aggressively toward the other net player.

Returner's Partner at the Net

The first duty of the returner's partner at the net is to neutralize the attack that the serving team has planned to execute against them. The net player should keep the eyes focused on the opposing net player and not on calling the serve in or out because the opponent at the net is looking to take the first volley directly at the returning net player. This player needs to stay low and try to volley back to the direction from which the opponent attacks.

As a rule, the net player on the returning team should try to stay about 30 feet (9 m) from the serving team's net player. After the net player sees that the partner has hit a successful return past the opponent at the net, then the net player should focus the eyes to the side of the court where the ball was returned. When the partner's return bounces on the opponent's side, the net player should move forward, taking as aggressive a position on the net as possible and be ready for the reply. If the ball is returned on the net player's side, the player needs to move backward and readjust the distance with the opposing net player's move forward to maintain the 30 foot (9 m) distance. If the pressure from the opponents is too great, the returner's partner can back up and start the point from the baseline along with the returner.

Server's Transition to the Net

Old school doubles tennis is based on players always serving and volleying off their serves in doubles. Current doubles play places a higher emphasis on hitting more groundstrokes and oftentimes not advancing to the net immediately off the serve; this is because of the power and precision of today's players. The net player on the receiving team is the most vulnerable player when a team serves and volleys, so it is best to hit it there when possible; this becomes a higher-percentage play.

When the server stays back on the serve, it could be because the server doesn't feel comfortable volleying off the serve and prefers to transition off a ball that allows more control. The server stays back and either transitions off a weaker return or begins a rally and transitions when gaining an advantage through effective use of groundstrokes. When transitioning to the net from the baseline, the player should approach crosscourt deep or more at an angle or, if in a good offensive position, the player can hit aggressively down the line.

Returner's Transition to the Net

Usually, if the returner is transitioning to the net, then that player is either trying to surprise the server or this is part of the returner's game. This game style is associated with the serve-and-volley style and, to a smaller degree, all-court play. The goal of the return and transition to the net is to put pressure on the serving team and potentially take away their advantage. This can be a risky play, especially if the serve is strong. However, if the returner is skilled and can execute a low return that puts the server on the defensive, it gives the returner the extra time to transition and a potentially easier next shot.

The returner can also use a lob to transition to the net when the lob is clearly over the head of the opposing net player or if the overhead is more defensive. When the returner transitions to the net on a good opportunity, the shift of power reverts to the returning team, and the goal would be to expose the serving team's net player, especially if that player is still at the net. If the net player has moved back, then the returning team should use percentage volleys and overheads to keep their offensive position.

The returner can also transition to the net later in the point rather than immediately after the return. In this case, the returner stays back at first and then transitions off a weak groundstroke from the opponent or transitions in a rally when they gain an advantage through the effective use of groundstrokes. For example, the returner could transition after pushing an opponent back in the court or wide. When transitioning to the net from the baseline, the player should hit the approach crosscourt deep or more at an angle; or, if in a good offensive position, the player can hit aggressively down the line.

Percentage Groundstrokes

In singles and doubles, the highest-percentage groundstrokes are played crosscourt. Of course, the difference in doubles is that a net player can potentially move in to try to intercept a shot. So, the goal in doubles is to keep it low or deep enough to prohibit the net player from becoming more active. In doubles play, the goal is to control the net, so players hitting groundstrokes should be focused on the best shots to transition to the net and on controlling the net. This can be groundstrokes that are hit angled and that stretch the opponent's defense, high and heavy shots that allow more time to transition, or an aggressive groundstroke down the line to expose the net player.

The crosscourt shot is generally used when in a groundstroke rally with the returner, but if the returner transitions to the net (so, both opponents are now at the net), then the highest-percentage play becomes the ball hit up the middle. When hitting up the middle, the ball must be kept low so the opponent at the net cannot poach across the net and put it away. This play sets up hitting toward the alleys. The down-the-line shot is the lowest-percentage play in doubles, especially when players are in a defensive position. However, if players are in an offensive position, then the percentages go up and it can be considered a good play.

The following general rules can also be helpful for percentage groundstrokes:

- **Keeping the ball low.** When a team keeps the ball low against another team, players force opponents to hit up or have to deal with tough shots that may produce a short ball. High balls hit in doubles need to be placed strategically (for example to an opponent's bad overhead or high volley). Low balls keep a team from being able to hit offensive shots, keep the situation neutral, and give more opportunities.

- **Lobbing a team that is close to the net.** Another high-percentage play in doubles is to lob a team that gets too close to the net. A team that closes tightly on the net is trying to get an upper hand in the rally and anticipating a drive by the other team. When a team can mix in lobs with drives, players are keeping the other team guessing or even out of position. Team players who feel as though they can position themselves closer to the net and stay successful either have good overheads, or it's possible that they know the other team doesn't lob very well.

High-Percentage Doubles Plays for Setting and Spiking

As noted previously, setting is placing the ball in a position so that the partner can put it away. Effective communication with a partner should include the direction of the serves as well as the movement of the net player and predominately what area to cover. For example, if the returner has a weak down-the-line shot, this may cause the net player to know they can cover more toward the middle. Conversely, if the returner has a good outside shot or the player likes to hit down the line, then the net player should shade more toward the alley. The same is true for high-level teams when returning. If a player signals or tells a partner that the player is about to go after the return with a dipping ball up the middle of the court, this can result in great setup shots that can be put away by a savvy volleyer.

Serving Side

The highest-percentage serve possible to set up the partner at the net for a put-away volley is a serve to the T on either the deuce or the ad side. This serve creates the least amount of angle on the return and shrinks the court so that both the server and server's partner can close in on the volley and attempt to control the net. The server who is coming to volley can take a little more of a direct path to the net with this serve because of the lack of angle that is created. If the partner realizes that the returner is stretched out to execute the return, the partner should look to pounce and volley away the return. The returner on the serve to the T must hit a well-executed drive to be able to hit it down the line and past the net player. This usually makes the server's partner at the net more confident to move and help out the server.

The serve to the body can be just as high a percentage play as the serve to the T, but a serve to the body that is not executed well can give the returner a more offensive position in which the returner can put the net player in a defensive position. A strong net player will welcome this challenge, but it is more prudent to get the opponents on defense. However, a well-placed and effective serve can be very successful if the serve jams the returner or catches the returner off guard. As a rule, when serving and volleying, the server should try to follow the serve in the same direction that the ball is travelling.

The serve out wide requires the net player to be more aware of covering down the line. The greater angle created by this serve can make it easier for a good returner to hit it down the line. For this reason the server's partner at the net may call fake to give the returner the impression that they are going to poach. A well-executed fake can set up the player at the net for a put-away by drawing the returner to hit the ball directly back to the volleyer at the net. The out-wide serve also gives the returner an easier opportunity to lob to the middle or down the line over the net player. The server's partner at the net should be told when the server is going to hit out wide because it is the lowest-percentage way to try to set a partner up for a put-away volley.

Return Side

Depending on the formation the returner is returning from, the returner can set up the partner to put the ball away. If the team is playing in a one up and one back formation, then a low-dipping return on an approaching server's feet can result in a popped up ball, which can be put away. If the opposing team is playing unfocused, then a hard-hit return at an unsuspecting net opponent may set up the player or partner for a short volley that can then be put away for a winner.

COURT POSITIONING GUIDELINES AND DOUBLES FORMATIONS

Doubles teams can use a variety of formations to defeat opponents. The three main options are one up and one back, both players up at the net, or both players back on the baseline. On the serve, the one up and one back formation can show some additional variety in the Australian and I formations, which are also added for challenging opponents. Following is a look at the serve and return positioning and tactics and the court positioning guidelines for the net player.

Serve Positioning and Tactics

When serving, the team's two most common court positioning tactics are to serve and stay back or serve and volley. Both tactics are important for keeping opponents guessing what the team will do next.

Serve and Stay Back

Serving and staying back is a relatively recent trend. Most players today prefer to use their groundstrokes to win points. This high-percentage play is used in most women's tennis matches and in quite a few men's matches. In this type of doubles play, players rally back crosscourt to each other, looking for the first opportunity to be aggressive with their shot or effectively transition to the net.

The server stands midway between the alley and the middle hash mark on the baseline. The net player stands in (or just in front of) the middle of the service box. For this tactic, the role of the server is to cover the other side of the court in case of a lob. The server needs to be able to rally crosscourt and put the opposing returner on the defensive to allow an opportunity to transition. On a ball that is easy to attack, the server can also go aggressively to the opposing net player. The server needs to control midway between the middle hash mark and the alley predominately near the baseline and look to join the net player at the net.

This type of doubles play requires the net player to develop keen and precise movement based on the shot hit by the partner. A shot hit wide and in the alley requires the net player to cover the down-the-line response. A powerful or deep shot can give the net player a greater license to be aggressive.

Serve and Volley

Serving and volleying puts the most pressure on a returning team because both players on the serving team transition to the net. Whether they maintain that pressure and control depends on their execution of well-placed or powerful serves and volleys, their positioning, and the location of their shots.

The server stands approximately midway between the hash mark and the alley. A server who is used to playing singles may prefer to stand and start the serve closer to the hash mark. Doing so is fine, but the server needs to be aware of the angle the opponent could create on the return. In other words, the server should be cautious of hitting a serve out wide and giving the returner a greater angle crosscourt that would be harder to cover. When serving from the normal midway position, the server will transition straight forward for a body serve and a T serve and cover the entire crosscourt area. If the server serves wide, the net player is forced to cover more of the line, so the coverage area would now include some of the middle that the net player may not be able to get to. The server needs to be aware of the court positioning and transition diagonally across from the returner.

When the returner hits an angled return, the net player who was standing in the middle of the service box should slide over approximately 2 to 3 feet (0.6 to 0.9 m) toward the angled shot to stay in position with the server hitting the volley. When the volley is hit crosscourt midway between the middle and the alley, the net player recovers back to the original position, and the server attempts to close further into the court. The server needs to be aware of lobs hit over the net player, so their position should be staggered initially; the server is slightly behind the net player. As the rally progresses, the server and net player can be positioned along the same line at the net, but both players must be conscious of a potential lob. If the server hits a ball down the line at the opposing net player, the server's partner at the net should slide toward the middle, approximately 2 to 3 feet (0.6 to 0.9 m).

The net player must not look back to watch the server volleying because doing so reduces the net player's reaction time if the opposing net player is poaching or hitting a volley. The net player should focus on the racket of the opposing net player and if there is any movement, the net player covers the middle. This move to the middle also serves to divert the eyes of the opponent net player while executing the shot.

Australian Formation

When a returning team consistently hits solid crosscourt returns, playing Australian formation is an effective way to break up the pressure put on the server. To play Australian formation, both partners on the serving team start on the deuce side of the court. The net player should be positioned approximately 1 to 2 feet (0.3 to 0.6 m) from the center line in the service box to the right. The net player stays in the same spot or signals to the partner the intention to fake.

The server serves from the normal singles serving position, 1 to 2 feet (0.3 to 0.6 m) from the middle hash mark. The server may transition to the net for the volley, but needs to be fast to cover and take control of the net and probably will have to transition off the return using a weapon. The server also needs to be aware of any lob hit over the net player, in which case the net player would shift back to the standard doubles net position (midway between the net and service line in the middle of the box).

Playing Australian formation takes away the crosscourt return and forces the opponent to hit down the line. This setup gives the returner less room to return because the middle is covered and they are essentially given the alley to return. This play works well if the server is positioned close to the center mark of the baseline and has a strong second shot (forehand or backhand) to reply when the opponents hit their return up the line. It also works well if the returner has shown difficulty returning down the line or has a weakness on the outside stroke (most commonly backhands for the right-handed players).

I Formation

The I formation is another way to force the opposing team to return down the line. The server in the I position stands close to the middle hash mark (similar to singles). The net player straddles the center line midway between the net and the service line and crouches low to avoid getting hit by the serve.

The net player and the server should communicate regarding the way the net player will move. If the net player stays in the middle and covers the crosscourt shot, then the server covers the shot down the line. The server can transition off the serve if this player is especially effective volleying, but usually the server crosses toward the other alley, stays near the baseline, and attempts to transition on the next shot. If the net player goes toward the normal volley position, then the server tries to follow the same path of entry similar to that for a normal transition of the serve. In this scenario, the server has to transition a little wider to make up for the serve position closer to the middle. For the server, keeping the ball up the T or jamming the opponent are the most effective plays for this formation.

Both Players Back

In this formation, the players position themselves on the baseline midway between the middle and the alley on each side. This formation is not a long-term strategy. It will not help players become better at doubles. In lower-level matches, this can be a useful play if the server's partner is not good at the net. So, for the short term, this formation may result in a win until a team can get a lesson on the volley. At the higher levels of play, this formation may be used to break the rhythm of a strong returning team. It can also be used on a day when one or both partners are struggling on serve. For example, in a situation in which the server is hitting weak serves and the net player is constantly being exposed, moving the net player back may be best.

Another use for this formation is when the serving team's groundstrokes are considerably stronger than their volleys and they prefer to allow the returning team to gain control of the net. It can also be a surprise tactic, especially when a returning team is dialed into their returns and placing their returns at the feet of the server or intimidating the server's partner at the net. The serving team can move the net player back, which effectively removes that particular target for the returning team, and the server can opt to hit groundstrokes instead of shoestring volleys. This formation can also be used if the returning team has considerably better volleys than the serving team. Again, though, this is not a long-term strategy. Using this formation exclusively can hamper doubles volley development and is not recommended when serving.

Return Positioning and Tactics

A returning team can use three court positioning tactics when returning: return and stay back, return and volley, or both players stay back. To become a tough team to beat when returning, players should practice using all three positions.

Return and Stay Back

In this formation, also known as standard doubles formation, one player is up and the other is back. When choosing to stay back, the returner needs a variety of returns to be successful. The returner should practice hitting returns from deep behind the baseline (against big serves), near the baseline, and from inside the baseline (against second serves).

On a point, the returner tries to set up the partner at the net to spike a volley away. This can best be done by keeping returns low and up the middle of the court or by hitting heavy and deep enough into the court to back up opponents, allowing the player and partner to storm the net. The returner can also try to keep the net player on the opposing team guessing by occasionally hitting shots down the line. This tactic keeps the opposing net player from getting too bold with net play.

If the server is transitioning to the net off the serve, the goal of the returner is to hit low at the server's feet or possibly hit it where the server is stretched out. These two shots give the returning side's net player the best opportunity to poach. The returner is responsible for his or her side of the court and any lob hit over the head of his or her partner at the net.

Return and Volley

For this formation, one player is up and the other is back. The returner moves in and takes the return early or hits the return from the normal return position. Then, after seeing a successful return, the returner transitions to the net. This tactic, sometimes called *crush and rush,* can be effective if the players are advanced or if they want to add a new dimension to their return game. Returning and volleying is a great play when a team is up in the score, receiving a second serve, or the players just want to throw something different at their opponents.

If the opponents are playing with one person up and the other back, one option is for the returner to hit the return deep into the opponents' court, move in, and hit a swinging volley or transition volley. Against the same formation, another option is to hit a lob over the server's partner at the net and rush up to the net for an easy volley put-away off what will be a defensive reply.

Against an opponent who is serving and volleying or coming forward after the serve, the returner can take the return very early in the court using a shortened backswing and put the ball at the opponent's feet. The following pop-up reply will be easy pickings for the returner and partner at the net. This is a risky play, though, especially if the server has a good serve. The problem with this type of return is that it is difficult to execute and often can lead to a mishit and easy volley winner for the serving team. Taking the ball on the rise and hitting the return up the line in an attempt to volley the reply is extremely low-percentage tennis and should only be attempted by advanced players or with a very large lead.

Both Players Stay Back

In this formation, both players stay on the baseline. It is a great strategy if a team wants to create a different look and a challenge for an aggressive net team. This is also a good play when the returner is having trouble making the returns and may benefit from some extra space to execute the return. This formation is also used when the serving team is better and more effective than the returning team at the net, and the returning team is losing a lot of net points. Using this tactic allows the returning team to use groundstrokes against the opponents' aggressive net play.

The returning team starts with both players on the baseline. After the returner hits the return, the team looks for opportunities to get the serving team out of position. Both players on the baseline should set themselves up for an opportunity to attack the net. The best way to do this is to hit dipping shots up the middle of the court or hit angles and then lob the ball or rip it at the attacking net players. The goal with this variety of shots is to get a short ball that the player and partner can then approach the net.

When both players are back, it is important that in the case of one of the players having an offensive ball, the partner should try to sneak in to the net. In this scenario, the back player needs to focus on hitting low and through the middle between the shoulders of both the net players, so the net player can advance. If the shot is effective and has the opponents stretched or hitting up, both players on the returning team can advance. The player who is back may go down the line, but needs to be on the offense.

Net Player Positioning and Tactics

Good net coverage is essential for success in doubles. The net player needs to be able to cover personal territory as well as any territory left open by the partner's movement. The following are four important guidelines for the net player to maximize net coverage.

- **Bounce and pounce.** In the staggered doubles position (one up, one back), any time a ball bounces deep on the opponents' side of the court, the net player moves forward and looks to gain better positioning. The net player moves from the middle of the service line up to the middle of the service box. It is important not to over-commit forward when a deep ball is hit because many players in that scenario would lob instead of return a ball crosscourt.

- **Ball in the air, then stay there.** In the one up and one back position, when the opponents are going to hit a shot in the air, the net player should hold the current position. In other words, when the other team is at the net, the net player and partner who is staying back should hold their positions and play for better position gained from a stronger next shot or a ball that bounces, allowing them to pounce.

- **Cover the Ts.** The Ts are the intersection of the singles sideline at the baseline. Assuming the staggered doubles position, when the net player covers the Ts at the net, the player should position the body so that the middle of the back is in line with the Ts. When the player is back, the T should be the player's base and a point of reference when moving.

  In a both players up formation, the net players should both position themselves so that the Ts are in line with the middle of their backs. In a situation in which the ball is hit straight ahead, it is easier to cover the Ts, but when a ball is hit at an angle or crosscourt, then both players should shift to cover the Ts.

- **Stagger at the net.** Another guideline for movement and positioning is the slightly staggered court position. The key here is the positioning of the net player who should be following where the ball has been hit. When a ball is hit to a particular side, the net player on that side is considered the lead volleyer and should be positioned slightly ahead of the other volleyer. This slightly staggered position allows the secondary net player to pay attention to any potential lobs. When a shot is hit to the other side, then the players shift positions so that the other net player becomes the lead volleyer.

Poaching Skills

Advanced doubles net coverage also includes being able to poach effectively. Poaching is when the net player moves from the position at the net (generally in front of the partner) and tries to intercept a crosscourt shot played by the opponent. In other words, the net player cuts across toward the partner's side to volley. In general, the net player is positioned in the middle of the service box when the team is serving and in the middle of the service line midway between the center line and the alley when the team is returning. However, the net player can poach in many different formations and positions.

Poaching is an effective way of disarming opponents and causes them to make errors. Poaching is also an effective way of being aggressive, and it's a great way to spike a partner's setup shot. The goal when poaching is to instill fear in the other team with aggressive play and the timing of the poaching so that the opponents worry about when the players will poach again. If the players' poaching inhibits their play, the opponents' game will deteriorate.

Poaching takes great coordination between players' vision and feel for where the ball will be hit, plus the proper timing and movement to execute a good shot. It is harder to poach when a ball is hit wide because the net player must maintain court position. It is easier to poach on balls hit to the middle or at the body. Low shots or shots where the opponent is on the defensive are best for poaching because these shots will likely be hit up or with less pace and they allow the net player more reaction time.

Types of Poaching

Net players can use two types of poaching against opponents. Another option is the fake poach, which is technically not poaching, but it also inhibits the opponent by using the threat of poaching.

- **Forward first poach.** One of the most effective ways to poach is to move forward first and then diagonally to the ball. The player moves forward first to get some attention from the opponent hitting the shot and gets the body's momentum moving forward in order to cut diagonally forward to intercept the shot. Often players move diagonally first instead of forward first. This can work if the move and the location of the shot are perfect. However, net players who cut diagonally first often turn their shoulders too much as they cross, which puts them out of balance for the poach if the ball is hit out of their reach. When moving forward first, a player can use outside leg movement more effectively and be in a better position for the poach.

  The forward first approach is also an effective way of poaching when working as the returner's partner because the player is getting in a better position to cut off an opponents' next shot. As the partner's return passes the player, the player should move forward toward the net. This gives the deception of covering the line (which the player is in position to do) and subconsciously makes the opponent want to hit the ball away from the player. This forward first movement can then be followed with a move diagonally if the net player can get to the ball.

- **Zigzag poach.** For this type of poach, the net player's movement is an initial move out toward the alley to make an opponent feel as though the player is covering the line, followed by a move diagonally toward the middle of the court to cut off a potential crosscourt return (see figure 11.1). The player can also zig in toward the middle when the ball is hit a little wider, giving the opponent the impression that the player is not covering the line, then zag out when the opponent is lured into returning down the line. This method is effective because often a player hitting a shot sees the movement of the net player, and a cat-and-mouse game ensues. The opponent is left to wonder whether the net player is moving or staying.

- **Fake poach.** A fake poach keeps the opponent guessing. This is a great play to help the partner hold serve or improve the player's return games because the player makes opponents uneasy with many movements. Two fakes are possible: For the deuce side, the move is fake right and

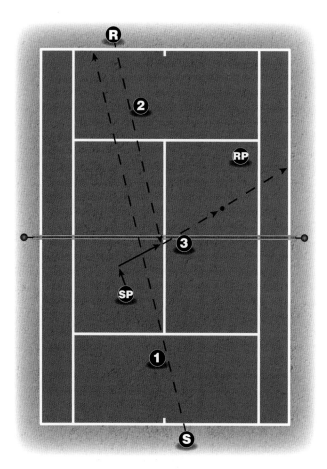

Figure 11.1 Zigzag poach.

cover left. For the ad side, the move is fake left and cover right. When the server's serve lands in the box, the server's partner makes a quick move as if to poach, but the move is a fake. If the player does a good job of acting, the reward is a return hit right toward the net player that can be volleyed away. This makes the net player an extremely effective partner. On the face poach, the player uses head movement, but the player's body and shoulders stay semi-open instead of turning. Advanced doubles players should poach or fake poach on every shot.

FOUR PHASES OF PLAY

The characteristics for the phases of doubles play are essentially the same as those already described for singles play in chapter 10 (see pages 193–195). The difference for doubles is that when deciding how to respond, players must account for the positions of two additional people on the court. The following descriptions provide some guidance in adapting the concept of phases of play to the doubles game.

Attack Phase of Play

Common doubles attacking shots include shots when a team can transition to the net or when a team can hit an aggressive shot with a lot of pace or spin that goes to a location deep in the court or at a sharp angle. When players are in the standard doubles formation (one up and one back) and the server and returner begin to trade groundstrokes cross-court, any weak shot hit by the opponents or any ball that lands near the service line can be attacked. Players can attack during these scenarios: when the returner has a return that can be used as a weapon or when the serve is weak. Another great way to attack is to transition to the net after a great return.

Doubles players should always be looking to transition to the net as much as possible because it can prove a more formidable front to an opponent. An attacking ball in doubles can be a ball hit at the net player, a winner, an approach shot, or a shot such as a high and heavy shot or a more angled shot that can push the opponent back off the court, allowing the player more time to advance toward the net.

Rally Phase of Play

Rally shots frequently occur in a couple of common doubles scenarios. One scenario is when both teams are in the one up and one back formation, after a team returns a ball crosscourt and begins to rally the ball with the opponents crosscourt. Another scenario is when a team has ventured to the net and the players are executing volleys for better positioning instead of going for a winner. The yellow light volley (see page 191) can force the opponents to go for too much on their shots. Shots for the rally phase of play usually include a high and heavy shot, a slice, or a drive hit with a little more loft than an aggressive drive.

Defensive Phase of Play

The defensive phase is when a doubles team is trying to keep the ball in play any way possible and players buy themselves time to regain the offensive. Common shots hit defensively include the lob, the high and heavy loop ball, the squash shot, and the slice backhand and forehand. When a player is stretched way outside the court, hitting a high lob can buy time to get back into position to hit another shot. Other times, just getting the ball back low and up the middle with topspin or slice can help a player regain the offensive.

Counterattack Phase of Play

The counterattack phase of play is when players display great hands or great anticipation or both. Counterattacking, or the orange phase of play (see page 191), occurs when a point appears to be shaping up to one team's advantage and then suddenly the other team is in the driver's seat. One example of how this can occur is when the serving team shoots across the net and blasts a volley right at the returner's partner. This player blocks the shot back behind the serving team for a winner. Another example is when one team smashes an overhead at a member of the opposing team and that player volleys it over their heads. As the first team goes scrambling back to recover, the player follows the ball to the net and puts the opponents' reply away. Volleys, lobs, groundstrokes, and returns are common shots for counterattacking.

DOUBLES STRATEGIES

One of the most rewarding aspects of playing doubles and incorporating strategy and tactics is that each player has a partner to help carry out the game plan. Players must be cooperative in carrying out strategies and employing tactics while meshing their strengths to build an effective game plan against an opposing team. How effectively partners can complement each other determines a team's success.

To start, ball control and overall consistency should be the number one doubles playing strategy. The same ball controls (consistency, depth, direction, height, spins, and pace or speed; see pages 189–191) that are essential to singles success are also important for doubles success. Players should continue to develop those ball controls in their singles game while focusing on the percentage plays, such as the serve to the T and the return hit crosscourt in doubles. On groundstrokes, players should rally crosscourt and look for the first opportunity to transition. At the net, players should keep the first volley down the middle of the court or deep crosscourt until able to move in to hit a second volley winner down the line or sharply angled crosscourt. Overall, players should focus on making their first serve and returns, especially second-serve returns.

Basic Strategy #1: Covering a Weakness

If one player has a weakness, the team should discuss how best to cover it. A player hides a weaker partner by having the partner play a side that gives the best opportunity to run around a weakness. One way to hide a weaker volleyer is to move the volleyer back when the returner is returning the serve. Another approach is to avoid long rallies in which the opposing team would have greater opportunity to find a weakness. The player can use the weakness to lob, allowing the stronger player to transition to the net.

A court positioning trick that maximizes a weaker player's strength and hides the weakness is for the partner to be positioned closer to the weaker player on the return. This positioning makes it hard for the server to get it to the weakness. For example, if a right-handed deuce player has a weak backhand, the ad player can be positioned close to center line of the service box on the service line or midway between the service line and the baseline. The returner on the deuce side is positioned close to the center, daring the server to serve out wide to the returner's weapon.

This strategy requires some additional accommodations. The partner of the weaker player has to poach more, cover more court, and be the leader of the team by telling (in an encouraging way) the weaker partner what to do, where to stand, and so on. Additionally, if the weaker player has a weak serve, the stronger partner must be ready to counterattack at the net. If the team continues to lose points, then the stronger player may need to back up further in the box to buy more time.

SWITCH GAME

Purpose: To practice switching positions.

Procedure: Four players are on the court in the standard doubles formation. A point is played out from the deuce side of the court; the two players on the baseline rally with one another crosscourt until one of the net players calls out *Switch* and poaches on the next ball (see figure 11.2). All four players play out the point. The next point is continued from the ad side of the court. Games are played until one team reaches 7 points.

Coaching Points: **The two net players have to keep their eyes focused on one another in this drill to be ready for the *Switch.***

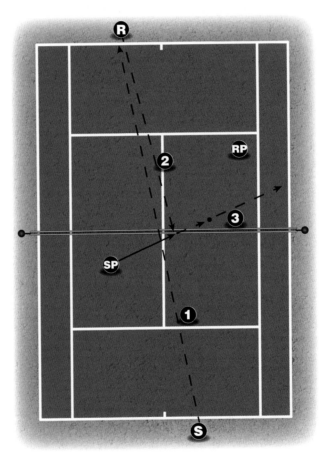

Figure 11.2 Poaching on the *Switch* call.

Basic Strategy #2: Weapon to Weakness

The next best strategy for doubles is to use weapons to the opponents' weaker player, position on the court, or stroke. Weapons in doubles include a big server combined with a net player who can poach and put away shots at the net, two great returners who can play great defense, or any combination of play that isolates a weakness in the opposing team. Sometimes, a team can win points just by hitting to the opponents' weaker player. However, a successful doubles team with a weaker and a stronger player has likely learned to hide weaknesses. The players may have superior movement, or they have learned how to move collectively and employ a good strategy.

Oftentimes, the stronger player protects the weaker one and picks up the slack for the team. If the stronger player moves a lot, one of the best strategies is to hit to the outside of or directly at that player to get the player focused on hitting the shot or staying in position. The next shot should be hit to the weaker player to get a better opportunity to win the point.

Common patterns of play: If an opposing player has a weak outside shot, the server should predominately serve out wide, and the partner at the net should pick off the weak return. To keep the opponent guessing, the server can mix it up by going to the T and having the partner at the net ready to pick off the easy response up the middle of the court. Returns should be hit to the weakness, which might include a down-the-line shot to expose a weak net player followed by an easy pass up the middle off the opponent's short volley (see figure 11.3), or, if the returning team doesn't play defense well, a lob followed by a quick close to the net.

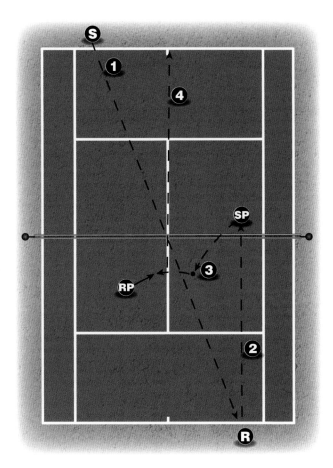

Figure 11.3 Returns hit to the weakness.

HOT SEAT

Purpose: To work on isolating one player or one shot from the opposing team. This drill provides a great opportunity for the hot seat player to work on counterattacking and defensive skills at the net.

Procedure: Four players on the court play a total of four games. For the first two games, each doubles team designates one player on the opposing team to be in the hot seat. In other words, the pair makes that player their primary target. After two games, the other player on each team becomes the new person in the hot seat for the opposing team.

Coaching Points: In this drill, most pairs start with targeting the player that they perceive to be weaker. Players discover that by doing a good job of picking on the stronger player, they break down the opponents' confidence even more. A returner may have a weakness in hitting in a particular direction. For example, if a returner doesn't have a good outside shot, then the net player can take more liberties and attack balls off the weaker return.

Basic Strategy #3: Through the Middle

For this strategy (also known as going through a team), a team aims every shot down the middle of the court. Hitting down the middle is a high-percentage play and keeps the ball in front of the players. In doubles, this strategy can be a very effective way to win points. This approach gives the opponent no angles to work with, and it can also lead to unforced errors as the opponent tries to create an angle or devise other ways to respond to this challenge. This is an aggressive style, and it can be very intimidating to an opponent.

Common patterns of play: From the baseline, a team can work this strategy by keeping the ball up the middle of the court until the players receive a short ball. One of the players can attack the short ball and drive it up the line or at the opponent at the net. Hitting through the middle is also very effective when the opposing players are at the net. Instead of hitting through the middle with power, the player can hit low at the opponent's feet with a topspin shot such as a short dipper, or a shot that makes both players move to the middle. When the opponents move in, the team can hit to the alleys or use a lob. Serving up the middle with a strong, deep serve in the box also eliminates angles. The server and the partner can anticipate the return coming up the middle of the court.

CHAMPS UP THE MIDDLE

Purpose: To work on hitting up the middle.

Procedure: This drill is for six or more players. Two players start on the service line; these players are kings (see figure 11.4). A coach stands behind them. Two additional players, the challengers, start across the net on the service line. The coach feeds the challengers the ball, and the point is played out. If the challengers lose the first point, they rotate out and the next pair steps up to challenge. The goal for the challenging pairs is to win 2 out of 3 points against the kings, or hit a winner up the middle between them to take their side of the court and become the new kings. The game is played for time, so at the end of the allotted time the players on the king and queen side of the court do not have to pick up the balls.

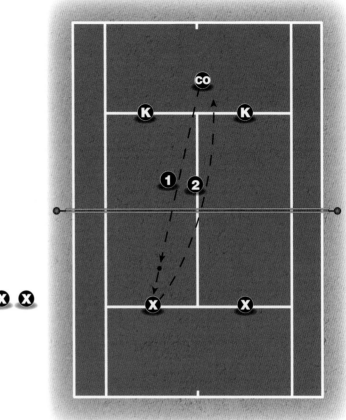

Figure 11.4 Start of first point.

Basic Strategy #4: Lobbing the Opponent Crazy

Most lobs in doubles are defensive, but using offensive lobs can be effective against an opponent, especially in situations in which the opponents don't hit good overheads. The lob is especially effective when net players try to be offensive and get too close to the net. The best time to lob is when the opposing players are recovering and they don't see it coming.

> **Common patterns of play:** The most common pattern of play is to bring a team closer to the net, intentionally deflating your shots by hitting topspin angles or drop shots and then lob them either crosscourt or down the line. A lob off the return is also a good play and can surprise the serving team, especially if the serve is out wide. Whenever a lob is hit, the player should watch the body position and effectiveness of the opposing player hitting the overhead to get an early read about what to do next. If the opponent is in trouble and the ball has gone over the opponent's head, the player should sprint to the net and look to put the response away with a countering volley or overhead.

HANDS

Purpose: To work on effective lobbing and reading the opponents' intentions on overheads.

Procedure: This drill is for six or more players. The game starts off on the baseline with two players designated as kings (see figure 11.5). A coach stands behind them to start. Two challengers are positioned on the other side of the net in the service boxes (one in each box). The coach throws a lob to the challengers and the point is played out. The challengers must hit overheads, and the kings must hit lobs unless the challengers let an overhead bounce and touch the court. If that occurs, then the kings have the option of hitting a passing shot. The goal is for the challengers to win 3 overhead points in a row. If they miss before 3 points, the next team of challengers replaces them. This game is played for time; the final kings are the team that collects 15 points. Points for the total may be won only on the kings' side of the court. Even challengers who knock out players, players' point totals remain the same until they return to demonstrate their great hands on the king side of the court.

Coaching Points: The kings look for body positioning and racket face when challengers are hitting their overheads. If they look as though they are in good position and hitting the overhead in front of them, challengers should be prepared for a big shot. If they are leaning back and reaching for the overhead, then challengers should move in for a more offensive shot on their defensive reply.

Variation: After the challengers hit the first overhead, the kings can hit whatever shots they like. The challengers can take the side in this variation by hitting an outright winner or winning 2 out of 3 points.

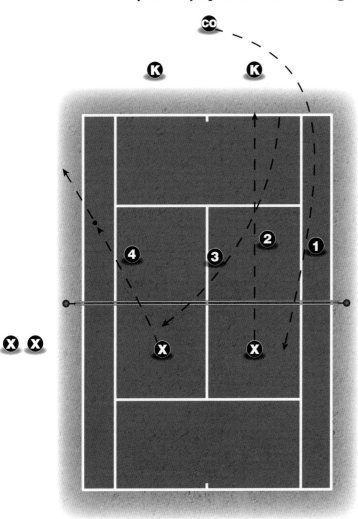

Figure 11.5 Hands drill setup.

Intermediate Strategy #1: Rush and Crush

Rush and crush is when a team decides to blitz the opponents, forcing them to come up with a good passing shot or lob. A team can implement this strategy by executing the serve and volley or the return and volley. Some opponents get nervous when a team applies constant pressure coming forward because it accelerates the pace of the point and doesn't give the opponents time to work themselves into the point. The players on the team using this strategy move forward together on their respective sides of the court and focus on executing a volley, advance forward, execute a volley, and advance forward until the point is won.

Volleyers advancing to the net should keep in mind that although they do want to advance forward, they must also move systematically; they hit the volley, take a couple of steps, and get ready to hit the next volley. Players should use two strategies to effectively move to any ball. One is to see where the opponent is hitting the ball and move there. The other is to anticipate where the opponent is going to hit the ball and start moving in that direction as the opponent is hitting the shot.

Common patterns of play: The most common pattern of play is to serve and volley at the same time the returner is returning and volleying. The best location for the player to rush and crush is to move forward on balls hit to the player or through the middle. The player should also hit to the middle or body while advancing until an opportunity presents itself. When the opposing team starts to lose a few of these points, it can undermine the team's confidence. Another rush and crush play is when the player and partner are back and the opposing team is up. The player hits a ball through the middle or out to the alleys and, as the opponent is reaching for the shot, the player and partner advance, hitting the ball to where they are not positioned. If both opponents are leaning to the middle, the player should volley down the line. If the opponents are leaning to the outside, then the middle of the court is open for the put-away.

KINGS

Purpose: To work on taking the net from two players already in position at the net.

Procedure: Two players start on the service line; they are the kings (see figure 11.6). A coach stands 3 to 5 feet (0.9 to 1.5 m) behind them, ready to feed balls. Two other players line up on the baseline on the opposite side of the net from the kings. The goal is for the challengers to win three points in a row against the kings. The teams play the first point from the baseline. They play the second point with both teams starting on the service line going volley to volley. On the third point, the kings retreat as the challengers get an overhead near the net from the coach. If the challengers win the third point, they take the opposite side of the court and become the kings. The winner is the team on the kings' side of the court when the allotted time is up.

Variation: Another way for the game to be scored is for each team to track their points while playing as the kings. The winner is the first team to win 15 points cumulatively on the kings' side of the court.

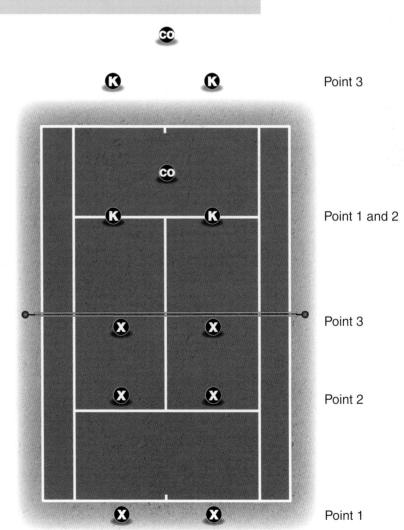

Point 3

Point 1 and 2

Point 3

Point 2

Point 1

Figure 11.6 Starting positions.

Intermediate Strategy #2: Butterfly Method

The butterfly method is an effective strategy for forcing an opponent out of position, and it can be an effective way to weaken an opponent's defense. To use this strategy, a team hits to the middle or to the outside alley first to get the opponent either protecting the middle or stretched out wide. Then the team hits the next shot to the opposite location. When a team attacks the middle of an opposing team, the opponents lean in, and the outsides are easier to attack. Similarly, when an opponent is pulled off the court, the middle is easy to attack. This in-and-out focus simulates a butterfly's wings.

Common patterns of play: When serving, the server can follow a slice serve or kick serve out wide with an attack up the middle (see figure 11.7). Conversely, the player can also hit a serve to the service T in order to then attack the outsides. Serving out wide and then attacking the middle is a higher-percentage play than serving to the Ts and attacking outside, but the latter is still effective. For the return, this strategy is used when the return is hit crosscourt and followed up with a shot or a poach to attack the middle. The player can also hit a return down the middle or at the net player to get a team leaning in and then attack the alleys with groundstrokes or volleys; this depends on court positioning.

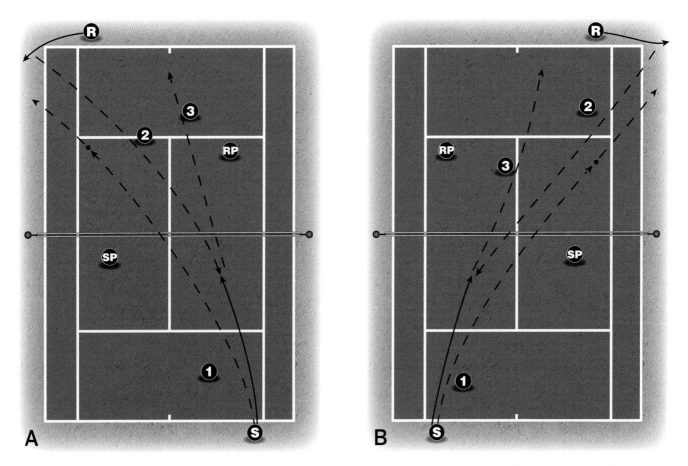

Figure 11.7 Using the butterfly method after a serve out wide to the *(a)* deuce side and *(b)* ad side.

BEST OF SEVEN

Purpose: To work on opening the court by hitting out wide or up the middle.

Procedure: Two players are at the net, and two are on the baseline; a coach feeds balls into play. No lobs are allowed in this game. The teams play up to 7 points. The first team (net players or baseline) to win 4 points wins, and then the teams switch sides.

Variation: If additional players are waiting to drill, they can play best of 5.

Intermediate Strategy #3: Pushing the Opponent Back

The other main strategy designed to pull a team out of position is to push a team back or get the opposing players thinking high in order to be able to attack them low and vice versa. This strategy is similar to the butterfly method except that this strategy uses changes in the height of the ball (high then low) to catch the opposing team off guard. This strategy is used off the serve, the return, groundstrokes, and net play.

> **Common patterns of play:** When serving and attempting to push a team back, a player uses kick serves that bounce high for the returner followed by low penetrating volleys. When the player is trying to push a team back off the return, the returner can hit a lob followed by his or her partner moving in to retrieve the defensive reply with a drop volley (see figure 11.8). Another option is a slice return that stays low, followed by a high and heavy shot that bounces high. A team can also use a lob to push a team back and follow it up with shot at the team's feet.

Intermediate Strategy #4: Dipping It

A great tactic in doubles is hitting the ball at the opponent's feet, getting the opponent to pop the ball up for an easy put-away. This tactic can be used on the return, as a groundstroke, or while playing at the net. On the return, the crosscourt return that lands at the feet of the oncoming server makes for a tough shot that can give the returning net player more time to anticipate and attack the half volley reply. A low ball hit down the line is a low-percentage shot unless executed extremely well; it is executed best when having a comfortable lead.

> **Common patterns of play:** There are three main options for the dip play. First is the dip and rip (see figure 11.9 on page 244), where a low ball is hit at the opponent's feet, down the middle of the court followed by a flat or topspin aggressive shot to the opponent's body or to the open court. Second is the dip and lob (see figure 11.10 on page 244), where the dip is hit close to the net to bring the opponents forward followed by a topspin lob over their heads. Third is the dip and angle (see figure 11.11 on page 244), where the low ball is hit to the middle of the court to bring the players to the middle, followed by an angled shot that stretches them out wide.

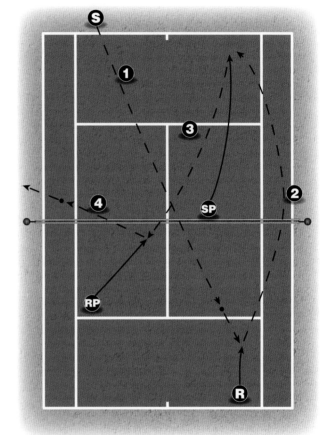

Figure 11.8 Pushing the opponent back in the court.

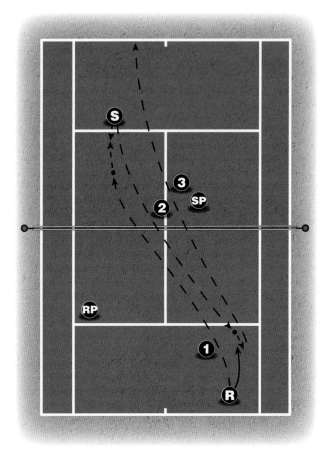

Figure 11.9 Dipping (shot 1) and ripping (shot 3).

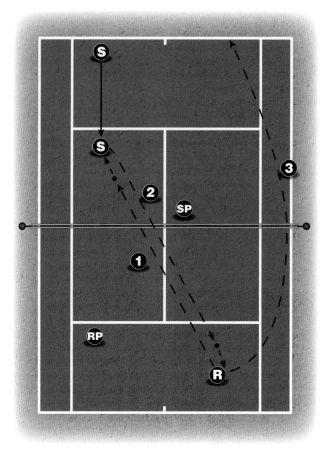

Figure 11.10 Dipping (shot 1) and lobbing (shot 3).

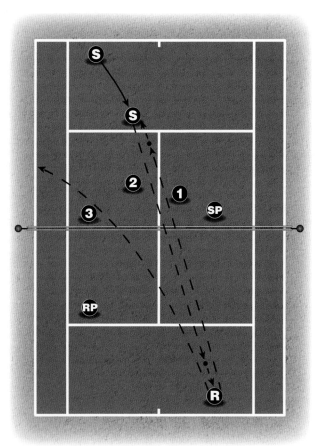

Figure 11.11 Dipping (shot 1) and hitting an angle (shot 3).

DIP, RIP, ANGLE, OR LOB

Purpose: To work on dipping, ripping, angling, or lobbing the ball.

Procedure: Two players start on the service line, and a coach stands 3 to 5 feet (0.9 to 1.5 m) behind them, ready to feed balls. Two other players line up on the opposite side of the net on the baseline. The coach feeds the ball into play, and the receiving team on the baseline dips, rips, angles, or lobs the ball. Once the ball is in play the two net players may move toward or away from the net, and the point is played out. Games are played to 7 points, and then players switch sides.

Variation: To practice a specific shot, teams can be required to hit a particular shot first and then play out the point.

Advanced Strategy #1: Inflating and Deflating or Deflating and Inflating

This strategy tests the opponents' ability to cover from the front to the back of the court. Moving a team backward first and then forward or vice versa can frustrate opponents and break down their defense.

Common patterns of play: To move a team backward first, a player hits a heavy deep shot or lob (inflating) and follows it with a drop volley (deflating). To move a team forward first, the player starts with a soft-angled return or a short-angled volley (deflating) to draw the opponents to the net and then lob (inflating) over them. With a good serve and aggressive net partner, a player can hit a topspin or kick serve that backs up the opponent, followed by a sharply angled drop volley when the player's partner poaches on the opponents' reply. The player can also volley deep into the court and then angle the next ball away.

FOUR SQUARE

Purpose: To practice hitting inflating or deflating shots to all parts of the court.

Procedure: Two players start on the baseline on each side of the net. Players should imagine the center line continuing to the baseline so that the court is divided into four squares (see figure 11.12). Once the ball is in play, each team must hit to a different square on the opponents' side of the court. Teams lose points if a ball lands in the same box twice in a row. Games are played out to 7 points.

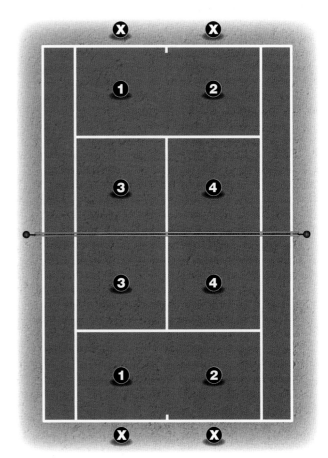

Figure 11.12 Inflate and deflate areas.

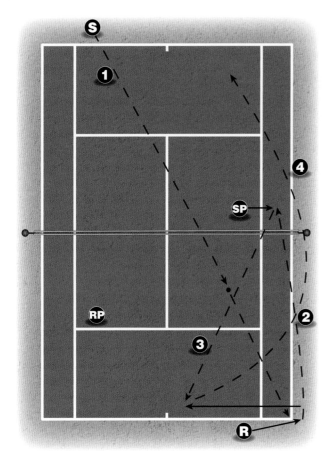

Figure 11.13 Intimidating a poaching opponent by putting a return straight down the line.

Advanced Strategy #2: Inflating and Inflating

In this scenario the players use two shots in a row that stretch the opposing team's defense and count on the fact that they will hit a shot, recover, and look for a middle shot. This tactic can be used early in matches to stop opponents from poaching, or it can be used late in matches to test the resolve of an opposing team at a crucial moment.

Common patterns of play: This strategy works well to try to break the opponent's serve. The goal is to intimidate and to keep the poaching opponent honest. The player takes the next return straight down the line with power and precision (see figure 11.13). Generally the first time doing this, the player should expect a shorter volley as the opponent defensively blocks the return back over the net. Depending on the hit, the players can either follow the down-the-line shot with a lob when the ball is hit deep, or expose the middle with a hard shot to the alleys again. Some defenses recover quickly from an attacking (inflating) situation, so the player may need to continue to inflate to spread them out before being able to deflate the ball (angle it off or hit it softly). In an inflating and inflating situation, players tend to overhit and go for too much on the shots to get an opponent in a stretched position. Players need to keep the speed of their shots within the limits that allow them to control the ball.

OFFENSE AND DEFENSE

Purpose: To practice the offensive and defensive situations played in doubles matches and establish optimum positioning and shot locations for all players.

Procedure: One team is at the net, and the other team starts on the baseline. A coach feeds a ball to one of two volleyers standing on the service line. The player receiving the feed hits the first ball back deep in the court toward the baseline. Net players may hit back crosscourt, down the line, or both. (These options should be predetermined and based on what the players need to work on.) After the initial ball is hit, the point is played full court and players can hit any shot anywhere they like.

Variations: To work on overheads and defensive replies from the baseliners, the drill can be started by feeding a lob to the net players. In this version, net players can hit their overheads anywhere in the court that they would like. The lob version can also be used with a high and deep lob that makes the net players retreat to the baseline for defense or has them reestablish their position at the net.

Advanced Strategy #3: Deflating and Deflating

Taking speed off the ball so that opponents must generate pace can result in a series of unforced errors. A team can lessen the pace by increasing underspin on the ball, or they can use a kick serve to create a slower ball that the opponents hit early or try for too much on. A player can use lobs, volleys that are softly angled or directly in front, or slices that stay low. When taking pace off shots, the player's goal is to locate them in spots where the opposing team finds it hard to be aggressive. This could be softer shots hit to a weakness or a lob that is tough for the opponents to put away.

> **Common patterns of play:** Common patterns include a slow kick serve followed by a drop volley shot, or a short dip to the middle of two net players followed by another short dip.

STRATEGIES AND TACTICS FOR DOUBLES STYLES OF PLAY

The game style of a doubles team is determined by the game styles of the individual team members. Any of the singles game styles can be combined on a doubles team, but players should bear in mind that the effectiveness of any combination depends on the strength of each partner's skills and tactics along with the ability to mesh the mental approaches and overall personalities of the two players. The various combinations of game styles create three types of teams: both aggressive (two aggressive player styles), both defensive (two defensive player styles), and salt and pepper (one aggressive and one defensive player). The characteristics of each type of team are discussed next.

Both Aggressive

This doubles style has two players of the following styles or any combination (hybrid teams) of the following styles: aggressive baseline players, serve-and-volley style players, and all-court players. When both players are aggressive, they constantly look for opportunities to be at the net and focus on applying pressure with their serves, returns, and poaching skills. This type of team favors the mentality of going through instead of around the opponent, so the players use lots of middle shots and shots at the body to help them advance forward. This combination is usually a power team, and the members are often big in stature. The players are likely to hit their overheads hard and mean to put their shots away.

Two Aggressive Baseline Players

In doubles play, aggressive baseline players like to make the action happen and typically hit big groundstrokes through the court or through the opponents. They try to intimidate with power and heavy spin. On a slow clay court, this team is a handful.

One of the strategies best suited to two aggressive baseliners is covering a weakness. Through their aggressiveness, these players make the opponents more concerned with defense than finding a weakness. This team should also attack the weakness of the opponents and use the aggressive strategies of through the middle, butterfly, the rush and crush, inflating and inflating, and pushing the opponent back in the court.

Besides these overall strategies, here are two other strategies commonly used by successful aggressive baseline players:

- Pinning their opponents to the baseline with balls that they hit through the court (ball bounces over the baseline) or off the court (ball bounces and goes over the doubles side line)
- Intimidating the net players by hammering groundstrokes directly at them

Two Serve-and-Volley Style Players

This team would serve and volley on every serve and try to attack every return and short ball. Their goal is to get to the net because they have good volleys and overheads, understand movement at the net, and obtain optimum volley location to stay on offense. This team will be formidable on quick hard or grass courts. The quickness and aggressive nature of this style of team tries to find the weakness of the other team and continually goes to it. Serve-and-volley style players look for the first opportunity to hit a power volley down the line exposing the net player. Serve-and-volley style players also use angled volleys to pull a team out of position so they can attack the middle.

The doubles strategies best suited to two serve-and-volley style players are the rush and crush and hitting through the middle. Return and crush works too, as does lobbing the opponents and taking the net as they retreat. Besides these overall strategies, other strategies commonly used by successful serve and volley teams include the following:

- **Playing Australian formation.** The server stands by the center hash mark to serve, and the partner lines up on the same side that the server is serving from.

- **Playing the I formation.** The partner at the net lets the player know which direction the partner plans to move after the player serves.

Two All-Court Players

A team of all-court Players is a pair of seasoned players. They must be so, because they can play any style whenever and on whatever surface that they like. Bob Bryan and Mike Bryan are the best all-court players that the doubles game has seen. They adjust effortlessly to all surfaces, and they specialize in a variety of ways to beat opponents.

Two all-court players can use any of the previously mentioned strategies. Consistency pays off for this team when the players are able to execute a variety of the doubles strategies. Hitting to a weakness is important because the all-court player team can execute it in different ways. This team can implement strategies based on what is working at the time. Besides these overall strategies, other strategies commonly used by successful all-court player teams include the following:

- Playing consistently but with a variety of styles to keep their opponents guessing

- Using their best styles to own the must-win points

One Serve-and-Volley Style Player or One Aggressive Baseline Player or One All-Court Player

The possible teams for these match-ups, include the following:

- One serve-and-volley style player and one aggressive baseline player

- One serve-and-volley style player and one all-court player

- One aggressive baseline player and one-all court player

These teams can be aggressive but might not commit to an all-out blitz on the net. This type of team also looks for opportunities but is mainly looking for a short ball to attack and then come to the net. These teams are dangerous on all surfaces, but especially on quicker surfaces. This team has power but partners must work together to combine one player's aggressive style of transition with a partner who likes to use groundstrokes or variety to transition. This combination works well when each partner can adapt slightly to the other partner's style.

The serve-and-volley style player uses the aggressive strategies of hitting to a weakness and rush and crush. The aggressive baseline player uses power on groundstrokes to ground and pound the opponents to transition forward. The all-court player uses any of the doubles strategies to get in good position. Besides these overall strategies, other strategies commonly used by successful all-court teams include the following:

- The serve-and-volley style player uses power and constant transition to affect the other team, and the aggressive baseline player or all-court player partner looks to transition off a weapon shot or a weaker ball.

- This type of aggressive doubles works best if the aggressive baseliner or all-court player thinks in terms of setting up the serve-and-volley style player.

Both Defensive

This team consists of two defensive baseline players. Since baseliners don't have big weapons, this team uses scrappy defense to make opponents hit a winner or put-away to end the point. The defensive team uses good defense initially to get the other team out of position and depth to keep opposing players back and prevent them from being more aggressive. Players on this team have good use of the lob and know how to position themselves to stay in the rally. On a slow clay court, this style of team can make it a long day. Opponents must be patient and get ready for long rallies.

The strategies best suited to two defensive baseline players are as follows:

- Consistency combined with great anticipation and speed can drive attacking teams crazy; it makes opponents always have to hit another shot.

- Lobbing is a way to really test the opposing team's ability to hit overheads. It is common in league play and can lead to victory.

Besides these overall strategies, other strategies commonly used by successful defensive baseline teams include the following:

- High percentage of first serves when starting the point

- Very high percentage of returns followed by deep groundstrokes and or lobs

One Aggressive and One Defensive

This team consists of a defensive baseline player paired with an aggressive baseline player, serve-and-volley style player, or all-court player. The partners in this type of team can complement each other if they work together. The aggressive player becomes the spiker, and the other player becomes the setter. All teams attempt to set their partners up for success, but this salt and pepper style of team is exceptionally good at it.

Depth by the baseliner is essential, and the ability to work in conjunction with a more aggressive partner means the least aggressive player must be able to join the more aggressive partner when the situation presents itself. The defensive player, whose preference of surfaces could make the difference, determines the best court surfaces. Opponents who keep pressure on the defensive player can eventually wear this team down because the aggressive player tries to take more on to finish the points.

In a salt and pepper team, one player uses the aggressive style of play with serve-and-volley play, rush and crush, and hitting through the middle. The other player uses lobs, uses the butterfly method, and tries to deflate shots or take pace off the shot. The other player could also be a defensive and aggressive player combination. Besides these overall strategies, other strategies commonly used by successful salt and pepper teams include the following:

- One player that inflates shots while the partner deflates.

- All-around players that deflate well together and then inflate together or vice versa.

ESTABLISHING A DOUBLES GAME PLAN

A doubles team should hold a meeting to discuss preferences such as shot, side, and surface. The following process can help doubles teams design a basic game plan.

1. **Identifying the playing style.** Players determine whether a team's playing style should be aggressive, defensive, or salt and pepper. Players test this out by playing practice sets against a variety of opponents.

2. **Prioritizing serve formations.** Players list in order of preference the formations that they like using. It is valuable to associate this with a score in mind, so players should write out all the possible scores and determine what they do best on differing scores.

3. **Assessing strengths and weaknesses within playing styles and formations.** Players review the information for their own playing style and evaluate which of the strengths, strategies, and patterns of play listed for the player type are strengths versus weaknesses. For example, if a team's style is two serve-and-volley style players, then both players agree that transitioning to the net is what they must do. They also agree that staying back for any long periods of time where their weaknesses could be exposed is not a good idea. So, their goal is to come in as soon as possible.

4. **Prioritizing patterns of play within the team's style.** The patterns of play are the partners' options, and they should prioritize their options for both the serving and receiving games. For example, for a team member using the serve-and-volley style and the other player who is using the aggressive baseline style, their service game options are as follows:

Option 1: Using T serves where the likely return will be down the middle or crosscourt. Serve-and-volley style players will come in off serves and sometimes stay back, mixing up their transitions to the net. Serve-and-volley style players will hit volleys and work their way in closer to the net. Aggressive baseline players will stay back and come to the net, but will be looking to be aggressive and go for a winning type volley.

Option 2: Serving out wide. This is tougher for serve-and-volley style players because they now have to cover more of the alley because of the angle created. Serve-and-volley style players will transition in and, if a high ball is hit, will direct their volley to the net player. Aggressive baseline players will look to stay back and run around their weakness off a serve out wide and hit their weapon to come in or rip it down the line.

Option 3: Using the jam serve. For a serve-and-volley style player, hitting this serve into the opponent's body could produce an easy put-away. Aggressive baseline players will look for a weak reply and transition to the net.

Following are the same team's options for the return games:

Option 1: Neutralizing the serve with a low ball hit crosscourt if the server is transitioning to volley, or using a high and heavy topspin if the server is staying back. The serve-and-volley style player may feel the urge to come in off the return or wait for the next ball. The aggressive baseline player will stay back and return the serve and then get positioned to hit a weapon crosscourt and transition to the net.

Option 2: Taking the opponent's second serve and hitting it up the line, coming to the net behind it for the serve-and-volley style player. The aggressive baseliner will pound groundstrokes crosscourt until they change direction and rip a shot down the line.

5. **Practicing style and options.** Players try to get some playing time by playing practice sets with the partner or at least with someone who plays the partner's game style. This gives players a better idea of what to expect.

6. **Playing practice sets and recording results.** Players play about three to five practice sets a week. They keep a journal on how they performed with their partner, how their styles affect each other's game, the strengths and weaknesses of the team, and how they can make it better.

7. **Playing under pressure.** Players enter a tournament or league competition. They should be diligent about playing their options under pressure. Competition is the test of players' perseverance and discipline.

8. **Evaluating matches.** After each match, the team considers whether anything that each team member did or didn't do might have helped the team play better. Players should do this for a month after each practice set, practice match, or real match. They will likely be amazed at what they learn about themselves and their game. This strategy can help a team create a blueprint for reproducible top performances.

Drill	Forehand	Backhand	Serve	Return	Net skills	Specialty skills	Singles	Doubles	Page #
Chapter 3: Forehand and Backhand Drills									
Call-out game	X	X							56
Straight-ahead short court	X	X							57
Diagonal short court	X	X							57
Competitive short court	X	X							57
Straight-ahead backcourt	X	X							58
Crosscourt backcourt	X	X							58
Release technique drill	X	X							59
Handcuff drill	X	X							59
Alternating open and closed stance	X	X							61
Back loading step	X	X							61
Forward movement	X	X							62
Side movement	X	X							62
Backward movement	X	X							62
Side-to-side movement	X	X							63

Drill	Forehand	Backhand	Serve	Return	Net skills	Specialty skills	Singles	Doubles	Page #
Backward-to-forward movement	X	X							63
Inside-out forehand movement	X	X							64
Random movement	X	X							64
Basic acceleration drill	X	X							65
Swinging volley drill	X	X							66
Moving acceleration drill	X	X							66
Hard hitting: out of the ballpark	X	X							67
Hard hitting: killer shots	X	X							67
Crosscourt flat shot	X	X							69
Down-the-line shot	X	X							69
High, heavy crosscourt and down-the-line shot	X	X							70
Shorter- and deeper-angled shots	X	X							71
Inside-out forehand	X								72
Slice		X							72
One shot	X	X							73

Drill	Forehand	Backhand	Serve	Return	Net skills	Specialty skills	Singles	Doubles	Page #
Serving fives			X						116
Flat serve (power)			X						117
Slice serve			X						118
Topspin or kick serve			X						118
Serve location scoring			X						119
Serving a game of pig			X						119
Billy ball				X					120
Short court to backcourt				X					120
Compact movement				X					121
Takeback and look				X					121
Return and release technique				X					122
Return acceleration and wrist snap				X					122
Aggressive flat or topspin return				X					124
Neutralizing return drill				X					124
Block return				X					125

Drill	Forehand	Backhand	Serve	Return	Net skills	Specialty skills	Singles	Doubles	Page #
Return location				X					126
Cricket				X					126
Target				X					126
Variety			X	X					127
Second serve game			X						127
First- and second-serve plus-minus game			X	X					127
Break, no break game			X	X					128
Goalie game				X					128
Chapter 9: Net and Specialty Drills									
Approach and catch movement	X	X		X	X	X			168
Block approach	X	X				X			169
Aggressive groundstroke approach	X	X		X		X			169
Swinging volley approach	X	X			X	X			170
Slice approach	X	X				X			170
Approach target	X	X		X		X			170

Drill	Forehand	Backhand	Serve	Return	Net skills	Specialty skills	Singles	Doubles	Page #
Multiple approaches	X	X		X		X			171
One-shot crosscourt pass	X	X		X		X			172
One-shot down-the-line pass	X	X				X			172
One-shot short dipper	X	X		X		X			173
Two-shot pass	X	X		X		X			173
Topspin lob	X	X		X		X			174
Backhand slice lob		X		X		X			174
Bunt lob	X	X				X			175
Lob target	X	X		X		X			175
Multiple lobs	X	X		X	X	X			175
Standard volley with leg loading					X				176
Moving volley					X				177
Volley tracking					X				177
Volley collar					X				177
High volley					X				178

Drill	Forehand	Backhand	Serve	Return	Net skills	Specialty skills	Singles	Doubles	Page #
Lob volley					X	X			178
Drop volley					X	X			179
Low volley					X				179
Half volley	X	X			X	X			179
Quick hands and quick feet volley					X				180
Deuce-ad volley game					X	X			180
Volley target					X	X			180
Live volley					X				180
Power overhead					X	X			181
Scissor kick overhead					X	X			181
Backhand smash					X	X			182
Overhead target					X				182
Live overhead					X				182
Drop shot target					X	X			182
Drop shot to drop shot					X	X			183

Drill	Forehand	Backhand	Serve	Return	Net skills	Specialty skills	Singles	Doubles	Page #
Drop shot technique					X	X			183
Forward running shot						X			183
Tweener shot						X			184
Slap shot						X			184
Double desperation shot						X			184
Approach, volley, and overhead	X	X			X				185
Approach and pass	X	X			X				185
Volley and lob	X	X			X				185
No winners					X				186
Coach Williams special	X	X			X	X			186
Chapter 10: Singles Strategy and Drills									
Three-quarter court drill							X		202
Alley drill							X		203
Walk-in drill							X		204
Running the opponent							X		205

Drill	Forehand	Backhand	Serve	Return	Net skills	Specialty skills	Singles	Doubles	Page #
First strike							X		206
Hitting shots to set up strengths							X		207
Deflate and inflate or inflate and deflate							X		208
Offensive inflation versus defensive deflation							X		209
Chapter 11: Doubles Strategy and Drills									
Switch game								X	236
Hot seat								X	238
Champs up the middle								X	239
Hands								X	240
Kings								X	241
Best of seven								X	243
Dip, rip, angle, or lob								X	245
Four square								X	245
Offense and defense								X	246

ABOUT THE AUTHORS

Joey Rive played on the ATP Tour for 8 years, competing in each of the 4 Grand Slams, and achieved a top 60 player ranking in singles and top 50 ranking in doubles. Rive also played Davis Cup tennis for Puerto Rico and practiced with the U.S. Davis Cup team. He was recently inducted into the hall of fame in Puerto Rico. Rive has been inducted into the Hall of Fame at Florida State University, where he won MVP honors for his team and conference as a player. He also received *Tennis* magazine's Sportsman of the Year Award.

After his successful playing career, Rive coached at Florida State University, the University of Alabama, and Texas Christian University. He produced multiple All-Americans, two conference titles, and one NCAA final four finish. During his tenure as a college coach, he was voted PTR College Coach of the Year. Rive also spent three years as a USTA national coach, working with Andy Roddick, Mardy Fish, Taylor Dent, Robby Ginepri, and Alex Bogomolov.

Rive is a USPTA, PTR, and USTA certified high-performance and sports coach. Currently, he is a teaching professional at T Bar M Racquet Club in Dallas, Texas.

For almost three decades, **Scott Williams** has been an internationally renowned coach working with players such as No. 2 ATP Tour player Tommy Haas and No. 1 ATP Tour doubles player Max Mirnyi. Williams is the author of *Serious Tennis* (Human Kinetics) and author and producer of the recently released *Spiritually Tough Tennis* DVD. He is president of Match Point Ministries and was voted the 2009 and 2011 Coach of the Year, receiving the Ace Excellence Award for his work with upcoming junior tennis players. In 2011 he led the Lady Scots to win the Florida State high school championships. Coach Williams was awarded coach of the year by the Florida Dairy Farmers, Sun Sentinel, and the Palm Beach Post.

Williams is currently the tennis director at Saint Andrew's School in Boca Raton, Florida. He is certified as a USTA high-performance coach, USPTA level 1 professional, and PSIA level III instructor.

Williams has been ranked nationally in both tennis and skiing and has played professional satellite and challenger events in Europe, South America, and the United States. He has won a total of 19 state championships in both tennis and skiing in Florida and Washington.

You'll find other outstanding tennis resources at

www.HumanKinetics.com/tennis

In the U.S. call 1-800-747-4457

Australia 08 8372 0999 • Canada 1-800-465-7301
Europe +44 (0) 113 255 5665 • New Zealand 0800 222 062

 HUMAN KINETICS
The Premier Publisher for Sports & Fitness
P.O. Box 5076 • Champaign, IL 61825-5076 USA

 **eBook**
available at
HumanKinetics.com